Thinking about Animals in Thirteenth-Century Paris

Exploring what theologians at the University of Paris in the thirteenth century understood about the boundary between humans and animals, this book demonstrates the great variety of ways in which they held similarity and difference in productive tension. Analysing key theological works, Ian P. Wei presents extended close readings of William of Auvergne, the Summa Halensis, Bonaventure, Albert the Great and Thomas Aquinas. These scholars found it useful to consider animals and humans together, especially with regard to animal knowledge and behaviour, when discussing issues including creation, the fall, divine providence, the heavens, angels and demons, virtues and passions. While they frequently stressed that animals had been created for use by humans, and sometimes treated them as tools employed by God to shape human behaviour, animals were also analytical tools for the theologians themselves. This study thus reveals how animals became a crucial resource for generating knowledge of God and the whole of creation.

IAN P. WEI is Senior Lecturer in the Department of History at the University of Bristol where he co-founded the Centre for Medieval Studies. He has been a Member of the School of Social Science at the Institute for Advanced Study in Princeton (2009–2010) and his previous publications include *Intellectual Culture in Medieval Paris: Theologians and the University, c.1100–1330* (2012).

Thinking about Animals in Thirteenth-Century Paris

Theologians on the Boundary Between Humans and Animals

IAN P. WEI
University of Bristol

Shaftesbury Road, Cambridge CB2 8EA, United Kingdom

One Liberty Plaza, 20th Floor, New York, NY 10006, USA

477 Williamstown Road, Port Melbourne, VIC 3207, Australia

314–321, 3rd Floor, Plot 3, Splendor Forum, Jasola District Centre, New Delhi – 110025, India

103 Penang Road, #05–06/07, Visioncrest Commercial, Singapore 238467

Cambridge University Press is part of Cambridge University Press & Assessment, a department of the University of Cambridge.

We share the University's mission to contribute to society through the pursuit of education, learning and research at the highest international levels of excellence.

www.cambridge.org
Information on this title: www.cambridge.org/9781108821728

DOI: 10.1017/9781108907552

First published 2020
First paperback edition 2024

A catalogue record for this publication is available from the British Library

ISBN   978-1-108-83015-7   Hardback
ISBN   978-1-108-82172-8   Paperback

For Raquel Rojo Carrillo, Betty R. Wei and Anne M. Wei

Contents

Preface

For scholarly advice and stimulating comments, and more generally for the intellectual companionship that makes thinking fruitful and fun, I have many people to thank. For some years I have taught a final-year undergraduate unit called 'Constructing the "Other" in Western Europe, *c.*1000–1400' at the University of Bristol, and this book owes much to the enthusiasm and insight of the students with whom I have had the privilege to work. Doctoral students, some co-supervised with colleagues at other universities or entirely by other colleagues at Bristol, have generously shared their ideas and excitement, and I am grateful especially to Owain Nash, Caitlin Naylor, Edward Sutcliffe and Teresa Witcombe. I am also immensely grateful for support and intellectual friendship to all my colleagues in the Department of History and the Centre for Medieval Studies at the University of Bristol, especially those who specialise in medieval and early modern history and history of art: Kenneth Austin, Fernando Cervantes, Lucy Donkin, George Ferzoco, Mark Hailwood, Anke Holdenried, Evan Jones, Carolyn Muessig, Ben Pohl, Richard Sheldon, Brendan Smith, Richard Stone and Beth Williamson. Colleagues fulfilling key leadership roles, formal and informal, in my Department and Faculty have also offered endless encouragement and assurance, and I must especially thank Robert Bickers, Helen Fulton, Ronald Hutton, Josie McLellan, Simon Potter and James Thompson. I also owe a particular debt of gratitude to some very special friends beyond the University of Bristol on whose generosity and expertise I can always rely: Peggy Brown, Rita Copeland, David Ditchburn, Marilynn Desmond, Sean L. Field, Robert Gibbs, Miri Rubin and David Wallace.

Throughout the writing of this book, it has been my pleasure and great good fortune to work with Liz Friend-Smith at Cambridge University Press. A fine historian and a wonderful editor, she has given warm encouragement and astute advice that has proved essential, and I am very grateful to her. I also thank the two anonymous readers who assessed the book for Cambridge University Press and gave excellent advice. Further thanks are due to Natasha Whelan and Atifa Jiwa at Cambridge University Press for their sympathetic and efficient support during the production of the book. I am also very grateful to Malcolm Todd who brought exceptional expertise and learning to its copy-editing. I give my thanks too to Laura Cleaver who helped find an image for the cover of the book.

My most important thanks must go to my family who give meaning to my life. To my wife, Raquel Rojo Carrillo, a fine medievalist and my most important intellectual companion as well as my closest companion in life. To my mother, Betty R. Wei. To my sister and her family: Anne, Phil, Alex and Beth. To my Venezuelan family: José Andrés Rojo, Andreina and Rafael, Laura and Danny. And although they are no longer with us, I thank as well as miss my father, Teh-Hsing Wei, and my mother-in-law, María Isabel Carrillo. Since Cambridge University Press published my last book, Raquel and I have had a daughter, Sarah, and a son, Andrés, and I have become acutely aware of how my wife, my mother and my sister hold the family together, so, in gratitude, it is to them that I dedicate this book: to Raquel Rojo Carrillo, Betty R. Wei and Anne M. Wei.

Introduction

This book seeks to understand what masters of theology at the University of Paris in the thirteenth century had to say about similarities and differences between humans and animals. It explores the ways in which they related similarities and differences to each other, holding them in productive tension, so as to construct a boundary between humans and animals, or to query and blur such a boundary.

In recent years some wonderful work has been published on the representation of animals in the vernacular literature of medieval Europe. Literary scholars have offered many insights into the ways in which animals and humans were understood in relation to each other. To give just three of the most outstanding and recent examples, Susan Crane, in her *Animal Encounters: Contacts and Concepts in Medieval Britain*, has argued that the 'binary conception' of a boundary between animals and humans 'must now melt into a multiplicity of intersecting and competing distinctions that better reflect medieval ways of thinking', pointing to 'the plurality and density of medieval thought about animals'.[1] She identifies 'an exploratory mode that takes man and other beasts to be unsettled categories coming into definition through relationship'.[2] Peggy McCracken has argued that medieval 'literary texts use human–animal encounters to explore the legitimacy of authority and dominion over others', and that 'human dominion over animals is revealed as a disputed model for sovereign relations among people: it justifies exploitation even as it mandates protection and care, and it depends on reiterations of human–animal difference that expose the tenuous nature of human exceptionalism even as they reinstate its claims', with the 'uncertain boundary

---

[1] Susan Crane, *Animal Encounters: Contacts and Concepts in Medieval Britain* (Philadelphia, 2013), p. 8.
[2] Crane, *Animal Encounters*, p. 169.

between animal and human' frequently 'at stake'.[3] Using literary
material for the most part, but also some scholarly and legal works,
Karl Steel has argued that such texts reveal the way in which 'acts of
violence and of differential allocation of care [...] are central to
distinguishing humans from animals and indeed to creating the opposing categories of human and animal', and he focuses on 'the violence
against animals through which humans attempt to claim a unique,
oppositional identity for themselves', violence that was individual,
systemic and linguistic.[4] There has been a tendency amongst both
literary specialists and historians to suppose, however, that medieval
theologians and philosophers, writing in Latin, all shared a very
straightforward view of animals as simply lacking reason, with all
other differences from the human arising from this deficiency. The
research for this book was stimulated by the hunch, informed by study
of many other areas of medieval intellectual culture, that learned men
were unlikely to be so out of step with vernacular writers. Nor indeed
did it seem probable that their approach to animals would be so much
more one-dimensional than their work on just about every other issue
they addressed. They did not all say the same thing about anything
else, so why would animals receive unanimous appraisal?

Very significant revision of our understanding of scholarly attitudes
to animals has been provided in recent years by the immensely valuable
work of historians of philosophy, notably Theodor W. Köhler, Tobias
Davids and Anselm Oelze.[5] In his monumental and magisterial
volumes surveying and collating thirteenth-century scholarly work on
issues of natural philosophy, Köhler has amply demonstrated that
attempts to define the human, frequently in relation to animals, were

---

[3] Peggy McCracken, *In the Skin of a Beast: Sovereignty and Animality in Medieval France* (Chicago, 2017), pp. 1, 161.
[4] Karl Steel, *How to make a Human: Animals and Violence in the Middle Ages* (Columbus, Ohio, 2011), pp. 14, 15; see 17 for a succinct discussion of the types of violence with which he is concerned.
[5] Amongst many publications, key works include: Theodor W. Köhler, *Homo animal nobilissimum. Konturen des spezifisch Menschlichen in der naturphilosophischen Aristoteleskommentierung des dreizehnten Jahrhunderts*, vol. 1 (Leiden, 2008) and *Homo animal nobilissimum. Konturen des spezifisch Menschlichen in der naturphilosophischen Aristoteleskommentierung des dreizehnten Jahrhunderts*, vols. 2.1 and 2.2 (Leiden, 2014); Tobias Davids, *Anthropologische Differenz und animalische Konvenienz: Tierphilosophie bei Thomas von Aquin* (Leiden, 2017); Anselm Oelze, *Animal Rationality: Later Medieval Theories 1250–1350* (Leiden, 2018).

far from uniform and that significant similarities between humans and animals were identified, many involving intelligent animal behaviour.[6] With regard to animal cognition, Oelze has shown 'the depth and diversity of the medieval discussion', and that it was the view of some medieval philosophers and theologians 'that certain highly developed species of nonhuman animals can engage in rational *processes*, such as basic forms of reasoning although they lack intellect and reason'.[7] Davids has revealed how, for Thomas Aquinas, the difference between rational humans and non-rational animals had transformative effects on the similarities that humans and animals shared as sentient beings.[8]

Despite these important contributions, there is more work to be done. Entirely understandably, these historians of philosophy focus especially on the relationship between medieval thought and ancient authorities, above all Aristotelian works that had recently become available, and they seek to identify dominant trends and the most original thinking. Oelze and Davids offer a process of critique, reconstruction and evaluation, piecing together what a scholar said in different works, assessing the plausibility of different versions that can be imagined, sometimes asking questions of medieval scholars that they did not actually consider, and often going beyond what the scholar actually said to make claims about what he must actually have thought. This approach is governed in part by a desire to relate medieval philosophy to contemporary philosophical concerns, and to evaluate medieval theories accordingly. These ways of interpreting medieval scholars are entirely legitimate and deeply fascinating, but

---

[6] Köhler, *Homo animal nobilissimum*, vols. 2.1 and 2.2, pp. 920 ('In ihren Untersuchungen stellen die Magister weitreichende Gemeinsamkeiten bzw. Kontinuitäten zwischen Mensch und Tier fest. Das ist naheliegenderweise vor allem in somatischer Hinsicht der Fall und auch in Bezug auf die (äußere) Sinneswahrnehmung, emotionale Reaktionen und soziale Verhaltensweisen nicht unerwartet. Darüber hinaus aber erstrecken sich die von ihnen angenommenen strukturellen Gemeinsamkeiten zum Teil durchaus weit auch in den Bereich intelligenter Verhaltensweisen hinein und weisen hier in Bezug auf einzelne Akte mitunter dichte graduelle Annäherungen an menschliche Intelligenzleistungen aus'), 923 ('Der Beitrag der einzelnen Magister zu den in ihren Untersuchungen behandelten Fragestellungen ist erwartungsgemäß kein einheitlicher, sondern insgesamt – auch bei gemeinsamen Grundpositionen – unterschiedlich und insbesondere auch von unterschiedlichem philosophischen Gewicht').

[7] Oelze, *Animal Rationality*, pp. xi, 235 (his emphasis).

[8] Davids, *Anthropologische Differenz und animalische Konvenienz*, pp. 215–16: 'die anthropologishe Differenz, rational/nicht-rational, verändert nämlich teilweise dasjenige, was Menschen und Tieren als Sinnenwesen gemeinsam ist'.

this book is more straightforwardly historical. My approach is based on extended close reading of texts, my concern is as much with how medieval theologians said things as with what they said, and, rather than focusing on any one philosophical or theological issue, I try to capture what they had to say about animals wherever it cropped up in their more wide-ranging works. In similar ways, my approach also differs from the work of scholars who seek to adapt and modify medieval thinking so as to incorporate modern scientific knowledge and construct theologically informed, especially 'Thomistic', theories relevant to current concerns about animals and animal rights.[9]

Several other historiographical trends are worth mentioning at the outset because they have been in my mind as I researched and wrote this book, and they perhaps therefore shape what I have written. First, many medievalists, literary specialists and historians, have suggested that, although they did not explicitly frame their work in these terms, thirteenth-century scholars were embarked upon a grand project to define the human, a project that extended beyond the universities. To give just a few examples, Alain Boureau has written that in the thirteenth century 'a new anthropology, derived both from naturalist knowledge and from Scholastic reflection, explored the strengths and weaknesses of human nature'.[10] For Shirin A. Khanmohamadi, 'the thirteenth century, an era of hope for the conversion of Asia to Christianity through missionary activity, was the age of elaborating the discourse of Christianity and defining the "human." In a range of discourses, both popular and elite, the thirteenth century evinces a heightened interest in establishing the contours of the human. New theorizations of what constituted the human emerged from scholastic thinkers like Albertus Magnus and Thomas Aquinas.'[11] Susan Crane refers to 'high medieval philosophy's ongoing project of delineating the human'.[12] Tobias Davids reflects that comparison with animals became an important philosophical method because the contours of

---

[9] See, for example, Judith A. Barad, *Aquinas on the Nature and Treatment of Animals* (San Francisco, 1995); John Berkman, 'Towards a Thomistic theology of animality', in Celia Deane-Drummond and David Clough (eds.), *Creaturely Theology: On God, Humans and Other Animals* (London, 2009), pp. 21–40.

[10] Alain Boureau, *Satan the Heretic: The Birth of Demonology in the Medieval West*, trans. Teresa Lavender Fagan (Chicago, 2006), p. 143.

[11] Shirin A. Khanmohamadi, *In Light of Another's Word: European Ethnography in the Middle Ages* (Philadephia, 2014), p. 20.

[12] Crane, *Animal Encounters*, p. 43.

the human appeared more clearly in contrast with the animal.[13] When considering why medieval theologians wrote about animals as they did, I have had this possible answer at the back of my mind.

I have also had in mind my own work on medieval academic discourse. When analysing quodlibetal disputations relating to money and to sex and marriage, I have previously argued that academic discourse was sometimes unstable, operating at different levels and offering much more than the grand normative statements that usually receive attention. Many ideas about money were understated or simply implied, built into the conclusions drawn when considering particular scenarios. Their means of denoting gender permitted considerable slippage in terms of focus on women and men. These strategies enabled them to respond to shifting social realities while respecting past authority.[14] This is why, in reading what the theologians had to say about animals, I have been as interested as much in how they expressed their ideas and arguments as the actual ideas and arguments themselves.

More generally, two other significant approaches must be mentioned, the cultural history of animals and critical animal studies. This book sits comfortably alongside, and indeed contributes to, the cultural history of animals which seeks to study animals 'as subjects in their own right', but fully recognises that their history is bound up with human history and must be researched chiefly through sources generated by humans, a point made explicitly and put into practice in Brigitte Resl's exemplary edited volume, *A Cultural History of Animals in the Medieval Age*.[15] Although, as will be apparent, Parisian theologians were not concerned with animals in their own right, their attitudes and ideas must be taken into account in writing the cultural history of animals in medieval Europe. This book does not, however,

[13] Davids, *Anthropologische Differenz und animalische Konvenienz*, p. 215. See also Köhler, *Homo animal nobilissimum*, vols. 2.1 and 2.2, pp. 911, 913.
[14] Ian P. Wei, 'Gender and sexuality in medieval academic discourse: marriage problems in Parisian quodlibets', *Mediaevalia* 31 (2010), pp. 5–34; 'Discovering the moral value of money: usurious money and medieval academic discourse in Parisian quodlibets', *Mediaevalia* 33 (2012), pp. 5–46; *Intellectual Culture in Medieval Paris: Theologians and the University c.1100–1330* (Cambridge, 2012), pp. 272–92, 348–55.
[15] Brigitte Resl (ed.), *A Cultural History of Animals in the Medieval Age* (Oxford, 2007); see esp. Resl, 'Introduction: animals in culture, ca. 1000–ca. 1400', pp. 1–26 at 1–3 for discussion of the aim to study animals 'as subjects in their own right' and the difficulties of doing so (quotation at 2).

make a direct contribution to critical animal studies. Outstanding work in this field, especially by Jeffery J. Cohen and Sarah Kay, has frequently stimulated my thinking and prompted me to define the nature of my endeavours more precisely, though not in ways that can be recognised in conventional footnotes.[16] Significant disciplinary and methodological differences divide us because for me as a historian the whole point is to try to explain past ways of thinking in their own terms. I trust that scholars in the field of critical animal studies will nonetheless find this book useful when they relate the ideas of medieval theologians to the conceptual frameworks that inform their own thinking.

With one exception, I have selected texts in which theologians tackled a broad range of theological issues, with the aim of exploring their treatment of the differences and similarities between humans and animals in varied intellectual contexts. Individual theologians and texts will be introduced more fully at the start of each chapter. Briefly, however, Chapter 1 looks at two works by William of Auvergne, a secular theologian and bishop of Paris, his *De legibus* and his *De universo*. Chapter 2 analyses two Franciscan works, the Summa Halensis and Bonaventure's *Commentary on the Sentences*. The third chapter focuses on works by two Dominicans, Albert the Great and Thomas Aquinas. Albert's *De animalibus* is the exception amongst the chosen texts because it is not straightforwardly theological, takes animals as its subject, and does not seek to address issues unconnected with animals. It seemed unwise, however, to neglect the work of the theologian most committed to the study of natural philosophy and animals as subjects in their own right, and he offers a distinctive strategy when placing animals and humans in hierarchical relationship. Two works by Aquinas are discussed, the *Summa contra gentiles* and the *Summa theologiae*.

It should be noted that when in Paris these men lived in what might be regarded as a very small world. They all worked in Paris while William of Auvergne was bishop, Bonaventure said that he was taught by Alexander of Hales, and Thomas Aquinas was definitely a student of Albert the Great. They must surely all have known each other

---

[16] See, for example, Jeffrey J. Cohen, *Medieval Identity Machines* (Minneapolis, Minn., 2003); Sarah Kay, *Animal Skins and the Reading Self in Medieval Latin and French Bestiaries* (Chicago, 2017).

because the Paris schools occupied a very small space, there were never more than ten to sixteen masters of theology at any one time in the thirteenth century, and they were all caught up in the complex institutional structures of the developing university. On the other hand, they were leading figures in an international community that trained men who taught, preached, heard confession and held high ecclesiastical office all over western Europe, and they shared a grand vision of themselves exercising authority at the summit of a hierarchy of learning with a duty to minister to the needs of the entire Christian world. Their words were potentially significant far beyond Paris itself.[17]

Finally, three points about terminology must be made. First, all Parisian theologians regarded humans as animals: the human species belonged to the genus of animals. It would therefore be most correct to distinguish between humans and non-human animals. For the sake of economy in writing, however, I have referred to non-human animals simply as animals, except where confusion might arise. Second, the Latin *homo* is gender neutral, though it was loaded with patriarchal assumptions that often meant that a man was envisaged. Without wishing to ignore those assumptions, I have as much as possible referred to humans and the human, making it easier to point up those occasions on which texts used gender specific terms like *mulier* and *vir*. Third, when the theologians discussed that part of the soul which was shared only by animals and humans (and not by plants), they referred sometimes to the *anima sensibilis* and sometimes to the *anima sensitiva*, and when they considered that part of the soul which was particular to humans, they sometimes called it the *anima intellectualis* and sometimes the *anima intellectiva*. Rather than standardise, I have referred to the 'sensible soul' or the 'sensitive soul', and to the 'intellectual soul' or the 'intellective soul', depending on the usage in the theological text under discussion.

---

[17] See Wei, *Intellectual Culture*, pp. 87–124, 174–84, 228–46; Ian P. Wei, 'The self-image of the masters of theology at the university of Paris in the late thirteenth and early fourteenth centuries', *Journal of Ecclesiastical History* 46 (1995), pp. 398–431.

1 | *William of Auvergne*

William of Auvergne was an immensely significant figure in the institutional development of the University of Paris in its first decades. He also played a crucial, though often underappreciated, intellectual role because he was one of the earliest Parisian theologians to make substantial use of newly translated Aristotelian works and related Arabic texts. All that is known of his early life is that he was born around 1180 or in the 1180s, and that he probably came from Aurillac. He was a secular cleric, rather than belonging to any religious order; by 1223 he was a canon at the cathedral of Notre Dame, and by 1225 a master of theology in Paris. When Bishop Bartholomew died in 1227, there was a disputed election and William went to Rome to appeal against the appointment that had been made. Pope Gregory IX resolved the issue by appointing William as bishop in 1228, which he remained until his death in 1249.

William continued to write prolifically while playing significant roles in secular and ecclesiastical politics. A prominent figure at the Capetian court and frequently acting on the pope's behalf, he was nevertheless highly independent and willing to stand up to both royal and papal power when he judged it necessary. His relationship with the growing University of Paris was highly fractious, not least because he sided with the royal authorities in 1229 when their heavy-handed response to student violence led to a strike and many students and masters departed from Paris, a dispute that was only resolved when Gregory IX issued the bull *Parens scientiarum* in 1231, granting the university privileges that significantly diminished the powers of the bishop of Paris. William nevertheless did much to shape the future of the university by giving crucial support to the friars just as they were seeking to establish themselves in the university. During the strike, while the secular masters were largely absent, the friars did not suspend their studies and even taught some secular students who had not joined the strike, and William made Roland of Cremona a master of theology, thus creating the first Dominican chair in theology. William was also responsible for the first Franciscan chair in theology when a secular master, Alexander of Hales, joined the Franciscans and William let him remain a master.[1]

William's *De legibus*, paired with a treatise *De fide*, and his *De universo* were parts of a vast work that William called his *Magisterium divinale et sapientiale*.[2] The *De legibus* sought to explain and compare Jewish, Christian and Muslim laws.[3] Especially in his discussion of Old Testament precepts, he had much to say about animals. The *De universo* was a wide-ranging discussion of the created universe, both material and spiritual, and animals featured in many different places.[4] William's writing is not always easy to follow. His use of images to

[1] The only monograph surveying William's life and works is Noël Valois, *Guillaume d'Auvergne, évêque de Paris (1228–1249): sa vie et ses ouvrages* (Paris, 1880). For more recent summaries of his life, see Steven P. Marrone, *William of Auvergne and Robert Grosseteste: New Ideas of Truth in the Early Thirteenth Century* (Princeton, N.J., 1983), pp. 27–9; Ernest A. Moody, 'William of Auvergne and his treatise De Anima', in his *Studies in Medieval Philosophy, Science, and Logic: Collected Papers 1933–1969* (Berkeley, 1975), pp. 1–109 at 1–6; Lesley Smith, 'William of Auvergne and the law of the Jews and the Muslims', in Thomas J. Heffernan and Thomas E. Burman (eds.), *Scripture and Pluralism: Reading the Bible in the Religiously Plural Worlds of the Middle Ages and Renaissance* (Leiden, 2005), pp. 123–42 at 123–4; Roland J. Teske, 'Introduction', in William of Auvergne, *The Universe of Creatures: Selections Translated from the Latin with an Introduction and Notes*, trans. Roland J. Teske (Milwaukee, Wis., 1998), pp. 13–29 at 13–14; Roland J. Teske, 'William of Auvergne', in Jorge J. E. Gracia and Timothy N. Noone (eds.), *A Companion to Philosophy in the Middle Ages* (Oxford, 2002), pp. 680–7 at 680. For comment on his close relationship with the Capetian court, see Lindy Grant, *Blanche of Castille: Queen of France* (New Haven, 2016), esp. pp. 187, 190–3, 210, 215, 267–8. For his relationship with the University of Paris and in particular the events of 1229–31, see Spencer E. Young, *Scholarly Community at the Early University of Paris: Theologians, Education and Society, 1215–1248* (Cambridge, 2014), pp. 40–43, 81–7, 100–101, 205–6, 222.

[2] On the nature of the *Magisterium divinale et sapientiale*, see Guglielmo Corti, 'Le sette parti del Magisterium divinale et sapientiale di Guglielmo di Auvergne', in *Studi e Ricerche di Scienze Religiose in onore dei Santi Apostoli Pietro e Paulo nel xix centenario del loro martirio* (Rome, 1968), pp. 289–307; Josef Kramp, 'Des Wilhelm von Auvergne "Magisterium divinale"', *Gregorianum* 1 (1920), pp. 538–616 and 2 (1921), pp. 42–103, 174–95; Teske, 'Introduction', pp. 14–17.

[3] For discussion of the purpose of the *De legibus*, see Smith, 'William of Auvergne and the law of the Jews and the Muslims', pp. 126–8.

[4] For an outline of the structure and content of the *De universo*, see Teske, 'Introduction', pp. 17–28; Teske, 'William of Auvergne', pp. 682–3.

argue by analogy can seem imprecise. Lengthy digressions can make it hard to be sure of any coherent structure. His Latin is idiosyncratic, with the subject of successive verbs often changing without being specified, though his way with words is often highly imaginative.[5] Writing about his work leaves the historian caught between offering a clarity that William did not himself present and replicating apparent confusion. Nevertheless, the breadth of his interests and his capacity to make surprising connections make the effort thoroughly worthwhile.

De legibus

Many of the Old Testament precepts that William of Auvergne sought to explain in the *De legibus* concerned animals, so he necessarily discussed the relationship between humans and animals in consider- able detail, and he consistently assumed or implied a hard boundary between them. In the first chapter, he stated very clearly that the law of Moses was elevated by having God as its author and maker. There was therefore nothing useless, pointless or absurd in it, and nothing in it, whether precept, prohibition, statute or story, that did not have rational cause and sufficient reason, whether hidden or manifest.[6] William then set out the main purposes that the laws served. Some laws were obviously useful because they honoured God or established the framework for human life. Others prevented bad things happening or ensured peace. Still others permitted but did not require various practices which were not in themselves desirable, thus ensuring that

---

[5] For comments on William of Auvergne's style of argument and expression, see Peter Biller, *The Measure of Multitude: Population in Medieval Thought* (Oxford, 2000), pp. 64–7; Marrone, *William of Auvergne and Robert Grosseteste*, pp. 30–32; Beryl Smalley, 'William of Auvergne, John of La Rochelle and St. Thomas Aquinas on the Old Law', reprinted in her *Studies in Medieval Thought and Learning from Abelard to Wyclif* (London, 1981), pp. 121–81 at 137–56 [first published in *St. Thomas Aquinas, 1274–1974: Commemorative Studies* (Toronto, 2 vols., 1974), vol. 2, pp. 11–72]; Smith, 'William of Auvergne and the law of the Jews and the Muslims', pp. 125–6.

[6] William of Auvergne, *Opera Omnia*, ed. F. Hotot (Orléans and Paris, 2 vols., 1674); *De legibus*, 1, p. 25A: 'Apparet igitur ex omnibus his legem Moysi Deo authore, et conditore editam esse. Quare nihil in ea inutile, nihil supervacuum, nihil absurdum. Nihil igitur in ea vel praeceptum, vel prohibitum est, nihil vel statutum, vel narratum, quod non habeat causam rationalem, et sufficientem rationem, sive occultam vel manifestam.' For a partial summary of the chapter, see Smith, 'William of Auvergne and the law of the Jews and the Muslims', pp. 128–30.

worse practices were avoided.[7] William then turned to what might have seemed like discrepancies or inconsistencies, and in so doing, he came to discuss the use and value of animals. He began by considering why some lesser evils were to be punished more severely than greater evils, and it soon became clear he had in mind that severe punishments were established for the theft of animals and not for theft of gold. According to William, the apparent discrepancy was doubtless because, although less serious, lesser evils occurred more frequently, and thus did more harm to the tranquillity of the people by their frequency than by their magnitude, and they were more difficult to stop because of the numbers involved. Furthermore, they were more easily committed because there were more opportunities; for example, it was easier to steal a sheep than the equivalent gold because a sheep was more easily found while gold was more closely guarded.[8]

There were still more significant differences between animals and gold, however. First, William compared animals and gold in terms of the sacrifices that God demanded. The laws required that some oxen and sheep be sacrificed to God, so that it was as if God owned part of flocks and herds. There was no precept, however, demanding that gold be offered, although it was used in the making of the tabernacle, the temple and its vessels. It was not surprising if God wanted more severe punishment for the theft of something of which part was necessarily owed to him than for the theft of something of which nothing was owed but was only offered voluntarily.[9] Second, William considered

---

[7] *De legibus*, 1, p. 25A: 'Etenim quae evidenter ad Dei honorificentiam, et vitae nostrae compositionem, et decorationem pertinent, per se manifestam habent utilitatem, et debita sunt per se [...]. Eodem modo evidens utilitas est in quibusdam, quae propter mala, quae de rebus alicujus provenire consueverunt, praecepta sunt [...]. Sunt et alia in quibus evidens est utilitas pacis [...]. Sunt et alia permissa tantum, nullomodo praecepta, permissa utique haec in lege non punita [...] quae utique ideo in lege permissa sunt ut majora mala declinarentur.'

[8] *De legibus*, 1, p. 25A–B: 'Quod autem quaedam mala licet minora quibusdam majoribus magis puniri praecepit, illa proculdubio causa fuit, quia licet minora frequentius tamen contingebant in populo illo. Et propter hoc plus nocebant tranquillitati, et paci populi ipsa frequentia sua, quam illa magnitudine sua. Propter hoc etiam, quia multitudine involvebantur difficilior erat eorum curatio. Amplius. Facilior erat eorum commissio propter oportunitates, sicut facilior est ovis furatio quam auri aequivalentis, et hoc est quoniam et ovis facilius invenitur, et aurum arctius custoditur.'

[9] *De legibus*, 1, p. 25B: 'De bobus, et ovibus sanctificabant Domino aliqua, et offerebantur in sacrificiis ex necessitate, et propter hoc quasi partem habebat Dominus in gregibus, et armentis. De auro vero nihil sibi sanctificari praeceperat,

the question of utility. Herds and flocks were not only useful but in themselves actually necessary for food and clothing, whereas gold was superfluous and useless in this regard. The theft of herds and flocks was therefore justly to be punished by more severe measures.[10] Third, William invoked what was to be a familiar theme throughout the *De legibus*, God's desire to establish practices that were very different from those of the Egyptians. The Egyptians believed that oxen and sheep should be treated as if they were sacred animals and almost worthy of divine honour, and maintained them because of the gods whom they worshipped, namely Seraphis and Ammon, who first appeared in the form of an ox and a ram respectively. God therefore wanted to show that these animals should be used very differently. He also despised the gold and all the superfluous riches of the Egyptians, and he reviled their avarice and cupidity through his laws.[11]

William then sought to explain why the laws seemed to value some animals more highly than others. Why was it that in Exodus 22:1 five oxen had to be given in restitution for the theft of a single ox, whereas only four sheep had to be given for the theft of a single sheep? Some believed the cause to be that a sheep had four uses, divided into two pairs: hide and flesh, offspring and fruit (meaning milk, cheese and butter), whereas the ox had these four uses plus an additional fifth, namely labour, either agricultural work or the transport of loads. Someone who stole an ox had therefore to answer for five losses, whereas for the thief of a sheep it was only four. William, however,

praeterquam in constitutione tabernaculi, et aedificatione templi, et fabricatione vasorum ipsorum. Quid ergo mirum si districtius ea custodiri voluit, et direptionem eorum ac furationem severius vindicari, de quibus ei pars de necessitate debebatur, quam ea de quibus nihil ei debebatur, sed voluntarie tantum offerebantur?'

[10] *De legibus*, 1, p. 25B: 'Armenta, et greges non solum utilia, sed etiam necessaria erant victui, et habitui, sive vestitui humano per semetipsa, aurum vero ad hoc superfluum est atque inutile. Merito ergo magis custodienda fuerunt, furtaque, et rapinae eorum severiori animadversione punienda.'

[11] *De legibus*, 1, p. 25B: 'Bobus, et ovibus tanquam sanctis animalibus, et poene divino honore dignis parcendum credebant Aegyptii, inter quos nutriti fuerant, propter Deos quos colebant, videlicet Seraphim, et Ammonem, quorum primus apparebat in specie bovis, alter in specie arietis [...]. Quia igitur nutriti erant in terra Aegypti, et inter Aegyptios, ostendit eis dominus non esse abominanda hujusmodi animalia juxta consuetudinem Aegyptiorum, et usum eorum necessarium ac multipliciter utilem. Aurum autem in parte ista, et omnes divitias superfluas non parum vilificavit, avaritiam etiam, et cupiditatem hoc facto suggilavit.'

considered it unlikely that God took account of the number of uses in drawing up his precept. Since another essential use for oxen was discovered in the promised land, namely the threshing of grain, God would have commanded that six oxen be given in restitution for the theft of a single ox if he had cared about the number of uses. It might be said that God did not regard the threshing of grain as distinct from agricultural labour, and since threshing was linked to agriculture, this was not unlikely. William considered it more probable, however, that here God took account of greater temerity rather than greater loss: there was greater temerity and improbity in the theft of an ox than in the theft of a sheep, so the former was to be punished more severely.[12] William noted, however, that these penalties were not inflicted unless the animals were eaten or otherwise consumed by the thieves. As Exodus 22:4 indicated, if the animals were found alive, the thieves were only obliged to restore double. This was because the consumption and eating of someone else's property were either new sins, that is to say new thefts, or at least great aggravations of the theft, and thus added penalties were deserved.[13] William went on to explain the

---

[12] *De legibus*, 1, p. 25B: 'Quod autem quinque boves pro furto unius, et quatuor tantum oves pro una restitui praecepit? Exod. 22. Illa creditur esse causa videlicet, quia quatuor commoda, sive utilitates habet ovis duas, scilicet pelles, et carnes, at alias duas, scilicet fructus, et foetus. Fructum autem intelligimus lac, caseum, et butirum. Has vero quatuor utilitates habet bos, et insuper quintam, videlicet laboris, sive agricolationis, sive evectionis onerum. Quia igitur quinque damna irrogat qui bovem furatur, quatuor vero tantum qui ovem, merito quinque boves pro uno restitui, et quatuor tantum oves pro una reddi praecepit dominus, verisimilius autem videtur non hoc attendisse dominum, quod diximus de numero utilitatem in hoc praecepto. Quoniam et invenitur alia utilitas bo[v]um in terra promissionis valde necessaria, videlicet tritura segetum, et ita sex boves pro uno restitui praecepisset, si huiusmodi utilitatum numerum attendisset. Si quis tamen dicat, quia utilitatem triturae segetum non reputavit aliam dominus ab utilitate agriculturae. Quoniam annexa est tritura agricolationi non improbabiliter dicet. Probabilius tamen videtur dominum in ista constitutione respectum habuisse ad majoritatem audaciae atque damni. Majoris enim audaciae, et improbitatis est bovem furari, quam ovem; ideo severius puniendum.'

[13] *De legibus*, 1, pp. 25B–26A: 'Debes autem scire, quia istae poenae non infligebantur, nisi cum animalia haec ab ipsis furatoribus vel comesta, vel aliter consumpta erant. Si enim inveniebantur apud eos viva, non nisi duplum restituere cogebantur, sicut legitur in praememorato capitulo, et hoc est, quoniam et consumptio et comestio res alienae, aut nova peccata erant, videlicet nova furta, cum essent novae contractiones rei alienae invito domino, aut saltem magnae aggravationes furtorum, et ideo merito ex superadditione addebatur, et poena.'

requirement to restore double when stolen goods were recovered undamaged, but this discussion did not bear upon animals in particular. He concluded with the general point that the overall aim was the avoidance of quarrels and homicides which easily arose in these circumstances.[14] In these early sections William treated animals as useful property for humans.

Having discussed the uses served by the laws given to Moses, William considered the nature of judicial discipline, and in calling for the utmost severity he compared humans and animals. Heresy had grown in his time and everything possible had to be done to destroy it. Those who held that children should not be corrected, at least with light flogging, abandoned them to all sins and insanities, and took less care of them than of dogs, asses and horses since such discipline was administered to animals of this kind. They sought the improvement of other animals through discipline, but neglected the punishment of their sons, thus abandoning them to deteriorate in every way.[15] Furthermore, humans were animals, and they were not spared discipline because they were animals, since on this basis no animals would be disciplined. The argument therefore had to be that humans should not receive discipline simply because they were humans. Humans were therefore neglected and valued less than other animals in this regard. It was manifest, however, that humans were 'incomparably more noble and more precious than other animals', and should therefore receive more instruction, and more care with every sort of protection and discipline.[16] William thus clearly stated his view of the relative

[14] *De legibus*, 1, p. 26A: 'Et hoc est, ut rixae, et homocidia, quae occasione hujusmodi factorum evenire facile poterant, declinarentur.'

[15] *De legibus*, 1, p. 26A: 'Et quia de fundo putei abyssi, hoc est de profundo diabolicae adinventionis exivit nostris temporibus haereticae garrulitatis ranunculus, audens coaxare contra Dei justitiam et legem. Quod nullo modo, nisi ex causa licet corporaliter occidere hominem, postquam in hoc devenimus, videlicet ut de lege talionis loqueremur, destruamus hunc errorem destructione qua possibile est, et convenit. Quaerimus igitur ab hujusmodi erroneis, utrum erudiendi sunt parvuli, et corrigendi, saltem quantumcunque levibus flagellis. Qui si responderint, quod non. Restat ergo ut dimittantur omnibus vitiis, et insaniis. Et propter hoc, ut minus curentur, quam canes, et asini, et equi, et minus etiam curandi sint, cum disciplina hujusmodi animalibus adhibenda sit, et non filiis, et melioratio per disciplinam quaerenda sit aliis animalibus, filii autem poenitus negligendi, et in omnem deteriorationem, et pessimationem abire dimittendi.'

[16] *De legibus*, 1, p. 26A: 'Cum homines etiam animalia sunt, non ideo quia animalia sunt, extra disciplinam erunt, quoniam ex hac causa nulli animalium

standing of humans and other animals, and it involved a hard boundary, with humans fundamentally superior.

William continued to argue in favour of disciplining humans, using
animals to make his case. Who doubted that the physical death of
humans, both children and adults, should be prevented, even if they
were unwilling to be saved, and that they should be dragged out of
water and fire, even if they threw themselves in? People made great
efforts to save brute animals, hauling them out of wells and pits, so
obviously even more vigorous actions should be taken to save humans
from physical death. When it came to the spiritual death of humans,
moreover, still more vigorous action had to be taken. To avoid physical death, humans should be removed and turned away from dangers,
even when they were unwilling and however much they resisted. To
avoid spiritual death, they should be incomparably more firmly
removed and turned away from spiritual dangers. It was therefore
obvious that humans should not only be removed from vices and sins,
but even kept away and thrust back from wicked crimes with zeal and
force.[17] William continued to labour his point. If your ass fell into
mud, surely it should be driven out with whips and goads? Surely it
should be dragged out with ropes if it refused to come out otherwise
and however much it resisted? How much more vigorously therefore
should a human be dragged from the lake of misery, from the mire of

esse impendenda disciplina, ergo propter hanc causam non erit eis impendenda
disciplina, videlicet quia homines sunt. Erunt igitur negligendi, et viliores
quantum ad hoc caeteris animalibus habendi, quo homines sunt. Manifestum
autem est ex hoc quia homines incomparabiliter nobiliores ac pretiosiores sunt
caeteris animalibus, magis igitur erudiendi, magis omni custodia, omni disciplina
curandi.'

[17] *De legibus*, 1, p. 26A–B: 'Quis dubitat, quin morti corporali hominum, tam
parvulorum, quam adultorum occurrendum sit, etiam eis invitis, et quin
extrahendi sint de aqua, et igne, ea videlicet violentia quam requirunt ista
pericula, et etiam ne in ea se praecipitent, aut aliter cadant avertendi? Si enim
morti corporali brutorum animalium tantopere succurritur. Si tanta sollicitudine
extrahuntur de puteis, aut foveis, aut praenominatis periculis, ut occurratur
morti eorum corporali. Quanto fortius ista facienda sunt, ut occurratur morti
hominum corporali? Multo fortius igitur ista adhibenda sunt, ut occurratur
morti eorundem spirituali? Inviti, et quantumlibet renitentes extrahendi sunt
de hujusmodi periculis, et avertendi ab eis homines propter mortem
corporalem, quare multo fortius incomparabiliter extrahendi sunt de periculis
spiritualibus, et avertendi ab eis propter mortem spiritualem. [...] Quare
manifestum est non solum extrahendos esse homines a vitiis, et peccatis, sed
etiam arcendos, atque repellendos cum studio atque vi a nephariis sceleribus.'

dregs, from deep slime with all zeal and force.[18] William concluded
that discipline must indeed be administered to humans, and he continued to justify the use of force and violence in the process.[19] The
validity of his argument depended on tacit acceptance of the lesser
worth of animals.

William resorted again to the use of animals in his arguments when
he justified the killing of heretics specifically. The comparison was now
between heretics and particular kinds of animal. If corporeal beasts,
namely wolves, lions, serpents and dragons, were to be exterminated
by sword and fire and every kind of warfare to save human bodies
which they ate and killed, how much more vigorously were 'spiritual
beasts' to be exterminated with every sword and by war to save souls
which they spiritually devoured and killed by seducing and subverting
them, separating them from God who was the life of souls? William
stressed that the comparison between material and spiritual beasts was
'most fitting' and appropriate in view of the savage power of heretics
and the poisonousness of pseudo preachers.[20] Furthermore, the

---

[18] *De legibus*, 1, p. 26B: 'Si asinus tuus in lutum cecidit, nunquid non flagellis, et
stimulis urgendus est, ut inde exiliat? Nunquid non funibus si aliter inde exire
noluerit quantumcunque renitatur, erit inde extrahendus? Quanto fortius igitur
homo de lacu miseriae, et de luto faecis, de limo profundi, cui non est substantia,
erit totis studiis, ac viribus extrahendus?'

[19] *De legibus*, 1, pp. 26B–27A. On William here arguing for 'the legitimacy of
capital punishment for heretics' and defining 'as heretical the very denial of the
legitimacy of such executions', see Sean Murphy, 'Pagans past and present:
righteousness and idolatry in academic discussions of ancient religion c.1130–
c.1230,' in Susanne Knaeble and Silvan Wagner (eds.), *Gott und die Heiden:
Mittelalterliche Funktionen und Semantiken der Heiden* (Berlin, 2015),
pp. 147–67 at 167. On William's hostility to the Cathars, see Alan
E. Bernstein, 'William of Auvergne and the Cathars', in Franco Morenzonni
and Jean-Yves Tilliette (eds.), *Autour de Guillaume d'Auvergne* (Turnhout,
2005), pp. 271–89; at 274 Bernstein suggests that 'his major work, the *De
universo*, may be considered an encylopedic refutation of Catharism, because
the purpose of this huge review of creation is to explain the right relationship of
the visible to the invisible world'.

[20] *De legibus*, 1, p. 28A: 'Si bestiae corporales, seu materiales, videlicet lupi, et
leones, serpentes, et dracones ferro, et igne, omnique genere debellationis
exterminandae sunt pro salute corporum humanorum, quae devorant, et
occidunt; quanto fortius bestiae spirituales pro salute animarum, quas
seducendo, et subvertendo spiritualiter devorant, et occidunt separantes eas a
Deo, qui vita est animarum, omni gladio, et bello exterminandae sunt. Et attende
comparationem bestiarum materialium, et spiritualium, quia convenientissima
est ac propria, si saevitiam potestatum haereticorum, si venenositatem pseudo
praedicatorum attenderis.'

incorrigible blasphemy of blasphemous preachers in the Church of God was like a contagious and diseased sheep in a flock, and like a cancerous limb in a body, the cancer being incurable and continually spreading. The word for spreading was *serpens*, creeping like a snake, so the animal imagery was maintained. William's point was that the same thing must be done with the blasphemous preachers to save the whole Church as had to be done with diseased sheep or a cancerous limb to save the whole flock or body; they had to be cut off or burned, removed by any means that was necessary.[21]

William continued to justify the extermination of heretics at length, invoking animals again at the end of the chapter. He was especially exasperated by those who wished to spare heretics in the hope that they might be corrected and become good Christians again. His view was that the conversion of heretics was difficult and rarely seen, whereas they very easily and often subverted the faithful. It was to convey the improbability of heretics' changing that William turned to animals. To argue that heretics should be spared in the hope of their conversion was like saying that a few wolves in the middle of a flock which they incessantly tore to pieces and devoured should be spared because perhaps God would make them sheep or lambs. It was as if to say that a few burning torches in the middle of a budding wood that they constantly set on fire should be ignored because perhaps God would turn them into fruiting trees. It was also as if to say that a few lepers in the middle of a healthy people which they infected unremittingly should be left alone because perhaps God would save them. Those who argued like this did not realise that it was easier for a wolf's rage to consume a flock than for the gentleness of a sheep to transfer to wolves, that fire spread more easily from torches to trees than fertility from trees to torches, and that the contagion of leprosy passed more easily from lepers to the healthy than health from the healthy to lepers.[22] In these passages, William characterised certain animals as

---

21 *De legibus*, 1, p. 28A: 'Quia blasphemus incorrigibilis blasphemiarum praedicator sic est in ecclesia Dei, sicut ovis contagiosa et morbida in grege, et sicut membrum cancerosum in corpore, cancerosum dico cancro incurabili, et jugiter serpente, ergo idem faciendum est de eo pro salute totius ecclesiae, quod faciendum esset de ove, et membro hujusmodi, pro totius gregis, et corporis salute. Quare resecandi, aut urendi, aut exurendi, modisque omnibus ex necessitate de modio tollendi.'

22 *De legibus*, 1, p. 29A: 'Hoc enim est ac si diceretur, ut paucis lupis in medio gregis existentibus, gregemque incessanter lacerantibus, ac devorantibus

hostile to humans, and then deployed them in metaphor and simile to denigrate heretics and justify their vigorous persecution.

At the beginning of the second chapter, William again stated that everything in the law had a rational cause; nothing was absurd or irrational. He did not propose to labour the point, but rather to consider the causes and reasons that lay behind the various precepts and prohibitions, taken literally, beginning with those pertaining to sacrifice and the altar, and then those relating to circumcision.[23] To this end, William thought it was worth asking why God wanted sacrifices to be offered to him, and more specifically why the death of innocent animals pleased him. After all, in itself the smell of a corpse had nothing of sweetness. The killing of the animals offered no utility, just their distress, terror and pollution. Moreover, what justice was there when only humans sinned and for their sins only utterly innocent animals died? How, for example, did an ox deserve this fate, an animal without deceit or anger?[24] William's questions thus depended on a characterisation of animals as innocents, incapable of sin, unlike the humans who slaughtered them.

---

parcatur, quia forte Deus facit illos oves, et agnes. Idem etiam est, ac si diceretur dimittendas esse paucas faces ardentes in medio silvae lignorum germinantium, ipsamque silvam incessanter exurentium, quia forsitan Deus faciet illas arbores fructiferas. Idem quoque est, ac si diceret quis paucos leprosos dimittendos esse in medio sani populi, assiduo contagio ipsum corrumpentes, et inficientes, quia forsitan Deus salvabit illos. Non attendunt, quod facilius saeviat rabies lupina in consumptionem gregis, quam mansuetudo ovina transeat in lupos, et incendium a facibus ad arbores facilius diffiliat, quam viror, et fertilitas ab arboribus ad faces, sic leprae contagium facilius a leprosis derivatur ad sanos, quam ab ipsis sanitas ad leprosos.'

[23] *De legibus*, 2, p. 29A: 'Revertamur autem ad id in quo eramus, et dicamus, quia postquam iam claruit nihil esse in tota lege, quod non habeat causam rationabilem, sive praeceptionis, vel prohibitionis, aut enarrationis. Manifestum nihil est absurdum, nihil irrationale in ea, et hoc in multis evidenter apparet, cum manifestae, vel honestatem contineant, vel utilitatem. Et propter hoc non oportet nos aliquatenus laborare. Incipiamus igitur in aliis, causas, et rationes praeceptionum, et prohibitionum, juxta literam aperire. Primum ergo de sacrificiis, et altari. Deinde de circoncisione.'

[24] *De legibus*, 2, p. 29A–B: 'Merito autem quaestionem habet, quare sacrificia sibi offerri voluit Deus, qua de causa placuit ei mors animalium innocentium. Nihil enim suavitatis habet per se nidor cadaverum. Nihil utilitatis carnificina illa animalium, sed solum laborem, horrorem, et inquinationem offerentium. Praeterea, quae justitia est haec, ut cum homines soli peccent, pro peccatis eorum sola animalia, et illa innocentissima moriantur? Juxta illud. Quid meruere boves, animal sine fraude doloque?'

William offered seven reasons why God wanted this kind of sacrifice both before and under the law.[25] The first and principal cause was giving honour and veneration to God, for all worship gave honour to God. What mattered was not the value of the offerings, but that God chose, instituted and accepted them, and also the obedience and devotion of those who made them. God had no wish to be worshipped by the inventions of humans, preferring rites of his own choosing because he always knew best what was pleasing to him.[26] The second cause was the powerful and strong impression of God's justice and mercy which this kind of sacrifice created. People were made aware that, for their sins, God could justly impose death upon them, and that their death was being exchanged for the death of animals. Their recognition of this and their awareness of God's severity and mercy were much more powerfully impressed upon them by the killing of animals than by words. Nothing was more salutary for humans than a vivid and steadfast memory that made them flee evil deeds in fear and pursue good things pleasing to God in hope.[27] The third cause was the recognition of divine beneficence. It was because of this that people kept part of what God had given them and offered part to God in acknowledgement that they received it all through God's blessing and

[25] For a summary, see Smith, 'William of Auvergne and the law of the Jews and the Muslims,' pp. 131–3.

[26] *De legibus*, 2, p. 29B: 'Prima igitur ac praecipua causa fuit Dei honorificentia, seu veneratio. Omnis enim cultus Deo honorificus est, quo ipse sibi serviri vult. [...] talibus ergo muneribus honorabatur Deus, non quidem pretiositate ipsorum, sed electione, institutione, et acceptione ipsorum a parte sua. Obedientia vero, et devotione offerentium a parte ipsorum. [...] Non enim coli voluit, neque colendus erat adinventionibus humanis, sed magis ritu electionis, et institutionis suae, ipse enim melius semper novit, quod et aequale ei servitium magis placet.'

[27] *De legibus*, 2, p. 29B: 'Secunda causa fuit justitiae suae, et misericordiae vehemens ac fortis impressio quam sacrificia hujusmodi faciebant, eo enim ipso, quod ad mortem hujusmodi animalia offerebant, mortique tradebant se ipsos morte dignos ostendebant, et Deum de justitia morte eis posse inferre, si secundum merita peccatorum suorum judicare vellet, expresse hujusmodi opere cognoscebant. In hoc vero quod mors eorum morte animalium commutabatur, mors inquam, quam meruerant Dei misericordiam erga se expresse legere poterant, vel etiam legebant, et erat fortior atque magis penetrans, magisque imprimens cognitionem, ac rememorationem severitatis, ac miserationis divinae hujusmodi operatio, quam posset esse sermo. Nihil autem salubrius fore poterat hominibus, quam vivax, et renax memoria, sive cognitio divinae severitatis et pietatis, ut timore, scilicet mala fugerent, et spe bona Deo placita sectarentur.'

largess.[28] The fourth cause was the sanctification of those who made the offering. By God's power and mercy, they were cleansed of contamination by sin.[29] The fifth cause was intimacy with and closeness to God. The offering of gifts and participation at the sacred table had this effect, drawing people into the family of God. William elaborated on the theme of eating together and family. The sacrifice of animals turned participants into the table companions of God, while eating together was the highest form of fellowship. God himself sent fire from heaven to consume his share of the sacrifices.[30] Pursuing this theme, the sixth cause was the union of the people of God. Just as the sharing of food literally produced one family or household, so the sharing of spiritual food and drink generated one spiritual family or household.[31] The seventh cause was attraction to the worship of God because nothing brought people together and made them gather in a particular place more than food and drink. The most wise and merciful God therefore wanted food and drink to be shared in his house so that the community of his people would be drawn there and bound more tightly. God also wished the food and drink to be sanctified so that the people took them not as their own goods but as gifts from God, not as common possessions but as something sacred, so that they

[28] *De legibus*, 2, p. 29B: 'Tertia causa, divinae beneficentiae recognitio, propter quod de ipsis donis ac datis suis, partem reservabant, et offerebant domino in recognitionem, quod de ejus benedictione, et largitione omnia receperant.'

[29] *De legibus*, 2, p. 30A: 'Quarta causa offerentium sanctificatio. Expediebantur enim, et emundabantur a contaminationibus peccatorum per hujusmodi sacrificia faciente Dei virtute, et misericordia.'

[30] *De legibus*, 2, p. 30A: 'Quinta causa familiaritas ad Deum, et appropinquatio, oblatio namque munerum, et participatio sacrae mensae, multam fiduciam praestant appropinquationis, et de familia Dei efficit participantes, ejus enim censetur esse familia a quo pascitur, et de cujus mensa vivit. Quare manifestum est hujusmodi sacrificia participantibus imprimere familiaritatem, et proximitatem ad Deum, dum eos Dei commensales quodammodo efficiebant. Commensalitas autem tanquam summa communio post commutationem causarum essendi, quae sunt pater et mater maxime effective est familiaritatis. Propter quod cum Deus non posset eis viceversa comedendo communicare, mittebat interdum ignem de coelo qui partem suam sacrificiorum comederet quasi vice ipsius.'

[31] *De legibus*, 2, p. 30A: 'Sexta causa, adunatio, sive unio populi Dei videlicet, ut una domus fieret, et una familia ex multis personis, unam enim familiam, et unam domum literalem maxime facit communio victualium. Sic et unam familiam spiritualem unamque domum maxime facit communio ciborum, et potuum spiritualium.'

should recognise God as their paterfamilias by whom they were fed and given life.[32] William evidently perceived animals as tools used by God to shape human behaviour.

William then considered why God chose to be offered oxen, sheep and goats of both sexes. He explained that this was because they were most necessary for human food and clothing, and because they were abundant. God therefore most wished to share with humans those things that they used most, and God wanted more recognition, gratitude and honour to be shown with regard to those things in which divine beneficence towards them was greater.[33] William then demonstrated a very practical turn of mind. It was also obvious, he explained, that amongst all quadrupeds, these were the tamest and they accepted death with the least resistance, so there was the least danger of their killing anyone. Moreover, people were used to slaughtering these kinds of animals because they were always eating them, especially after the flood.[34] Furthermore, amongst quadrupeds, these were the cleanest; they lived with the cleanest pasture, and even their impurities were clean.[35] Moreover, not only did these animals provide humans with necessities, with food and clothing, they were the only animals without which humans could not live. Humans could live without other animals such as pigs and dogs; they were superfluous with regard to

[32] *De legibus*, 2, p. 30A: 'Septima causa fuit attractio ad Dei cultum, nihil enim magis aggregat homines, et convenire facit ad locum aliquem, vel factum, quam cibus, et potus [...]. Voluit ergo sapientissimus et misericordissimus Deus, ut in domo sua et altari esset communicatio cibi, et potus, ut communitas populi sui per hoc et illuc attraheretur, et ibidem astrictius teneretur, voluitque hujusmodi sibi sanctificata esse, ut populus non tanquam bona propria, sed tanquam Dei dona, nec tanquam communia, sed tanquam sacra illa sumeret, ut Deum patremfamilias suum, a quo pasceretur, et animaretur agnosceret.'

[33] *De legibus*, 2, p. 30A: 'Si quis autem quaerat quare ista tria animalium genera sibi offerri elegit de quadrupedibus videlicet, bovem, ovem, et capram in utroque sexu. Respondemus, quia haec sunt maxime necessaria victui humano, et vestitui, maxime, quia apud patres abundabant, in his ergo quibus ipsi maxime utebantur, maxime voluit communionem, et participium habere cum eis, et de his in quibus largior erat beneficentia ejus erga eos, voluit sibi majorem recognitionem, regratiationem et honorificentiam exhiberi.'

[34] *De legibus*, 2, p. 30A–B: 'Manifestum etiam est, quia inter omnia quadrupedia, ista mansuetissima sunt, et minori rebellione sustinent mortem, et ideo minori periculo occidentium. Praeterea assueti erant interfectioni hujusmodi animalium, utpote qui eis incessanter vescebantur, maxime post diluvium.'

[35] *De legibus*, 2, p. 30B: 'De quadrupedibus ista mundissima sunt, quia et mundissimis vivunt pastibus, et eorum immundiciae etiam mundae sunt.'

the necessities of life. God wanted to be offered and honoured with animals that were necessary and not those that were unnecessary.[36]

This left William with more explaining to do because later God added the turtle-dove and the pigeon to Abraham's sacrifices in Genesis 15. Why? In part it was obvious that God wanted his share of clean, tame and useful creatures that could fly as well as those that could walk. Moreover, as well as being clean, tame and useful to humans, a quasi-conjugal chastity was found in pigeons and something like the chastity of a widow in the turtle-dove. Moving beyond the literal description of their qualities, William explained that God thus made one think that if he required behaviour of this kind in brute animals which he chose to be sacrificed to him, how much more strongly must he require it of humans. And if God rejected vices contrary to this behaviour in brute animals, in which there was nothing reprehensible, culpable or punishable, so that he would not have them in his chosen part, how much more strongly must he detest and condemn these vices in humans, who could be culpable and deservedly punished, so that those who were contaminated and disfigured were not admitted into God's part?[37] William then noted that the sparrow was added to the sacrifices. This was easily explained because the sparrow nested in holes in houses and flew in flocks, and was therefore

---

[36] *De legibus*, 2, p. 30B: 'Ista sunt, quae totum quod sunt, et vivunt, necessitati hominum sunt et vivunt, hoc est victui, atque vestitui, sola enim sunt sine quibus homines vivere non possunt; sine animalibus enim aliis possunt vivere homines, quemadmodum sine porco, cane, et quo. Si igitur vitae humanae necessitas respiciatur, sola ista de animalibus necessaria sunt hominibus. Caetero vero superflua quantum ad necessitatem vitae. Quare eo ipso, quod voluit talia sibi offerri in sacrificiis, abstulit nobis occasionem quaerendi non neces[s]aria, dum eis honorari noluit, neque ea sibi offeri.'

[37] *De legibus*, 2, p. 30B: 'Postmodum vero addidit turturem, et columbam in sacrificiis Abrahae, sicut legitur Genes. XV, in quibus praeter hoc, quod munda et mansueta, et utilia usibus humanis sunt, etiam castitas quasi conjugalis in columbis, et quasi vidualis in turturibus invenitur. Manifestum igitur est, quia partem suam gressibilium et volatilium mundam, mansuetam, et utilem voluit esse dominus Deus, exceptis aliis, quae diximus. Inquo etiam iuxta literam quales sint, qui in partem eius atque sortem transeunt, intelligentibus insinuavit, si enim huiusmodi mores requirit in animalibus brutis, quae in partem suam elegit, quanto fortius in hominibus? Et si moribus istis vitia contraria eo usque repellit in brutis animalibus, ubi reprehensibilia non sunt, nec culpabilia, nec punibilia, ut in parte electionis suae ea esse non sustineat, quanto fortius in hominibus ubi culpanda sunt, et poena dignissima vindicandi, ea detestatur, et reprobat, ut eis qui contaminati, ac deturpati sunt, in partem Dei nullatenus admittantur.'

very similar to the pigeon in habitation and feeding.[38] William ended
his discussion by explaining that God chose so few types of animals for
sacrifice because the killing of all kinds was linked to idolatry, auguries
and magic, as was apparent in the multitude of sacrifices performed by
the Egyptians, although idolatry had not given rise to sacrifice because
there were sacrifices before there was idolatry.[39] He then added just
one more reason for sacrifices: the sustenance of priests who had to be
free from worry about acquiring food so that they could conduct
worship and teach the people.[40] William thus emphasised again that
animals were useful, and some even necessary, for humans. Moreover,
whereas he had characterised some animals as hostile to humans,
others were now presented as modelling human virtues. By accepting
these animals in sacrifice and not those which, though incapable of sin,
behaved in ways that were sinful in humans, God used animals as
symbols from which humans were to learn.

In the third chapter, William discussed circumcision, observing that,
on the face of it, circumcision served no purpose except the good of
obedience. He explained, however, that it had other literal causes and
benefits, and one of his arguments involved animals.[41] Having referred
to the sins of the peoples who previously inhabited the lands that God
was giving to the people of Israel, William explained that circumcision
was an insult to the sacred rites of Venus and Priapus in which the
penis and sexual activity were not a little honoured and cultivated.
Moreover, the penis was the part of the flesh that most fought against
the spirit, as was still very much the case. It hugely contaminated the

---

[38] *De legibus*, 2, p. 30B: 'Passer autem superadditus est in lege [...], de quo
manifestum est, quod multum similis est columbis, habitatione scilicet et pastu,
nidificant enim in foraminibus domorum, et gregatim volant, ut columbae.'

[39] *De legibus*, 2, p. 30B: 'Haec sibi tam pauci de tot generibus animalium elegit
dominus, et sibi appropriavit, quasi reliquias, quia omnia genera, ut idolatrae
sacrificiis suis execrabilia fecerant, aut augures vanitate observationum suarum
profanaverant, aut magi veneficiis suis, et maleficiis odibilia reddiderant, sicut
apparet ex multitudine sacrificiorum Aegyptiorum [...]. Clarum etiam est ex his,
quod idolatria non dedit occasionem sacrificiis, cum ante idolatriam sacrificia
fuerint.'

[40] *De legibus*, 2, p. 30B: 'praeter has autem causas sacrificiorum quas diximus,
nonnulla fuisse videtur alimonia, seu sustentatio sacerdotum: hoc est virorum
divino cultui, et eruditioni populi vacantium, quibus duobus officiis, ut libere
vacarent, liberos eos esse oportuit a sollicitudine acquirendi victus'.

[41] For a summary of William's arguments and a different reading of the argument
referring to animals, see Smith, 'William of Auvergne and the law of the Jews
and the Muslims', p. 132.

peoples of those lands so that they rushed into all shameful acts, not only with other men, but also with brute animals. William then quoted Leviticus 18:27: 'For all these detestable things the inhabitants of the land have done, that were before you, and have defiled it.' William was evidently expressing hostility to same-sex and bestial intercourse because in Leviticus this quotation comes after a list of forbidden sins, the last two of which are sex between men and sex with animals: 18:22, 'Thou shalt not lie with mankind as with womankind: because it is an abomination'; 18:23, 'Thou shalt not copulate with any beast: neither shalt thou be defiled with it. A woman shall not lie down to a beast, nor copulate with it: because it is a heinous crime.' William further commented that these shameful practices fed the idolatry of the peoples who inhabited the promised land before the arrival of the sons of Israel.[42] Unsurprisingly, William did not think that humans should have sex with animals; there was a boundary that should properly be maintained.

The issue of sex came up again in Chapter 12 when William sought to explain the prohibition of sex between different types of animal, offering eight reasons. The first was so that the order of nature was commended to the people of God as natural law.[43] The second, so that every sodomitical disgrace was shunned.[44] The third, so that the people of God should be unlike the most impure peoples who were ejected from the promised land before them.[45] The fourth, so that a modesty and suppression of concupiscence more pleasing to God would be shown, in that he wished the limits and rule of nature to be

---

[42] *De legibus*, 3, p. 33A: 'Quarta [causa] in suggillationem sacrorum veneris, et priapi, in quibus pars illa tanquam pars, et occupatio veneris in corpore humano, non parum ornabatur, et colebatur. Haec autem est pars carnis, quae maxime pugnabat contra spiritum sicut et maxime adhuc. Maximeque contaminaverat populos terrarum illarum, ita ut in omnia flagitia non solum masculorum, sed etiam brutorum animalium proruebant, sicut legitur Levitici [1]8: "Omnes execrationes illas fecerunt accolae terrae, qui fuerunt ante vos et polluerunt eam". [...] Haec etiam plaga effrenatae ac flagitiosae libidinis, gentes illas septem execrabiles quae terram promissionis ante adventum filiorum Israel inhabitaverant, in idolatria nutriebat, ac postissimum detinebat.'

[43] *De legibus*, 12, p. 43B: 'Prima ergo causa fuit, ut ordo ipse naturae commendaretur populo Dei, tanquam jus naturale, ejusdemque statutum.'

[44] *De legibus*, 12, p. 43B: 'Secunda causa, ut flagitium omne sodomiticum declinaretur.'

[45] *De legibus*, 12, p. 43B: 'Tertia causa, ut spurcissimis illis gentibus, quae ante Dei populum ex terra promissionis ejiciendae erant, dissimularetur.'

regulated even in brute animals.[46] The fifth, to 'repress the nefarious actions and magical evils which are procured with the offspring generated by such mixtures'. William noted that it was possible to read about such deeds in the book of Neumich which was entirely about this kind of mixing and was called the *Laws of Plato* because it was against the laws of nature.[47] Sixth, it was an insult to the cult and idolatry of Venus and Priapus whose adherents used such mixing to further their idolatry.[48] Seventh, William noted the view that the prohibition existed lest humans should be contaminated by making these acts happen. Animals of diverse species very rarely and scarcely desired each other unless a human did something to arouse this desire. William agreed that it was unworthy and indecent that a human should do anything to arouse this kind of desire and procure sexual intercourse.[49] Eighth, this kind of mixing could hardly occur except in the sight of one or more humans through whom it was procured. This kind of sight was dangerous, however, because it was provocative of desire and for similarly nefarious mixing.[50] William added that the

---

[46] *De legibus*, 12, p. 43B: 'Quarta causa, ut modestia, et pressio concupiscentiae ex hoc Deo acceptior esse ostenderetur, quod etiam in animalibus brutis ad limites, et normam naturae eam esse regulatam volebat.'

[47] *De legibus*, 12, p. 43B: 'Quinta, ut nefanda opera, et maleficia, quae de fecibus ex hujusmodi commixtione procreatis fiebant, declinarentur; et haec opera leguntur in libro qui dicitur, Neumich, sive Nevemich, et alio nomine vocant leges Platonis, qui liber totus est de hujusmodi commixtionibus, et vocatur leges Platonis, quia contra leges naturae est.' See Maaike van der Lugt, '"Abominable mixtures": the "Liber Vaccae" in the medieval west, or the dangers and attractions of natural magic', *Traditio* 64 (2009), pp. 229–77, esp. 231, 251–2, 256–9, 261–3, 268–9 (the translated passage is taken from 256); Sean Murphy, 'The corruption of the elements: the science of ritual impurity in the early thirteenth century', in Jack P. Cunningham and Mark Hocknull (eds.), *Robert Grosseteste and the Pursuit of Religious and Scientific Learning in the Middle Ages* (Cham, 2016), pp. 103–16.

[48] *De legibus*, 12, p. 43B: 'Sexta causa, suggillatio culturae, sive idolatriae veneris, et priapi, hujus enim commixtiones in ampliationem hujusmodi idolatriae faciebant homines perditionis.'

[49] *De legibus*, 12, p. 43B: 'Septima causa, ut ait quidam, erat, ne homines hujusmodi operibus contaminarentur, eis immiscendo se, animalia quippe diversarum specierum rarissime, et vix se invicem concupiscunt, nisi homo aliquid opere suo, vel operis adhibeat ad appetitum hujusmodi concitandum: hoc ergo indignum homine valdeque indecens ipsum judicavit iste, et non immerito videlicet, quod homo aliqua operatione sua appetitum hujusmodi concitaret, et commixtionem procuraret.'

[50] *De legibus*, 12, p. 43B: 'Octava causa, quia hujusmodi commixtio vix fieri potest, nisi in conspectu hominum, unius, aut plurium, per quem aut quos

same reasons explained the prohibition of different kinds of animals being joined together in work; he cited Deuteronomy 22:10: 'Thou shalt not plough with an ox and an ass together.' He added a further explanation, however. People joined different kinds of animals together in work according to the conjunctions of the planets and constellations, believing that their work would be successful as a result. God wanted to remove the vanity of this credulity from their hearts because it was the root of idolatry, lest they should abandon their creator and be drawn into servitude to the stars.[51] William's belief that God had imposed laws to distance his people from idolatry was again much in evidence, as was his view that God used animals as tools with symbolic functions to shape human behaviour. His concern that witnessing sex between different types of animals would arouse human desire to participate pointed again to the sexual boundary which had to be maintained between humans and animals. William also expressed a further concern about the use of animals in magic, about which he had more to say later on. All this supposed a hard boundary between humans and animals, except insofar as sinful transgression might arise from sexual desire.

William again associated animals with what he regarded as sinful when he embarked upon what he called 'the destruction of the absurdities and insanities of Muhammad'.[52] After presenting a historical account of Islam in Chapter 18, in Chapter 19 he focused on its notion of paradise.[53] William opened the chapter with the statement that he intended to destroy 'the radical errors by which Muhammad seduced

---

procuretur, ut diximus. Periculosos autem est conspectus hujusmodi, provocatorius enim est libidinis, similisque nefariae commixtionis.'

[51] *De legibus*, 12, pp. 43B–44A: 'et istae eaedem causae fuerunt prohibitionis conjunctionis hujusmodi animalium in aliquo opere, sicut et illa prohibitio: "Non arabis in bove et asino," quae legitur Deut. 22[:10]. Scito tamen, quia istas conjunctiones animalium diversorum generum, in operibus suis faciebant juxta conjunctiones planetarum, et quasdam alias constellationes, credentes ex hoc, opera prosperari, voluit ergo Deus removere vanitatem credulitatis ipsius a cordibus eorum, tanquam radicem idolatriae, ne per eam, creatore relicto, ad stellarum servitia traherentur.'

[52] *De legibus*, 18, p. 49B: 'accedemus juxta promissum ad destructionem deliramentorum, et insaniarum Macometi'.

[53] See Winston Black, 'William of Auvergne on the dangers of paradise: biblical exegesis between natural philosophy and anti-Islamic polemic,' *Traditio* 68 (2013), pp. 233–58 at 248–56; Smith, 'William of Auvergne and the law of the Jews and the Muslims,' pp. 138–40.

that *brutal* people', the adjective surely invoking the animal.[54] After briefly listing the carnal and impure pleasures that he said Muhammad had promised for paradise, he quoted Cicero, *Paradoxa Stoicorum*, 14, perhaps a little approximately: 'those seem to be the voices of cattle, not of humans'.[55] In Cicero's work, this referred to the view that 'pleasure is the highest good', and Cicero went on to mock an outlook that would entail complete lack of difference between humans and animals: 'Will you, to whom god (or nature, the mother of all things as I call her) has given a thing more excellent and divine than anything else, a soul, so abnegate and degrade yourself as to believe there is no difference between yourself and a four-footed animal?'[56] After invoking this authoritative account of a hard boundary between humans and animals, and having complained that nothing more than the goods of this life were on offer, William condemned a vision of a paradise that was so close to the present life, and so base, that even brute animals partook. Muhammad virtually equated paradise with the present life, which William regarded as much better, even though it was shameful, than a happiness in which Muhammad made humans almost equal with brute animals. Muhammad offered humans no other happiness than one which brute animals could share with them.[57] Throughout the chapter, William returned to this theme. In Muhammad's paradise, for example, humans 'would be animals speaking to animals, thinking neither of their true home nor of its joys'.[58] He concluded that

---

[54] *De legibus*, 19, p. 50B: 'Radicales autem errores quibus gentem illam brutalem seduxit, in hoc loco destruere intendimus.'

[55] *De legibus*, 19, p. 50B: 'ut ait Tullius, voces istae pecudum videntur esse, non hominum.' Cicero, *Paradoxa Stoicorum*, 14: 'Quae quidem mihi uox pecudum videtur esse non hominum'; Michele V. Ronnick, *Cicero's "Paradoxa Stoicorum": A Commentary, an Interpretation and a Study of its Influence*, Studien zur klassischen Philologie 62 (Frankfurt am Main, 1991), p. 109.

[56] Ronnick, *Cicero's 'Paradoxa Stoicorum'*, p. 138, and p. 109 for Latin text.

[57] *De legibus*, 19, p. 51A: 'Summa igitur est ratiocinationis nostrae in hoc, quod intentionem, et veritatem Paradisi, et foelicitatis non intellexit, qui tam propinquam vitae praesenti eam posuit, et tam vilem, ut in ea etiam bruta animalia communicent. In hoc ergo fere aequavit eam vitae praesenti, ut nos docebimus in sequentibus, quod longe melior est vita praesens, etiam flagitiosa, quam foelicitas illa, quae in hoc etiam homines brutis animalibus similiter pene coaequavit, dum non aliam foelicitatem hominibus posuit, quam cujus et bruta animalia possent esse consortia.'

[58] *De legibus*, 19, p. 52B: 'Unde animalis iste homo, animalibus loquens, nec patriam, nec foelicitatem patriae cogitavit'; as translated by Smith, 'William of Auvergne and the law of the Jews and the Muslims,' p. 139.

Muhammad's vision of paradise was not only impossible but ridiculous, and part of the problem was that it envisaged happiness appropriate to animals. Muhammad's paradise would be a place for pigs to roll around and its speech would be that of cattle, not humans.[59] William thus invoked a hard boundary between humans and animals to construct a boundary between Christians and a human 'other', and to condemn the beliefs of that other.

Although hostility to idolatry was a dominant theme throughout the *De legibus*, a number of chapters were devoted directly to it, and animals featured in a number of ways. One of William's first points was that those who transferred the honour due to God to quadrupeds and reptiles sinned more execrably than those who transferred it to humans; and those who transferred that honour to images of humans or animals sinned more execrably than those who transferred it to humans or animals. This showed the extent of the injuries done to God: not only had honour and glory been transferred to the smallest and most vile creatures, but even to images of them.[60] He went on to illustrate his point by condemning books of magic which attributed powers to images of animals. To images of flies sculpted under a certain constellation, they attributed the power of repelling flies from wherever they were located. Similarly, images of scorpions were held to drive away all scorpions from the city or region in which they were buried, and images of various animals were supposed to give powers to catch the actual animals.[61] William again took for granted that the status of animals was vastly inferior to that of humans.

---

[59] *De legibus*, 19, p. 54A: 'Declaratum igitur est tibi evidenter ex his, quia non solum impossibile est carnalem esse paradisum, et foelicitatem sensibilium delitiarum, sed etiam ridiculosum. Et quia somniata ista foelicitas non est nisi brutorum animalium, nec esse potest. [...] Manifestum est etiam, quia paradisus iste non est nisi sicut volutator porcorum, et quia vociferatio ipsius vox pecudum est, non hominum.'

[60] *De legibus*, 23, p. 65B: 'Execrabilius enim peccaverunt, qui honorem istum in quadrupedes, aut reptilia transtulerunt, quam qui in homines; et qui in imagines hominum, aut animalium, quam qui in homines, aut animalia. [...] Vides igitur ad quantas Dei injurias, et contumelias deducti sunt insipientissimi homines, ut non solum in minimas vilissimasque creaturas honorem et gloriam creatoris transtulerint, sed etiam in imagines earum.'

[61] *De legibus*, 23, p. 67A: 'et hoc expresse legitur in libris eorum quos de praestigiis, et imaginibus, aliisque sacrilegis maleficiis scripserunt. Quidam enim imaginibus posuerunt virtutem praestandi honores, seu dominationes, atque praelationes, aut artes, aut eloquentiam; et imagini muscae sub certa constellatione sculptae, attribuerunt virtutem fugandi muscas ab omni loco in

When William attacked the idolatry of demons in particular, animals were again an important part of the discussion. The idolatry of demons, William explained, was based on human ignorance and misunderstanding. In general, it depended on the erroneous belief that demons had power not only over humans and human things, but over the elements.[62] With regard to natural magic, humans wondered at what demons could do and even saw them as omnipotent because they did not appreciate that demons simply used powers of nature.[63] As examples, William cited the spontaneous generation of frogs, lice, worms and other animals. This was an entirely natural process, but it was stimulated by the demons so that the work of generation was accelerated. To those who did not know what was happening, it seemed not to be a work of nature, which usually occurred more slowly, but rather that nature was subject to the command of demons.[64] Demons could even bring forth new and previously unseen types of animal by mixing seeds in new ways, as was clearly taught 'in Emuth', by which William meant the *Liber vaccae*.[65] The birth of lower forms of animal was thus potentially subject to demonic interference, and William envisaged animals as the tools of demons, as well as of God and humans.

Having explained the root and all the causes of idolatry, William moved on to discuss the impiety and madness of idolatry, intending to

quo ipsa esset. Similiter, et imagini scorpionis fugandi omnes scorpiones a civitate, vel regione in qua sepulta esset; eodem modo, et imaginibus quorundam animalium posuerunt virtutes congregandi ea.'

[62] *De legibus*, 24, p. 69A: 'Huic autem error ille causam dedit, quo credebant decepti homines daemones habere potestatem, non solum in homines, et res humanas, sed etiam in elementa.'

[63] *De legibus*, 24, p. 69B: 'Et de operibus hujusmodi est magia naturalis [...]. Haec igitur mirifica homines ignari scientiae istius, quae natura operabatur virtutibus sibi a creatore inditis, credebant daemones operari, et propter hoc non solum potentiam magnam, et mirificam eisdem attribuerunt; sed etiam omnipotentiam.'

[64] *De legibus*, 24, p. 69B: 'De hujusmodi autem operibus, est subita generatio ranarum, et pediculorum, et vermium, aliorumque animalium quorundam, in quibus omnibus sola natura operatur, verum adhibitis adjutoriis, quae ipsa semina naturae confortant, et acuunt adeo, ut opus generationis in tantum accelerant, ut ab eis qui hoc nesciunt, non opus naturae videatur, quae tardius talia consuevit efficere, sed potius vis naturae cujuspiam imperantis.'

[65] *De legibus*, 24, p. 70A: 'Non erit igitur dubitandum in novis seminum commixtionibus, et ipsorum adjutoriis, nova animalia, et necdum visa posse gigni, sicut aperte docetur in Emuth.' See van der Lugt, '"Abominable mixtures": the "Liber Vaccae" in the medieval west', pp. 261–2.

destroy it completely, leaving no shadow of a doubt.[66] In a long list of points, several included reference to animals and hinged on William's assumptions about them. If, for example, someone said that worshippers received benefits from their gods in return for small and large gifts, one had to ask whether the gods *needed* these gifts or not. If they needed them, William pointed out that anyone who needed the blood of moles, bats and cows was extremely weak. Kites and owls who took these kinds of animals freely everywhere and without any kind of exchange were more fortunate. Even more fortunate and powerful were wolves and lions who caught animals as they wished in order to eat their flesh and drink their blood. If, however, the gods did not need this kind of gift but demanded them in return for their favours, their goodness and favours clearly amounted to nothing. Venality was to be detested in humans, who were not permitted to require gifts which they needed in return for services, so it was even more wrong for those who did not need any gifts to demand them. William explained that anyone in need could seek help from someone who enjoyed abundance, and that person should simply give to the other, not in return for something, otherwise this person was selling the gift and descending into trade. The key point was that a gift only stemmed from true goodness if nothing were required in return, especially when the giver did not need anything in return. So, if gods were truly good, it was impossible that they should require, desire or even permit recompense from their worshippers. A good man ('vir') would blush and be horrified to have this stain on his glory, and would not allow something that should stem freely from goodness to be extracted or extorted as a sort of payment; otherwise, his deed would stem not entirely from goodness, but from empty, arid and foul cupidity.[67] Gods who took offerings

---

[66] *De legibus*, 24, p. 70A: 'Jam igitur declaravimus tibi radicem intimam idolatriae, et causas omnes [...]. Post haec igitur dicemus impietatem ipsius, atque vesaniam, et haec dictio erit destructio ipsius plana et evidens, et nullum habens penitus nubilum dubitationis.'

[67] *De legibus*, 24, p. 71A: 'Quod si dixerit, quia in hoc locum habet gratia, et beneficentia apud Deos, quia a cultoribus suis parva recipiunt, et magna eis tribuunt, quaerimus iterum, an indigeant muneribus nostris, an non indigeant. Quod si indigent, miserrimi sunt omnium, et in extremo inopes, qui sanguine talparum, et vespertilionum, atque vaccarum indigent; et feliciores eis sunt milvi, atque bubones, qui gratis, hoc est absque mercimonio aliquo, hujusmodi animalia ubique accipiunt: feliciores etiam, atque potentiores lupi, atque leones, qui pro desideriis suis animalia, quorum carnes esuriunt vel sanguinem sitiunt ut sua ubique capiunt: si vero non indigent hujusmodi muneribus,

were thus either venal if they did not need them or weaker than various animals if they did, an argument that derived its force from the assumption that animals were of low status.

Still discussing offerings made to the gods, William noted that it might be claimed that they were necessary to placate the gods who would otherwise be angry with mortals. William therefore queried the reasons for this anger. If the gods were angry for some reason other than the sins of the people, the gods were plainly unjust and therefore sinners; not only were they not gods, they were evil devils. If the gods were angry with mortals because of their sins, they should be appeased when the mortals abandoned their sins. If, however, mortals relinquishing their sins did not appease the gods, but rather inflamed their anger, unless the flesh and blood of animals were offered to them, it was manifest that this kind of anger was not the anger of gods but rather the anger of snakes, lions or other roaring beasts while they caught their prey. Moreover, they were not gods, but devils infested with natural malice towards humans, like snakes and other beasts. And if they were only to be feared because of rage and savagery, they ought to be treated as nothing other than serpents and lions, and thus not accepted as gods. Nothing therefore remained but to forsake, destroy and remove them like serpents and lions. Indeed, no animal was so furious and savage that it could not be placated or softened by taking away its food.[68] Once again, William's invective, relentlessly likening

apparet ex hoc nulla esse bonitas eorum, vel beneficia, quando munera hujusmodi pro beneficiis suis exigant. Si enim detestanda est venalitas in hominibus, ut nec liceat eis ex beneficiis exigere munera, de quibus indigent: quanto fortius non licebit exigere munera etiam quibus non indigent? Pro indigentia siquidem sua potest unusquisque petere ab eo qui abundant, ut ei tribuat aliquid, non pro beneficio, alioquin vendit beneficium, et deturpat illud in mercimonium. Summa igitur ratiocinationis haec est, quod veri nominis bonitas pro beneficio, quod ex illa est, non patitur unquam aliquid exigi; et maxime quando eo, hoc est munere, vel retributione non indigetur. Quare si vere boni Dii sunt, impossibile est quod retributionem a cultoribus suis, vel exigant, vel intendant, vel quod eam etiam patiantur: vir enim bonus, et erubescit, et horret hanc maculam poni in gloria sua, nec ullo modo sustinet, ut quod gratis ex bonitate debet effluere, retributio extrahat inde, vel extroqueat, alioquin non de plenario bonitatis opus effluit, sed de vacuo, et arido, tetroque cupiditatis.'

[68] *De legibus*, 24, p. 72A: 'Quod si dixerit quis, quia placandi sunt Dii, quia interdum irascuntur mortalibus: quaerimus ab eis propter quid irascantur mortalibus? Si etiam alia de causa irascuntur, quam propter peccata ipsorum, injuste irascuntur illis; injusta enim est omnis ira, si non est contra peccatum, aut proprium, aut alienum. Si enim non propter peccata eorum irascuntur

gods to animals, took for granted the low status of animals. Moreover, some animals were again held to be naturally hostile to humans, comparable even to devils in this respect, although more readily subjected to human control simply by denial of sustenance.

Continuing his attack on idolatrous offerings, William raised a point that did not immediately concern animals but eventually took him back to the issue of animal sacrifice. What if someone said that good gods helped us with their intercessions and advocacy, obtaining many favours for us from the highest God? In this case, they were honoured only as patrons and advocates, not as judges higher than God and not as gods. William's reply was that it was then obvious that neither sacred rites, sacrifices nor other honours should be established for them; only super-eminent and sublime divinity required these. But what if someone then said that it was no great thing to kill an ox, ram or any animal in honour of any god because many animals were licitly killed even to honour a friend, and especially if animals, great and small, were given to kings and princes, who were assuredly humans, and even to all sorts of humans, to express adoration and service? Why then should these things not be done for gods who were more to be honoured and served than humans, being more exalted and more eminent? William replied that although animals could licitly be given to and killed for humans, they could and should not be *sacrificed* for humans. He went on to explain the nature of sacrifice as a sacred rite that sanctified the giver of the gift as well as the recipient. The person making the sacrifice attributed to the recipient the power to sanctify and to cleanse from sin; this power, however, only belonged to

mortalibus; manifestum est, quia injuste irascuntur eisdem, et ideo injusti ipsi ex necessitate sunt et peccatores; quare non solum Dii habendi non sunt, set potius diaboli mali. Quod si propter peccata eorum solum irascuntur mortalibus; tunc maxime placantur, cum mortales a peccatis recesserint; contrariorum enim contrarias causas esse necesse est. Quod si justificatio mortalium, elongatioque a peccatis non placat eos, sed exardescit ira eorum, donec offerantur eis carnes, et sanguis animalium: manifestum est, quia ira hujusmodi non est ira Deorum, sed potius ira serpentum sive leonum aut aliarum bestiarum rugientium, donec aliquid praedae ceperint; et hujusmodi substantiae non Dii sunt, sed Diaboli naturali militia infesti hominibus, ut serpentes, aut aliae bestiae. [...] quod si propter rabiem, et saevitiam timendi tantum sunt, nihil curandi sunt nisi ut Serpentes, atque Leones, et ideo nec Dii habendi: non restat igitur nisi ut deficiamus, destruamus et exterminemus eos, ut Serpentes, atque Leones. Nullum enim animal est adeo rabidum, aut saevum, quod escarum oblatione placari non possit, atque mitescere.'

God most high. Someone who sacrificed to another god therefore recognised this god as the all-powerful creator and god most high. It was obvious how great an injury and insult this was to the true creator since it took away his incommunicable and singular glory and passed it to some other. To make the nature of this impiety clearer, William set out the intentions that underpinned sacrifices. Someone who sacrificed an animal thereby in effect said the following seven things, which William voiced in the first person and which mirrored very approximately the seven reasons that William had previously given for God wanting animals to be sacrificed. First, by this offering or sacrifice, I confess you to be the author of sanctity, and I invoke your powers of sanctification. Second, just as this animal is in my hands, to kill if I wish or spare if I so please, so we are in your hands, to kill through justice because of our sins if you wish or to spare through your mercy if you so please. Third, just as this animal is in my power to kill or save, so we are in your power to destroy or save. Fourth, just as this animal dies, so every sin dies in me through this sacrifice. Fifth, just as this animal by my offering becomes yours, so that henceforth it lives and dies for you, so do I. Sixth, just as from this table or altar I receive corporeal refreshment, so I also receive spiritual refreshment. Seventh, through this communal sacrifice, by which I am admitted to this table with your other worshippers, I profess that I belong to your family and am one of your worshippers. William declared that it was obvious that none of these could be said except to the omnipotent and most merciful God, and it was therefore blasphemy seven times over to make sacrifices to others.[69] Animals thus served, in William's estimation, as

---

[69] *De legibus*, 24, p. 72A–B: 'Si vero dixerit quis, quia boni Dii interpellationibus suis, et patrociniis nos adjuvant impetrantes nobis apud Deum altissimum multiplicia beneficia: honorandi igitur sunt tantum, ut patroni, et advocati; quare non ut judices ante Deum, et ideo neque ut Dii. Manifestum igitur est, quia nec sacra, nec sacrificia constituenda sunt eis, nec alii honores, quos sola requirit supereminentia, et divinitatis sublimitas. Quod si quis dixerit, quia non est magnum occidere bovem, aut arietem, aut aliquod animal in honorem seu pro honore cujuscunque Deorum; quia etiam pro amico honorando multi animalia licite occiduntur: praeterea si regibus, et principibus, qui utique homines sunt, et etiam cujuscunque generis hominibus dantur animalia, et parva, et magna, et hoc ad adorandum eos, et serviendum ipsis; cur non de his liceat talia fieri cum magis honorandi sint, quam homines, et magis eis serviendum, quam hominibus, utpote sublimioribus, atque praestantioribus? Respondemus, quia etsi dati possunt animalia licite hominibus, et occidi pro hominibus, non tamen sacrificari possunt, vel debent hominibus. Sacrificium

a crucial means by which humans established their proper relationship with God.

William once again drew upon the characterisation of animals as angry and hostile when he countered a view that evil gods had to be placated lest they savage mortals. William insisted that such 'substances' were not gods but beasts, first because a beast was something that, lacking wisdom, grew angry to the point of savagery, and was placated by food, and second if they were placated by offerings and were angry with those who did not make offerings and sacrifices, so that they permitted only their worshippers to live.[70] William then

enim est munus, quod offerendo sacrum sit, et sacrum efficit offerentem, quantum in eo est, et etiam illum pro quo offertur, et hoc est proprie sacrificare, ipsum scilicet munus offerendo, sacrum facere, et tam offerentem, quam eum pro quo offertur, sanctificare. Quapropter sacrificans eo ipso quo sacrificat, virtutem sanctificativam, et emundativam a peccatis attribuit ei, cui sacrificat; haec autem virtus non est, nisi altissimi Dei. Attribuit etiam eidem tantam virtutem sanctificativam, ut eo ipso munus sanctum, seu sacrificium sit, quod eidem offertur. Qui Deo alii, quam Deo altissimo sacrificant, jam facto ipso illud, quicquid ipsum sit, sanctificationem et offerentis, et muneris, et ejus etiam pro quo offertur, esse confitentur; et propter hoc consequenter, omnipotentem creatorem, ac Deum altissimum. Manifestum igitur est tibi quanta injuria, quantaque contumelia creatoris sit, incommunicabilem, ac singularem eius gloriam eidem auferre, et in aliud quodcunque transferre: eodem modo de aliis intentionibus sacrificiorum, quas supra memoravimus, se habet. Haec autem impietas, ut amplius elucescat, et manifestior tibi fiat, nominabimus et numerabimus tibi intentiones sacrificiorum, et vires. Qui igitur sacrificat animal, idem est ac si diceret, et revera opere illo sacrificii haec dicit. Tibi offero, vel sacrifico, auctorem sanctitatis confiteor, et ad sanctificandum invoco, sanctificandum autem illum, pro quo hujusmodi sacrificium tibi offero. Secundo, sicut animal istud in manibus meis est, ita ut ipsum occidam, si voluero, vel parcam eidem si mihi placuerit; ita in manibus tuis sumus ut nos occidas per justitiam propter peccata nostra si volueris, vel parcas nobis per misericordiam tuam, si beneplacitum tuum fuerit. Tertio, sicut in potestate mea est animal istud ad occidendum, vel salvandum; ita in potestate sua sumus ad perdendum, et salvandum. Quarto, sicut moritur istud animal ita moritur in me per istud sacrificium omne peccatum [...]. Quinto, sicut istud animal oblatione mea tuum officitur; ita ut de caetero tibi vivat, et tibi moriatur: ita et ego. Sexto, sicut de hac mensa, sive altari corporalem refectionem recipio, ita et spiritualem. Septimo, per hanc immolationum communionem, per hoc quod ad mensam istam admittor cum aliis cultoribus tuis; de familia et cultoribus tuis me esse profiteor. Manifestum autem est tibi, quia nihil horum dicendum est, nisi omnipotenti, ac misericordissimo Deo; ipso enim facto sacrificij septemplicis in ipsum blasphematur.'

[70] *De legibus*, 24, p. 74B: 'Quod si dixerit quis, quod propter insipientiam suam, atque malitiam placandi sunt ne saeviant in mortales, error iste multis viis destruitur; primum, quia hujusmodi substantiae non dii sunt, sed belluae.

asked whether their power was such that they were free to attack
whomever they wished however they wished, or whether their power
was bound and limited. William evidently considered them subject to
another power which controlled whom, how and when they attacked.
It was this power alone that had to be placated with offerings and
sacrifices, not this kind of beast whose malice counted for nothing
except insofar as this other power desired and permitted. Who, to
avoid being attacked by a beast that someone was holding back,
adored and honoured the beast rather than the person controlling it?
It was certain, however, that God most high bound and limited their
power, so he alone was to be prayed to, adored and honoured to
contain the anger and savagery of beasts of this kind, not the beasts
themselves.[71] William thus associated animals not only with ferocity
and hostility to humans, but with lack of freedom to decide upon
their actions.

Lack of reason was the quality that he associated with animals when
he turned his attention to idolatry of the stars and light. Either this
idolatry was directed at inanimate bodies or animate bodies which
were animals. If the latter, they were necessarily irrational animals,
and it was therefore pointless to serve them since they could not
recognise and would not reward service.[72] William further commented

> Bellua enim est, quae sine sapientia irascitur ad saeviendum, et placatur esca:
> secundo, quia hujusmodi ne dicam dii, sed belluae, si placerentur muneribus,
> irascentur non offerentibus munera, sed sacrificia eorum contemnentibus, et ita
> non sinerent vivere nisi cultores suos.'

[71] *De legibus*, 24, p. 74B: 'Aut est eis potestas haec libera, ut saeviant in quosque, et
quantumcunque voluerint; aut est in eis ligata, et limitata [...]: si vero non eis
libera, sed ligata ac limitata, est igitur in potestate, et beneplacito ligatoris, ac
limitatoris, in quos, et quantum, et quando saeviant. Ipse igitur solus placandus
est muneribus, et sacrificiis, non hujusmodi belluae quarum malitia nihil habet,
nisi quantum ipse vult, et sinit. Quis enim videns aliquem tenentem bestiam
ligatam, adoret, vel honoret ipsam bestiam, ut in ipsum non saeviat, et non
potius renentem illam. Certam autem est, quia solus Deus altissimus, et ligator,
et limitator est hujus potestatis; quare ipse solus orandus, et adorandus, et
honorandus est contra iram, atque saevitiam hujusmodi bestiarum, non ipsae
bestiae.'

[72] *De legibus*, 25, p. 77A-B: 'Dicemus igitur, quia idolatrae hujusmodi aut
intendebant huiusmodi cultu servire corporibus inanimatis, aut corporibus
animatis, quae etiam animalia essent. [...] Si vero corporibus animatis, vel
animalibus, necesse est hujusmodi animalia esse irrationabilia, et non
intelligibilia. Vane igitur et ignominiose eis servitur, cum neque ipsum
servitium agnoscant, neque servitor es, et propter hoc in remunerationem
eorum nullatenus intendant.'

that it was insane to pay divine honour to brute animals because every rational animal was incomparably more noble, excellent and sublime than every irrational animal. To subject oneself to the stars was therefore to subvert the order of nature.[73] The irrationality and therefore the inferiority of brute animals were taken as given.

Towards the end of the treatise, William returned again to animal sacrifice, stating baldly that sacrifices of animals were manifestly useless in themselves and had no power to placate God or to obtain his grace, nor had they ever done so, except as gifts. This was because the sacrifice of animals did not entail the death of human sins, and their consumption did not mean the consumption of human sins. Nor was it in any way necessary that the sufferings of sacrificed animals should be followed by similar sufferings in the souls of those performing the sacrifice, or that there should be any change in the souls of those making the offering or for whom the animals were offered because of anything that happened to the animals. It was obvious therefore that by their own power killings and burnings of animals could not benefit the souls of those making the offerings or of those for whom they were offered, either by cleansing them of sins or by seeking grace. The gifts could achieve nothing with God, except through his satisfaction or the fervour of the giver. That the animals themselves gave God no satisfaction was clear from what he himself said, and William quoted Psalm 49:13: 'Shall I eat the flesh of bullocks? or shall I drink the blood of goats?' For the animals themselves had nothing that ought to be or could be pleasing except use for sustenance, sweet taste for pleasure, value for wealth, or a kind of beauty for ornament, but all these were nothing to the creator, and so could never give direct satisfaction to God. If the animals were ever to please God, it had to be because of those who offered them, and because of their devotion, or obedience, or some other quality.[74]

[73] *De legibus*, 25, p. 77B: 'Brutis animalibus divinum honorem impendere manifestae insaniae est. Omne namque animal rationale nobilius est, atque praestantius, sublimiusque incomparabiliter omni irrationabili; incomparabiliter igitur inferiori, atque ignobiliori se subditum animal rationale est. Eis enim, scilicet hujusmodi animalibus, ut dicunt coelestibus, per adorationem, et culturam se subdit, quare ordinem naturae intolerabili perversitate subverti.'

[74] *De legibus*, 28, p. 96B: 'Post haec transibimus ad sacrificia et dicemus in primis, quia sacrificia animalium per se esse inutilia manifestum est, et nullam habere virtutem ad placandum Deum altissimum, vel impetrandam gratiam ipsius, nec habuisse unquam, nisi quemadmodum munus apud receptorem ipsius.

William then listed ways in which animals were sacrificed, noting that these cooking methods were never in themselves pleasing to God, which allowed him to expand on what was pleasing to God. He repeated that God was pleased by the devotion or obedience of those making the offering, adding that he was also pleased when such practices served as occasions for remembrance, teaching people that they ought to please God, or keeping them involved in divine worship. For these killings did not a little to bring people to worship of the creator, just as the fat of sacrificed beasts and the wine of libations kept many in idolatry, and just as happened in the confraternities of William's day which few or none would attend if there were no meals, which were also important for the sustenance of priests. William expanded on how getting rid of or killing sins and evils was in itself always pleasing to God and an acceptable sacrifice. Indeed, because the mortification of sins was not only always pleasing to God, but also necessary for humans, it was a sacrifice in itself and essentially, and a just sacrifice that was owed of necessity. William now referred to evils and sins as 'spiritual animals' ('spiritualia animalia') that had to be killed; these kinds of spiritual sacrifice were always necessary for those who offered them, whereas the literal or material sacrifice of animals was never necessary. William stated clearly that the obligation to

> Manifestum enim est non esse eam ligationem, seu vinculum inter animas immolantium animalia ipsa, quae naturalia cogat, vel exigat, ut propter mortem animalium sequatur mors peccati, quod totum in anima vel in animabus est, et propter consumptionem eius, quod in sacrificio de animali immolato consumitur, vel sequatur consumptio peccati, vel peccatorum. Neque ullo modo necesse est, ut passiones rerum immolatitiarum sequantur similes passiones in animabus operantium, vel aliquid immuretur aut innovetur in animabus offerentium sive eorum pro quibus offeruntur animalia, propter aliquid quod sit in animalibus. Quare manifestum est mactationes, vel combustiones animalium ex propria virtute prodesse non posse animabus offerentium, vel eorum pro quibus offeruntur, vel ad mundationem a peccatis vel ad gratiarum inquisitionem, munera vero apud receptorem nihil possunt, nisi vel placore suo, vel fervore donantis: et quidem quod placorem nullum apud Deum habeant animalia in se manifestum est, sicut ipsemet dicit. "Nunquid manducabo carnes taurorum, aut sanguinem hircorum potabo?" [Psalm 49:13]. Nihil enim habent propter quod placere debeant, vel possint, nisi aut utilitatem ad reficiendum, vel suavitatem gustabilem ad delectandum, vel pretiositatem ad ditandum, vel pulchritudinem aliquam ad ornandum: de his autem omnibus nihil ad creatorem, quare propter proprium placorem nullatenus placere potuerunt umquam creatori. Restat igitur si unquam ei placuerint, quod hoc fuerit propter offerentes propter devotionem, seu obedientiam offerentium, vel propter aliam utilitatem eorum placuerunt Deo altissimo talia, quantumcunque placuerunt.'

make animal sacrifices had ceased and indeed they were forbidden to Christians. They offered Christians none of the benefits that had previously accrued and therefore could not please God in any way at all. Now they would be simply burdensome and pointless. William noted an objection that all Jews and many Christians were still carnal by nature, so carnal sacrifices were still necessary for them. He replied that they should be compelled to become more spiritual, and carnal sacrifices would feed their carnality. Such sacrifices should not be brought back lest they create a split in the people of God.[75] In this analysis animals were again useful to humans as food and property, and an ornamental function was also added in passing. They were also valuable because their slaughter constituted a means by which humans could demonstrate their qualities, thus establishing the proper relationship between God and humans. Their relative lack of worth was apparent, however, when they were deployed metaphorically: sins were 'spiritual animals'.

William then considered a point that took him back to the requirements of the Old Testament. Why had God ordered the killing of pure animals when he wanted that which was pure to be conserved and increased by humans, and these pure animals signified the gifts of God's grace and power? William replied that humans were never so pure that that they did not need purification or that they could not be improved. And although the animals were pure in that they were not polluted by idolatry or sorcery, they nevertheless had 'natural impurities' by which the spiritual impurities of humans were signified. Thus, in the bull there was stubbornness, and in the ram wildness, which in humans signified pride and contentiousness respectively. Pure animals were killed for the sake of justice. Those who made the offering knew that they could not give God his due other than by offering him pure animals, they could not themselves come to God other than by spiritual fire and sword, and they could not themselves live for God other than by killing these offerings. Therefore, just as these animals became God's part by corporeal death, so all the elect did so by this kind of

---

[75] *De legibus*, 28, pp. 96B–97B. I have summarised a passage that is too long for quotation. See Sean Eisen Murphy, 'On the enduring impurity of menstrual blood and semen: Leviticus 15 in William of Auvergne's *De legibus*', in José Martínez Gázquez and John Victor Tolan (eds.), *Ritus Infidelium: Miradas Interconfesionales sobre las Prácticas Religiosas en la Edad Media*, Collection de la Casa de Velázquez 138 (Madrid, 2013), pp. 191–208, at 204.

spiritual death.[76] Animals were again characterised as incapable of sin in that they were pure, and as gifts from God, but they were also taken to exhibit qualities with negative connotations, 'natural impurities' as William termed them here, which signified sins in humans.

William had a great deal to say about animals in the *De legibus*, and not only when they featured in the Old Testament laws that he was seeking to explain. When comparing them with humans, explicitly and implicitly, his emphasis was almost entirely on difference. Humans were more noble and unquestionably superior in status. Unlike humans, however, animals were innocent and pure, lacking the capacity to sin, though some animals were nonetheless characterised as ferocious and hostile to humans. Unlike humans, animals were irrational and lacked free will, though these differentiating features received slight attention. William only suggested similarities when condemning some humans: humans who witnessed sex between different species of animals might be sinfully aroused to have sex with animals; animal similes and metaphors were deployed to attack heretics and Muslims. For William in the *De legibus*, animals existed chiefly as tools. God used them to shape human behaviour, both by demanding sacrifice and by granting them symbolic meaning. Demons used them in natural magic. Humans used them as valuable and sometimes necessary property in pursuit of survival, and to ensure proper relations with God. The boundary between humans and animals was consistently strong and unproblematic.

[76] *De legibus*, 28, p. 97B: 'Si quis autem quaerat, quare animalia munda occidi sibi dominus praecepit, cum ea quae munda sunt in hominibus teneri, conservari, roborari, et augeri velit, et munda illa animalia significent dona gratiarum suarum, et virtutum. Respondemus, quia nihil adeo est mundum in hominibus, quod non mundatione indigeat, vel quod emendari non possit. [...] Vel quia illa animalia, etsi munda essent, id est non polluta idolatriis, vel sortilegiis gentium, tamen habebant immunditias naturales quibus nostrae immunditiae spirituales signantur, ut in tauro est cervicositas, in ariete efferitas, hoc est cornibus feriendi levitas, spiritualia nostra significant, scilicet superbiam, id est cervicositatem, seu contentiositatem: vel occidebantur munda animalia pro impetranda, seu conservanda, roboranda, et augenda justitia, ut propter hoc eo ipso agnoscerent qui offerebant, non aliter in Dei partem transire nisi mundos se eidem offerent, et non aliter ad ipsum pervenire posse, nisi per ignem spiritualem et gladium, quibus ingressus paradis primis parentibus prohibitus est, vel quod est sublimioris significantiae, ut non aliter se vivere Deo posse, nisi sibi morerentur offerentes agnoscerent. Sicut igitur animalia illa per mortem corporalem pars Dei efficiebantur, sic et omnes electi per hujusmodi mortem spiritualem.'

De universo

Matters were much more complicated in the *De universo*. When differences were advocated, as they were strongly at many points in the work, there was much more emphasis on human rationality and animal irrationality than in the *De legibus*. Moreover, similarities were frequently identified, especially in relation to processes of knowing and the will, that rendered the boundary between animals and humans far from clear.

An example of William emphasising difference and insisting on a hard boundary occurred when William attacked the doctrine of the transmigration of souls, denouncing the many 'inconvenientia' to be found in the Pythagorean view. Several of his many points reveal the strength of the divide that he saw between humans and animals, and that this divide was between the rational and the irrational. He argued, for example, that the doctrine of the transmigration of souls implied that all brute animals had reason and intellect, so that all animals were rational. This was because a human was only rational because of a rational soul, and not because of the body. If rational souls, specifically human souls, were in the bodies of brute animals, brute animals were rational for the same reason as humans. It could be objected that humans were different because they possessed not only reason, but also the use of reason, to which William replied that in fact many humans did not have the use of reason, for example morons and people in the grip of fury, and yet they were still regarded as both human and rational. If it were then objected that reason did not function in these people because of the evil disposition of the body, the same would have to be said about brute animals: only the disposition of the bodies of brute animals, because it was not congruent with human souls, impeded the use of reason by brute animals. Those who advocated the transmigration of souls were therefore obliged to concede that brute animals were rational.[77] That this was an argument against the

---

[77] William of Auvergne, *Opera Omnia*; *De universo*, 1.2.14, p. 704B: 'Pythagorae vero accident inconvenientia multa et inopinabilia. Primum est, quia omnibus animalibus brutis erunt ratio, et intellectus, et propter hoc omnia animalia erunt rationalia. Homo enim nec est, nec dicitur animal rationale, nisi propter animam rationale, et nullo modo propter corpus. Cum igitur animae rationales, hoc est, animae humanae sint in corporibus brutorum, eadem de causa erunt bruta animalia rationabilia. Quod si dixerit, quia hominibus liberum est uti ratione,

transmigration of souls depended on William's assumption that brute animals were irrational, and his confidence that readers would share it.

William argued further that either God had created some brute animal bodies into which human souls were not transmigrated, or he had not. If God had done this, and there were some brute animals with brute souls, these were true brute animals and necessarily of a different species from those brutes that had human souls. Moreover, humans who owned brute animals would not know whether they possessed true horses, asses and oxen, or if they had false ones which ought to be considered humans more than brute animals. Even more worryingly, it would be abominable for anyone to impose servitude on brute animals or to beat them, because when driving oxen or spurring on horses, or inflicting various other labours upon them, one might be attacking the souls of one's parents, brothers or other relatives. If, however, all brute animal bodies had or would have human souls, clearly no genuine brute animal had been created by God, and no animal was truly irrational.[78] Again, the force of the argument depended on sure conviction that animals were irrational, as well as belief in animal servitude.

William noted also that the intellectual power did not operate in or through the body, so human souls that had transmigrated to animals

> et non solum habent rationalitatem, immo et usum ipsius: respondeo, quia multi non habent usum, nec facultatem uti ratione; quemadmodum illi, qui vocantur moriones; similiter et furiosi omnes tempore furoris sui, nihilominus tamen et homines, et animalia rationalia sunt, et dicuntur. Si vero dixerit, quia non per naturam ligata est ratio in hujusmodi hominibus, sed a casu per malam dispositionem corporis; hoc ipsum necesse habet dicere et in hujusmodi brutis. Sola enim dispositio brutalium corporum, quia non congruit animabus humanis, impedit in eis usum rationis: aliam enim causam fingere non possunt, quare necesse habent concedere bruta hujusmodi animalia esse rationabilia.'
>
> [78] *De universo*, 1.2.14, pp. 704B–705A: 'Aut creavit Deus corpora brutorum aliqua, in quae non sunt translatae aliquae animae humanae, aut non creavit. Si creavit aliqua, quae habent animas brutales ex illis: cum animabus suis brutalibus sint vere animalia et ex necessitate alterius speciei, quam illa bruta, quae habent animas humanas, quare nescient homines, qui habent animalia bruta, an habeant veros equos, veros asinos, veros boves, an falsos, aut si magis homines reputanda sint, quam bruta animalia: et ita nepharium erit unicuique hominum uti servitute brutorum animalium, et affligere illa, ne forte stimulando boves, aut equos urgendo calcaribus, aut affligendo aliis variis laboribus, grassetur in animas parentum suorum, aut fratrum, aut cognatorum. Si vero nulla creavit corpora animalium brutorum Deus, in quibus non incluserit, vel inclusurus sit animas humanas; tunc manifestum est nullum vere brutum animal creatum esse a Deo, et nullum animal vere esse irrationale.'

would not be prevented by the brute animal bodies that they inhabited from philosophising and contemplating abstract spiritual matters. Philosophising about corporeal and material entities was aided by the senses, however, and some brute animals had senses that were superior to human senses. This was why animals had advance knowledge of storms and could foretell many things from them, and why dogs were able to track and catch robbers, apparently seeming to imitate prophetic splendour, a point on which he elaborated later in the work, as we will see. It was manifestly a consequence of the transmigration of souls that brute animals could philosophise and make prophecy.[79] Indeed, William seemed to suggest that their superior senses might make them better philosophers and prophets, a conclusion so absurd that William did not feel the need to point it out.

William further noted that no one had yet dared to say that brute animals sinned, but it was obvious that humans did. It therefore had to follow from the transmigration of souls that brute animal bodies were better than human bodies for the expiation and purification of human souls. Human bodies were entirely unsuitable for the purification of human souls because souls were corrupted in so many ways in them, although they resisted. In brute animal bodies, however, they could not be corrupted in any way.[80] William did not comment further, but once again he manifestly held the implications of transmigration of souls to be absurd, here because it was beyond doubt that animals were incapable of sin.

---

[79] *De universo*, 1.2.14, p. 705A: 'Virtus intellectiva non operatur in corpore, nec per corpus operatur suam nobilem operationem, ut sunt intelligere, et ratiocinari de substantiis sublimibus spiritualibus abstractis: quare non prohibebuntur a parte corporum bruta animalia philosophari de talibus, et contemplari in eis: ad philosophandum autem de corporalibus, et materialibus adjuvantur sensibus: et multo nobilius, atque sublimius adjuvantur quibusdam sensibus quaedam, quam homines. Unde et tempestates praesagiunt, et multa ex eis, et per ea praenoscuntur, sed et canes qui latrones investigant et deprehendunt splendorem propheticum evidenter imitari videntur. Manifestum igitur est consequens esse, animalia bruta et philosophari, et prophetare posse.'

[80] *De universo*, 1.2.14, p. 705B: 'Nemo adhuc ausus est dicere de brutalibus, quod peccent: de hominibus autem manifestum est, quoniam absque mensura, et numero peccant quare aptiora expiationi, et sanctificationi animarum humanarum sunt corpora brutorum, quam corpora humana: immo quod plus est, corpora humana omnino inepta sunt istis purificationibus animarum nostrarum, cum in eis tam multipliciter inquinentur, licet renitentes, et invitae. In aliis autem inquinari nullatenus possunt.'

Musing further on whether human souls were supposed to migrate to all or only some animals, William pointed out that if human souls were in all animals, they must be in the bodies of fleas and flies. That meant that every day innumerable thousands of human souls were hunted by swallows. Every day a single swallow hunted more than two thousand flies. Every day, therefore, innumerable thousands of human souls were returned simply from the bodies of flies. Plato, however, had asserted that as many human souls had been created as there were stars, but it was clear that there were not as many stars as fleas and flies, nor therefore as many stars as human souls. If, however, it was claimed that human souls transmigrated only to some animals, one ran into a problem that William had already considered: there would be some true animals which had souls naturally suited to their bodies, and some false animals which had human souls and brute bodies. There would be genuine horses and horses that were not genuine, and the same with lions.[81] William did not elaborate, but plainly he considered this to be manifestly absurd.

Having ridiculed the notion of transmigration of souls by pointing to a series of untenable consequences, William argued against it on the grounds of utility. The transmigration of human souls into brute bodies served absolutely no purpose and was damaging in many ways. Souls could not be made wiser or better than they were in human bodies. Rather, they would be made foolish and entirely resistant to wisdom and honesty. Transmigration would be thoroughly useless with regard to expiation or correction because souls could not possibly

[81] *De universo*, 1.2.14, p. 706A: 'Quod si dixerit, quod in corporibus omnium animalium ergo in corporibus pulicum, et muscarum quare quotidie exibunt a corporibus hujusmodi innumerabilia millia animarum humanarum per solum venatum hirundinum. Omni enim die unaquaeque hirundo venatur plusquam duo millia muscarum. Quotidie igitur revertuntur innumerabilia millia animarum humanarum ad compares stellas de solis corporibus muscarum. Amplius. Manifestum est non esse tot stellas in coelo, quot sunt pulices, et muscae. Cum enim nota sit magnitudo coeli, et declaratum sit unamquamque stellarum fixarum visibilium, et notabilium, majorem esse tota terra: manifestum est musculas, et pulices numero excedere stellas omnes, quare et omnes animas humanas. Plato autem posuit animas humanas creatas esse ad numerum stellarum. Si dixerit, quod in aliquibus animalibus stat opinio Platonis, et Pythagorae, [. . .]: illa igitur sola erunt vera animalia, utpote habentia animas naturali aptitudine congruentes corporibus suis: ex anima enim humana, et corpore brutali, non potest esse verus asinus, aut verus leo, et ita de aliis. Erunt igitur quaedam animalia brutalia vera, et quaedam falsa, quod est dicere, equi veri et equi quidam non veri, et de leonibus similiter.'

be corrected in brute bodies. Moreover, it could not be argued that transmigration was inflicted as punishment by divine justice, with souls being transferred from noble human bodies to more ignoble bodies because of their sins, because it was unknowable: no one felt the punishment and no one was deterred from crime because they feared it. Transmigration was so unknowable that it was not revealed by prophecy. Pythagoras had not discovered it by his senses or reason, while the Manichees were simply stupid and wrong.[82]

William then considered the view that human souls transmigrated only to human bodies. This would mean that humans were not true animals. Rather, they would be said to be animals equivocally, and the human soul would be said to be a soul equivocally compared with brute souls, for the brute soul would be fully a part of the brute animal, as its form and the perfection of its body, the natural inhabitant of its body, and its brute body would be its proper home. The human soul, however, would naturally, from its creation, have being outside the body, and it would be in the human body as a guest and a stranger. This would mean that the most noble species of all the animals, that which was like their head, namely the human, would be missing from the *universitas* of animals. But it was not fitting that the creator should leave the *universitas* of animals imperfect, and so hugely detruncated,

---

[82] *De universo*, 1.2.14, p. 706A–B: 'manifestum autem est, quia translatio animarum humanarum in corpora brutorum, nihil omnino habet utilitatis, plurimum vero habet noxietatis. Si enim cucurreris per omnes vias utilitatis quantum ad ipsas animas, nullam prorsus invenies, quia nec ibi sapientiores, aut meliores effici possunt, quam essent in corporibus humanis; immo prorsus desipiunt ibi, et indociles sapientiae, et honestatis omnino efficiuntur; ad expiationem vero, vel correctionem, sive emendationem penitus inutilis est hujusmodi translatio. Impossibile enim est eas corrigi, vel emendari in brutalibus corporibus. Quod si dixerit, quia ex ordine divinae justitiae, videlicet ad poenam, propter delicta sua transferuntur a nobilibus corporibus humanis ad ignobilia, et viliora, et hoc ipsum vanum est, quia poenam hujusmodi non sentient ipsae, vel aliae, quas metus hujusmodi poenae deterrere posset, et arcere a similibus delictis. Inutilis autem est manifeste poena omnis, quae nec patienti, nec aliis prodesse potest, talis est autem omnis poena incogniscibilis. Haec autem adeo incogniscibilis est, ut nec prophetis revelata sit, nec a tantis prophetis potuerit inveniri. Quod si dixerit, quia a Pythagora inventa est: respondeo, quia non est inventum, nisi quod vel sensu, vel ratione irrefragibili verum esse declaratum est, nisi forte creatoris revelatione fuerit ostensum. In hujusmodi enim rebus opiniones hominum, non inventiones, sed somnia reputanda sunt, nisi sint certis probationibus, aut saltem verisimilibus finaliter approbatae. Si vero dixerit, quia Manichaei invenerunt hanc translationem, reminisci debes imbecillitatis, et erroneitatis ipsorum.'

or rather decapitated. If humans were not to be part of the *universitas* of animals, William could not accept brute animals as perfect; rather, the whole class of animals was rendered incomplete and lacking its head.[83] Moreover, William argued that the human body was not naturally less harmonious than brute bodies, nor did it have less natural aptitude. On the contrary, the human body was incomparably greater with regard to many operations, as was clearly apparent from the production of sculptures, drawings and innumerable constructions and artifices. For William, it was inconceivable that the creator should not provide the human body with the natural perfection that was congruent with it and was its due.[84]

William's refutation of the idea of transmigration of souls thus invoked a catalogue of differences separating humans and animals. Animals served humans, and humans could legitimately inflict pain upon them. Animals could not sin. Humans were the most noble species of animal. Human bodies were superior to animal bodies, although some animals had more effective senses. Above all, humans were rational while animals were not, and animals could not philosophise. A hard boundary between humans and animals was consistently taken for granted.

Absolute difference was again to the fore when William considered what would happen to the sublunary world after the Last Judgment.

---

[83] *De universo*, 1.2.14, p. 706B: 'Si vero dixerit, quia stat in solis corporibus humanis hujusmodi translatio animarum humanarum, ut manifestum est, quia omnia animalia bruta, et vere animalia, et vere bruta sunt: soli autem homines, nec veri sunt homines, nec vera animalia, immo aequivoce animalia dicuntur, et anima humana aequivoce dicitur anima ad animas brutorum, cum anima brutalis omnis pars sit ipsius animalis bruti, ut forma ipsius, atque perfectio corporis ejusdem, et ut ita dixerim, naturalis inhabitatrix corporis ejusdem, et corpus brutale habitaculum ipsius, anima vero humano econverso: unde naturaliter, hoc est, ex ipsa creatione sua habet esse extra, juxta positionem Platonis, et Pythagorae, et sit in corpore humano, tanquam hospes, et advena limitatae hospitationis. Secundum hoc nobilissima species omnium animalium deesset universitati animalium, et quod est in ea velut caput, videlicet homo: hoc autem non decuit creatorem, videlicet, ut universitatem animalium relinqueret imperfectam, et tam enormiter detruncatam, immo decapitatam, ut aptius loquar.'

[84] *De universo*, 1.2.14, p. 706B: 'Cum corpus humanum non minus organicum sit naturaliter, nec minoris aptitudinis naturalis, immo evidenter incomparabiliter majoris, quam corpus brutorum ad operationes multiplices, quod manifeste apparet in sculpturis, figuris, et innumerabilibus fabricationibus et artificiis, quomodo creator non providit hujusmodi corporibus naturalem perfectionem eis congruentem, et debitam, ut est perfectio naturalis?'

He explained that because animals and plants, and other things that humans used in this life, were not necessary except because of humans, they would cease to be of use when humans moved to the places where they would be everlastingly, and so generation and corruption of animals and plants would necessarily cease.[85] Making the same point another way, he argued that land and water could not continue to be adorned by terrestrial and aquatic animals unless they were either immortal or continued in perpetual generation and corruption. There did not appear, however, to be any utility in the immortal life of animals. Those animals that were only useful as food and clothing for humans served both uses through death. Animals would not be of any use for carrying or as the basis for medicines because the bodies of glorified humans would not be burdened by work or weariness, or by illness and wounds, while the bodies of the damned would be bound in a misery that was entirely incurable. Nor would animals be of any use to children who had not sinned while alive because divine protection would prevent any suffering. It followed that if animals had only been created for the uses of humans, they ought not to exist and could not exist once these uses had ceased. That they were created for the uses of humans was indicated by nature itself.[86]

---

[85] *De universo*, 1.2.39, p. 741B: 'Cum enim animalia, et vegetabilia, similiter metalla, et alia quibus utuntur homines in habitatione ista, non sint necessaria, nisi propter ipsos: translatis autem hominibus in loca perennium habitationum suarum cessent utilitates rerum hujusmodi, necesse est esse cessaturam tunc generationem et corruptionem ipsarum.'

[86] *De universo*, 1.2.39, p. 742A–B: 'Quod si quis ornatum aquarum dicat pisces, et alia animalia, quae generantur in aquis, et vivunt in eis: dico, quia similiter idem potest dicere, quod ornatus terrae est animalia terrestriae, et uterque ornatus revera pulcherrimus, atque nobilissimus, et nec terra, nec aqua potest habere praestantiorem. Quia igitur not potest hoc esse, nisi alterutro duorum modorum, videlicet ut immortalia sint utraque animalia, terrestria, scilicet, et aquatica, aut ut continuetur in perpetuum generatio, et corruptio. Nulla autem apparet utilitas immortalis vitae animalium. Ea enim, quae ad esum, et victum hominum tantum utilia sunt, per mortem utrique usui deserviunt. Ad vectiones vero, et medicinas nulla erit utilitas eorum, cum glorificandorum hominum corpora nulli oneri, vel taedio sint eis futura, cum laborem, et lassitudinem apud eos foelicitas illa procul ab eis inaccessibiliter faciat. Medicinae vero nullus locus ibi esse poterit, ubi nec morbi, nec vulnera, ubi tanta foelicitas, et firmitas, ut confortationem, vel meliorationem non recipiat, corpora quoque damnatorum miseria omnino immedicabili, et irremediabili teneantur. De corporibus vero parvulorum qui actualiter non peccaverunt, dum hic viverent, quoniam immortalitate stabilienda sunt, et divinae protectionis impassibilitate munienda, sicut dixi, et qualiter dixi, manifestum est, quod nullus usus

William then noted the objection that unless the generation and corruption of animals continued in perpetuity, land, water and air would be empty and serve no purpose. He simply reminded his reader that he had already explained that there had to be an end to generation and corruption, and to all change and movement that took place in time. He repeated that the generation of animals necessarily ceased once all their uses ceased. William was willing to countenance the possibility that water and air, and presumably land, would be purified, and that God might honour and reward those whom he had chosen and whom he loved not only in themselves but also in all that they had used in obedience to him, and he recognised that some learned Christians took just this view. But he utterly rejected the suggestion that this argument might apply to animals and vegetables, insisting that they would not be able to receive reward because they would be dead beyond revival and irreparably corrupt. If it were suggested that they ought to be resuscitated to receive due reward, he said this was impossible because neither water nor land would be able to take them, and he had already shown in many ways that they could not and should not be perpetual.[87] Entirely unlike humans, animals therefore lacked any kind of eternal future.

animalium apud ea locum habebit. Quapropter consequens est, quia si propter usus, et utilitates hominum solummodo vel creata vel creanda essent hujusmodi animalia, ea nec debere, nec posse esse, cum usus isti, et utilitates cessaverint. Quod vero propter usus, et utilitates hominum creata sunt, ipsa natura testificatur, quae homines omnibus uti docet, et suggerit.'

[87] *De universo*, 1.2.39, p. 742B: 'Si vero dixerit quis generationem, et corruptionem animalium continuandum esse in perpetuum, ne habitationes istae, terrarum scilicet, et aquarum, et aeris vacuae sint, et perpetua otiositate inutiles: reminisce debes eorum, quae praecesserunt in isto tractatu, quorum unum est, quia necesse est finiri generationem, et corruptionem, aliasque mutationes omnes, et motus, qui in tempore habent fieri, finiri, et cessare cum tempore, et diffinitione temporis, de quo non est tibi relicta dubitatio. Aliud vero est, quia generatio animalium cessatura est ex necessitate, cum ejus omnis usus, et utilitas cessabit. Quod si dixerit, quia deputabitur aqua, quemadmodum, et aer, depurabitur inquam ab immunditiis suis, quae sunt alienae commixtiones, non improbabiliter dicit, neque incredibile est eam esse largitatem, et magnificentiam creatoris, ut electos suos, atque dilectos, non solum in se ipsis, sed etiam in omnibus suis, hoc est, quibus in obsequium creatoris bene usi sunt, honorificet, atque remuneret, quemadmodum supra dixi de ipsis corporibus ac de corporalibus virtutibus animarum hoc est, quibus operantur per corpora. Propter hoc igitur non immerito sentiunt doctores christianorum, extendendam esse mercedem, sive remunerationem largitatis creatoris, non solum in servitores ipsius, sed in ea etiam, quibus bene utendo eidem laudabiliter servierunt, et propter hoc in terras, et aquas, et aera, quasi non

William did much more to justify the belief that animals had been created for use by humans when he discussed God's providence in the third part of the first principal part of the *De universo*. At the beginning of the second chapter, he noted the benefits that humans and other animals gained from the movements of the heavens and the stars, from the changes of the seasons, and from the generations and corruptions that followed from these seasonal shifts. He argued that, for the intelligent, these benefits were clear proofs of God's care and providence because God would have created humans, other animals and plants uselessly if he had not provided them with food and other things that they needed to survive. William emphasised the significance of regular patterns in the created world. Frequency, perpetuity and universality, he maintained, were the most certain proofs of care and providence, eliminating chance. That all humans died, for example, proved with certainty that death befell humans through the care and providence of the creator. William was presumably concerned that his audience might rely too much on their limited knowledge of the created world because he immediately stressed that while rarity and particularity were certain proofs of chance for us, chance simply did not exist for God. This had to be borne in mind especially when considering all types of animals. The generation of feet, wings, feathers and scales in all the animals that naturally possessed them necessarily stemmed from the care and providence of the creator because it was perennial, lasting as long as the creator provided that animals be here, and universal for each kind of animal. So, for William, it did not matter that some animals might seem strange or unfamiliar to humans; consistent features in each animal species demonstrated the workings of providence.[88]

frustra, neque in vanum tot, et tanta commoda, sive servitia electis, et dilectis Dei aer, aqua, et terra, impenderint, quoniam prout decet largitionem creatoris magnificam, inde remunerabitur. Si vero dixerit quis, quia secundum hanc rationem, et causam, extendenda est remuneratio, sive merces in alia animalia, et etiam in vegetabilia: respondeo, quia non sunt receptibilia remunerationis, cum irresurgibiliter mortua sint, et irreparabiliter corrupta. Si vero dixerit, quia resuscitari debent, ut sibi congruentem remunerationem recipiant, dico, quia nec hoc possibile est, quia nec aquae, nec terrae ea capere possent. Et jam alias patefactum est tibi, nec possunt, nec esse debent perennes, et multae viae ad declarationem hujusmodi ostensae sunt tibi.'
[88] *De universo*, 1.3.2, p. 755B: 'De motibus autem coelorum, stellarum, et luminarium, et de vicissitudinibus temporum, et de generationibus, et corruptionibus, quae vicissitudines temporum sequuntur propter curam,

William continued the chapter by insisting that everything, even the smallest, had been created through God's care and providence, and God continued to care for them now. Furthermore, because God had created each thing to have certain uses, it was necessary that he direct and lead them to the fulfilment of those uses and to the end because of which he had wanted them to exist. To avoid making God responsible for the actions of bad humans and bad angels, William was careful to add that God directed every thing insofar as it was appropriate for him to do so.[89] William was very clear, however, that God had created animals for the use of humans, and that they were put to human use through the 'skills and arts' which God had given to humans for this purpose. William explained that it was thus through humans as intermediaries that animals were led to their end, which was their creator, for whom they existed. He then articulated the axiom that the cause of a cause, provided it was the same kind of cause, was the cause of what was caused. Applied to this case, the creator caused human ability and desire to use animals, and this caused the use of animals by humans, from which it necessarily followed that this use was the work and gift

et providentiam creatoris, sunt indicia manifesta intelligentibus utilitates, quae inde proveniunt hominibus, et aliis animalibus, quae nullo modo provenire possent, nisi per curam, et providentiam creatoris. Inutiliter enim hujusmodi, hoc est, homines et alia animalia, atque vegetabilia creasset creator, si non eis alimenta, et alia, sine quibus durare non possunt, providisset. [...] Frequentia similiter, sive perpetuitas, et universalitas indicia certissima sunt curae, et providentiae, et removent casum, et temeritatem, [...] quia mors accidit hominibus universaliter, et semper, quandiu sunt hic: haec igitur duo sunt indicia certissima, quod per curam, et providentiam creatoris mors est in hominibus. Econtrario vero raritas, atque particularitas, indicia sunt certissima casus, et temeritatis, quantum ad nos, quantum autem ad creatorem, neque casus, neque temeritas aliquid est, et istud tibi attendendum est diligenter in omni genere amimalium; generatio enim pedum, alatum, et etiam plumarum in omnibus animalibus, quae naturaliter habent membra hujusmodi, vel adjumenta, sicut plumas, et squamas, ex necessitate per curam, et providentiam est creatoris, quoniam perennis est, ut ita dicam, hoc est durans quantum creator hic esse animalia providit. Est etiam universalis unicuique generi animalium hujusmodi.' See also William of Auvergne, *The Providence of God regarding the Universe: Part Three of the First Principal Part of the Universe of Creatures*, trans. Roland J. Teske (Milwaukee, Wis., 2007), pp. 33–4. I am much indebted to this fine translation.

[89] *De universo*, 1.3.2, p. 757A: 'Cum propter certas utilitates unumquodque eorum, quae sunt, creaverit, necesse est, ut ea dirigat, et perducat ad illas utilitates, quantum in eo est, et ad finem, propter quem eas esse voluit, quod dico propter homines malos, et angelos malos.' See William of Auvergne, *The Providence of God*, p. 38.

of the creator. Moreover, whatever was caused or given by him in this way was caused or given through his care and providence. The use of animals by humans therefore stemmed from the care and providence of the creator.[90] So, not only did the existence of animals prove God's providence, but it was through that same providence that they existed for the use of humans.

At various points in the *De universo*, William showed himself to be keenly aware that animals might seem physically superior to humans: some were bigger, and others could do things that humans could not. He was keen to stress, however, that this did not mean that that they were superior in their souls, or even in their bodies. When discussing the movement of the heavens, for example, he made the point that the greater magnitude of a body did not indicate that the soul inhabiting and ruling that body was naturally more noble. This was apparent in the horse, the elephant and the human: it was manifest that the human soul was more noble than that of the elephant or horse since the human body was 'much better' than the bodies of animals of this kind.[91] And if size did not matter, nor did the ability to fly. The movement of birds was the most noble of animal movements, and in this specific regard birds were the most noble of all animals, but they were not more noble in their souls.[92] Elsewhere, to give just one further example, William

[90] *De universo*, 1.3.2, p. 757A–B: 'Animalia quoque, quae sunt ad usum hominum creata, per industrias et artes, quas ipsemet dedit hominibus ad hoc, convertuntur in usus hominum; quare, licet per homines medios, ad finem perducuntur, ad creatorem, ad quem sunt. Jam enim alibi dixi tibi, quod quicquid est causa causae per se in eodem genere causae, est etiam causa causati, et intelligo causa causae per se. Cum igitur industria hominum, et voluntas utendi animalibus hujusmodi, a creatore causatae sint efficienter, sive effective, et ipse causet usum hujusmodi eodem modo causandi, necessario et usus hujusmodi opus est creatoris, et donum, atque beneficium. Quicquid autem est causatum ab eo ita, vel donatum, est causatum, vel donatum ab eo per curam, et providentiam ipsius. Quare usus animalium hujusmodi erit per curam, et providentiam creatoris.' See William of Auvergne, *The Providence of God*, p. 39. See also *De universo*, 1.3.4, pp. 762B–763A; William of Auvergne, *The Providence of God*, pp. 54–5. I have not identified the source of the axiom cited by William.
[91] *De universo*, 2.1.7, p. 814A: 'dico in hoc, quia magnitudo corporis non indicat naturaliter nobiliorem esse animam inhabitantem, ac regentem ipsum, sicut apparet in equo, et elephante, et homine. Manifestum enim est nobiliorem esse animam humanam, quam sit equina, vel elephantina, cum corpus humanum longe melius sit corporibus hujusmodi animalium.'
[92] *De universo*, 2.1.7, p. 814A: 'Quod si dixerit, quod inferiores coeli tardioris motus sunt, quam superiores, et propter hoc coelum lunare tardissimi motus est

pointed out that the souls of dogs and spiders were said to be able to do many things that human souls could not. He doubtless had in mind that dogs could track thieves and spiders could weave webs and catch flies, capacities that he discussed at length in passages to be analysed shortly. Despite this, William was clear that their souls were naturally incomparable to the human with regard to nobility and perfection.[93] Humans were more noble and more perfect than animals, however impressive the bodies or abilities of animals might be.

The boundary between humans and other animals was sometimes equally strong when William considered cognition. When he compared human souls, angelic substances and the souls of brute animals, he found that the greater the unity, simplicity and indivisibility of human souls, the greater their capacity for cognition. The souls of brute animals only had cognitions that were sensible, imaginative or in the memory, the latter left from sensible and imaginative cognitions, and not all brute animals had even these, for some of them lacked the power of memory, so that they were untrainable. Human souls, however, were receptive to all sciences, as were angelic substances to an even higher degree.[94] In this part of the *De universo*, William was very clear about differences between animals and humans when it came to knowing.

A similarly hard boundary was sometimes also evident when the question of freedom of will arose, as it did when William attacked the

inter omnes coelos mobiles [. . .]: respondeo, quia neque hoc indicium est certum majoris nobilitatis vel in coelis, vel in animabus eorum, sicut apparet in praedictis exemplis elephantis, et equi, et hominis. Evidentius autem apparet in volatilibus, quorum motus inter motus animalium nobilissimus est. Nam quoad hoc ipsa volatilia inter omnia animalia nobilissima sunt.'

[93] *De universo*, 2.1.32, p. 834A: 'cum audiveris jam saepius animas canum, et aranearum, multa posse, quae non possunt animae nostrae, licet nobilitate, atque perfectione sint eis naturaliter incomparabiles.'

[94] *De universo*, 2.1.46, p. 843B: 'Fac considerationem comparativam animarum nostrarum, et substantiarum angelicarum, animarumque brutalium, et invenies evidenter, quia animae nostrae, quanto unitiores sunt in se, majorisque simplicitatis, atque impartibilitatis, tanto sunt majoris capacitatis, quantum ad cognitiones. Animae quippe brutales solas capiunt cognitiones sensibiles, et imaginativas, ac memorativas, quae relinquuntur ex sensibilibus, et imaginativis, et has etiam non habent omnia animalia bruta, quadam enim ex illis carent virtute memorativa: propter quod nec disciplinabilia sunt [. . .]. Animae vero nostrae receptibiles sunt omnium scientiarum, angelicae vero substantiae similiter omnium verum tanto magis, et majorum, ac sublimiorum scientiarum receptibiles sunt, quanto a natura corporeitatis, atque partialitatis, naturali nobilitate sunt elongatiores.'

view that angels did not move the heavens but rather helped with the speed of their movement, as if the heavens did not move fast enough unless the angels helped. Before addressing the question of will, however, he stressed the inferior status of animals, and indicated the value of understanding their nature. It was manifest, William insisted, that the creator gave every mobile thing, whether its movement was voluntary or natural, powers that were sufficient for the movements that were fitting for them and congruent with their natures. William turned to brute animals to illustrate his point. It was just as could be seen with the swallow, to which the creator gave the power of flight that was sufficient for it to catch its food. Similarly, the creator gave hares fleetness of foot so that they could escape capture, though not from all animals because the creator gave other animals, such as dogs, tigers and eagles, much greater speed so that they could capture hares. How then, William asked rhetorically, could the most wise and best creator not provide the heavens with powers that sufficed for the movements that befitted them?[95] William's point was that if the creator provided adequate powers of movement to brute animals, it was inconceivable that he should fail to do so at the hierarchically superior level of the heavens. So, this was more than just illustration: by studying animals lower down the hierarchy, it was possible to work out what it must be like higher up.

Later in the chapter, however, William built his case not on the powers of animals but on their lack of free will, their subjection to passions like desire and fear, and their lack of reason. He argued that if the souls of the heavens could not themselves moderate the speed or vehemence of the movements of the heavens, their movement would not be in any way voluntary; rather they would be either natural or

---

[95] *De universo*, 2.2.97, p. 951B: 'Si autem dixerit, quod angeli isti non movent coelum, neque signa motu novo, sed adjuvant velocitatem motus ejusdem, quasi non satis velociter moveretur, nisi ipsi velocitati suum adjutorium adhiberent, et hoc iterum non nisi vanissime dici potest. Manifestum est enim, quia creator unicuique mobilium, sive sint mobilia voluntarie, sive sint mobilia naturaliter, dedit virtutes motivas sufficientes ad motus convenientes eisdem, et congruentes naturis eorum: quemadmodum vides in hirundinibus, quibus dedit volatum, et volandi virtutem, quae sufficit ad acquisitionem victus earum; similiter et leporibus levitatem pedum ad effugium, et evasionem captionis, non quidem ab omnibus animalibus, quoniam et quibusdam aliis, et quibusdam canibus, et tigribus, et aquilis, longe majorem velocitatem dedit: propter quod et eos capiunt. Qualiter igitur et ipsis coelis non providit sapientissimus, et optimus creator virtutes, quae sufficerent ad motus convenientes ipsis coelis?'

'brutal'. It could not, however, be natural to have too much of something since nature never did anything superfluously because it did
everything as established by the creator, and it did not have the power
to do anything else or to do it differently. William cited the maxim that
nature acted as a servant, one with a limited mandate that could not be
transgressed. But the souls of the heavens could not be 'brutal' either.
That would mean that they moved by some necessity and not by free
will. It would mean that, driven by passions like brute animals, as if
seized by desires or repelled by fears, they could not in any way restrain
themselves and had to be held back by force. The souls of the heavens
would therefore be deeply ignoble if they were 'brutal', and if their
movements were not rational but precipitated and unconsidered. It
could not be believed that the most-wise creator acted so improvidently
and foolishly as to grant the governance of the entire sublunary world
and of all animals, both brute animals and humans, to heavens that
were like brute animals. It could not be believed that an ass was ruled
by another ass.[96] After elaborating on the ludicrousness of supposing

---

[96] *De universo*, 2.2.97, pp. 951B–952A: 'si enim animae coelorum per semetipsas
non possent motuum coelorum velocitatem, vel vehementiam moderari, non
esset voluntarius motus earum ullo modo, sed esset vel naturalis, vel brutalis;
naturalis autem non potest esse nimius, vel superfluus, et hoc est, quoniam
natura nec superflue quicquam, nec diminute unquam aliquid operatur, cum
omnia agat, prout ei ab ipso creatore constitutum est, nec in potestate habet vel
aliud vel aliter operari; sicut enim saepius audivisti: ipsa operatur per modum
servientis, vel potius per modum servi, limitatum mandatum habentis,
limitatione, scilicet intransgressibili, de brutali quoque anima non oportet
doceri te, quin quadam necessitate moveat, et non libera volunte, et quin
impetu passionum ita ferantur bruta animalia, et quasi rapiantur post
concupiscentias suas, vel repellantur timoribus, nullo modo autem refraenant
se, nisi moderentur, aut retrahantur, sed potius, ut dixi, repelluntur quasi vi, et
impetu necessario, et non libertate. Ignobiles igitur essent valde animae
coelorum, si brutales essent, et motus eorum non essent rationabiles, sed
praecipites, et inconsiderati; sed et ipse creator omnino improvide, et
insipienter tam nobilia, ac sublimia tam ignobilibus animabus commisisset, aut
credidisset, qualiter autem coelis, qui utique animalia bruta essent secundum
hoc, totius sublunaris mundi gubernationem, et omnium animalium tam
brutorum, quam hominum, creator sapientissimus, et optimus tradidisset? Nec
enim uni ex asinis alius asinus regendus unquam creditus est, vel commissus.' On
the maxim that nature operates in the manner of a servant, which William owed
to Avicenna but attributed to Aristotle, see Michael Miller, 'William of
Auvergne and the Aristotelians: the nature of a servant', in John Inglis (ed.),
*Medieval Philosophy and the Classical Tradition in Islam, Judaism and
Christianity* (Richmond, 2002), pp. 263–76.

that the souls of the heavens were 'brutal,' William concluded firmly that angels were not constituted in the supernal regions to carry out the alleged duties. His arguments depended on what made animals different: their inferior position in a hierarchy, their lack of reason, and especially their lack of free will.

Thus far it might seem that William's attitudes to animals were very clear, with a firm boundary between humans and animals much in evidence. Frequently in the *De universo*, however, similarities came to the fore, and William's certainty about how humans and animals differed was apparently much diminished. It was when he delved deeper into questions about processes of knowing and the will that the boundary became decidedly blurred.

When William discussed God's providence, for example, to facilitate 'more lofty consideration of the care and providence of the creator in small matters', he considered how animals learned the behaviours that were characteristic of their species. He invited his reader to 'consider and investigate where spiders learn or learned to spin, make threads, or weave their webs or nets, likewise where they learned that flies would fall into their webs, and that flies should naturally be their prey or food before they saw their mothers making threads, before they knew of either threads, webs, or nets, and before a fly was seen by them'.[97] Similarly, William asked his reader to think about ducks 'which, as soon as they see water, immediately jump into it and begin to swim although they had seen no living being swim', asking 'Where did they learn to swim and that water is their abode, that is, one most suitable for their nature?' The behaviour of ants raised similar questions: 'Where did they learn to store grain away, and what is more amazing, where did they learn that grains of wheat would germinate if left

[97] *De universo*, 1.3.3, p. 757B: 'Ut autem erigam te, atque dirigam, ad sublimiorem considerationem curae, ac providentiae creatoris in rebus minimis, considera, et investiga, ubi discunt, vel didicerunt araneae nere, sive filare, et telas suas, atque retiacula texere, ubi didicerunt similiter casuras esse muscas in retiacula earum, et quod muscae praedae earum esse naturaliter debeant, et esca, antequam vel matres filantes viderent, antequam cognoscerent vel fila, vel telas, vel retiacula, antequam appareret eis musca aliqua.' The quotations are from William of Auvergne, *The Providence of God*, p. 40. For partial summary of *De universo*, 1.3.3 with regard to natural philosophy, see Theodor W. Köhler, *Homo animal nobilissimum: Konturen des spezifisch Menschlichen in der naturphilosophischen Aristoteleskommentierung des dreizehnten Jahrhunderts*, vols. 2.1 and 2.2 (Leiden, 2014), pp. 113–15, 118.

whole, and for this reason they divide them in pieces?'[98] And how was it that the magpie could build a nest 'which no carpenter or architect can copy', and that 'swallows and certain other birds seem to use the art of masonry for that structure'? 'And who taught chickens and other egg-laying animals to generate other living beings of their species by nesting on their eggs?' 'And who taught bees to build their combs in hexagons?'[99] In the opening section and later in the chapter, William also challenged his reader to explain the behaviours of partridges, beetles, ostriches, the phoenix, the toad, vultures, cats, horses, fish, eagles, ravens and scorpions.[100]

William claimed to have asked others about such matters in a playful way and always to have received the same answer, that it was nature that taught animals these kinds of arts and skills, a response that he proceeded to ridicule. Was this nature a book or a master? If a book, what kind of book and in what kind of script, how big was it, and who wrote it? His victims did not know how to reply. If a master, where did he learn these skills, or did he not have to learn them because he was in fact the creator? And, whether a book or a master, it was remarkable that nothing similar had yet been found amongst humans. If it was the creator, why did he give these skills to animals and not to humans who had greater need of them? There was a much stronger case for humans receiving natural skills, at least those that were necessary, so that they did not have to work so hard to learn them. If it was a book, how did animals read it? If there were letters, they could not be natural because

[98] *De universo*, 1.3.3, p. 757B: 'Similem considerationem fac de anatibus, qui quam cito aquam vident, in eam statim insiliunt, et natare incipiunt, cum nullum animal natare viderint, ubi natare didicerunt, et aquam esse habitationem suam, hoc est naturae suae convenientem? Similis est quaestio, ac consideratio de formicis, ubi didicerunt thesaurizare, et quod est mirabilius, ubi didicerunt grana tritici germinatura, si ea integra relinquerent, et ideo dividunt ea in frusta?' The quotations are from William of Auvergne, *The Providence of God*, p. 40.

[99] *De universo*, 1.3.3, p. 758A: 'Sunt et alia innumera artificia animalium, quale est artificium picae, quo compingit nidum suum, quem nemo carpentiorum, vel architectorum effigiare potest. Dicitur autem et illud mirabile, quod fateor me non probasse, quin etiam pluries restiti, structura illa, arte etiam caementariorum quadam uti videntur hirundines, et quaedam volucres aliae. [...] Denique quis docuit gallinas, et alia animalia ovantia, superincubando ovis suis, generare animalia suarum specierum? [...] Quis vero docuit apes, ut favos suos per exagonos operarentur?' The quotations are from William of Auvergne, *The Providence of God*, p. 41.

[100] *De universo*, 1.3.3, pp. 757B–762B. William of Auvergne, *The Providence of God*, pp. 40–53.

letters were not read naturally by humans, and natural letters could only be natural signs, but where were they marked and by whom? Finally, William invoked Aristotle's view of nature as not being itself a subject, but rather existing in a subject, as an accident therefore. It could not be maintained that an accident could know or teach anything, except in the sense that whiteness taught through sight or heat through touch, but this was far from the types of cognition that were seen to exist naturally in animals.[101]

Thus far William had only mocked the views of others, not offering a firm statement of his own position. Now he presented what seemed to be a more valuable explanation, though his language retained a hint of reservation: 'It seems, therefore, that one should say that ...'. It seemed that one should say that, just as being flowed – from the first and universal font of being – over being caused by him, and just as goodness, beauty and other things called good flowed over all created

---

[101] *De universo*, 1.3.3, p. 758A–B: 'Super hujuscemodi igitur jocose multoties aliquos interrogavi, et est una responsio omnium, quod natura docet animalia hujusmodi artes, et artificia. Postmodum autem quaero ab eis, utrum natura haec liber sit, an magister, et iterum cujusmodi liber, cujusmodi literis scriptus, et quae quantitas, et cujus voluminis, et de scriptore interrogo eos, et nesciunt mihi respondere. Quod si dixerint mihi, quia magister est: quaero iterum, ubi magister ille tot, et tanta artificia didicerit, si didicit, quoniam si non didicit, hoc est, si scientiam hujusmodi ab alio non habet, necesse habent confiteri, quia magister iste creator est, cum solus creator scientiam ab alio non habeat, et quicunque habent, ab eo habeant. Mirabile autem valde est, quod similis artifex, et magister, aut similis liber apud nos nondum inventus est. Quod si creator ipse est, qui docet hujusmodi artifices, quibus nulla est artificiorum necessitas propria comparatione indigentiarum, et necessitatum nostrarum; quanto magis in nos deberet esse tantae divinae bonitatis largitas, ut in hominibus essent istae artes naturaliter, vel saltem artes necessariae, ut non cogerentur homines tantis vigiliis, et laboribus, artificia sibi necessaria discere, et acquirere? Mirabile autem est, si sit liber, in quo legunt isti artifices artificiorum suorum scientiam, qualiter ibi legere possunt, et videtur quod literae illae non sint naturales, si literae ibi sunt, quoniam nullae literae naturaliter leguntur ab hominibus, et literae non possunt esse naturales aliud, quam naturalia signa: sed et haec signa, ubi impressa sunt, et quis impressit? Amplius. Natura, quae ita docet hujusmodi artifices, si non est subjectum, sed in subjecto, quemadmodum docet Aristoteles qualiter docet, cum ipsa nihil scire posse videatur? Quis enim opinetur accidens, vel scire aliquid, vel docere, nisi quemadmodum quis dicat albedinem, vel alium colorem per visum, et calorem per tactum, et unumquodque aliorum sensibilium docere sentientem se per sensum, sive per sensionem sui. Modus autem iste multum longe est a cognitionibus, quae videntur esse naturaliter in animalibus antedictis, et in multis aliis.' See William of Auvergne, *The Providence of God*, pp. 41–2.

and generated beings, according to the creator's will, 'so also from the light of the wisdom of the creator there naturally descend or flow down in accord with his good pleasure the lights of the previously mentioned sorts of knowledge, as their necessity and usefulness requires'. William was now able to link his discussion to the theme of providence with which he had begun. In this way, a 'certain light of providence' flowed over the ant when it did what it needed to do to survive. Similarly, 'a certain cleverness in hunting' descended 'like another light' on the spider, and, because this would not be sufficient on its own for the spider's survival, 'another light, namely, of spinning and making thread and weaving its webs' was added 'by the providence of the creator'.[102]

When William turned to the abilities displayed by dogs, he likened the light which some of them received to prophecy and divination: 'in dogs not only is the sense of smell more noble than in many other animals, but is also like a certain light of prophecy or divination naturally given to certain dogs by the creator so that they search out, recognize, and apprehend by this light both thieves and men in hiding'. This was because dogs were created to guard humans and their property. They showed this by their friendliness and by the barking and biting with which they strove to drive off what seemed to them to be harmful to their human masters or their possessions. This kind of light, which was like that of divination, was given to dogs because robbers and murderers in hiding greatly harmed humans and their property. It was given to very few dogs, however, either because of the nobility of the light or because of the rarity of the disposition (*dispositio*) that made them receptive to this light. According to one view, this was just like prophecy and humans: someone, and William gave no name, had

---

[102] *De universo*, 1.3.3, p. 758B: 'Dicendum igitur videtur, ut quemadmodum fluit esse a fonte primo, et universali essendi, et pro beneplacito ipsius, super esse causatum ab ipso; et quemadmodum bonitas, et pulchritudo et alia quae vocantur bona, sunt bonitate sua super omnia creata, et generata; sic et a lumine sapientiae creatoris descendunt, sive fluunt pro beneplacito ipsius naturaliter lumina praedictarum cognitionum, prout requirit necessitas, et utilitas eorum; quemadmodum super formicam lumen quoddam providentiae, quia hoc requirit necessitas vitae ipsius: [...] sic quaedam venandi astutia, velut aliud quoddam lumen, descendit super araneam: manifestum enim est, quoniam venatione muscarum vitam suam sustentat aranea: et quoniam hoc lumen in ipsa inutile esset per se, superadditum est ei ex providentia creatoris aliud lumen, videlicet nendi, sive filandi, et retiacula sua texendi.' The quotations are from William of Auvergne, *The Providence of God*, p. 42.

said that 'the splendour of prophecy' was very rarely found in humans because sufficient goodness of disposition (*complexio*), receptive of this splendour, was rarely found. William, however, disagreed about the nature of prophecy in humans. The splendour of prophecy had nothing to do with disposition, but was given to many because of the merit of their sanctity, to many so that they could instruct others and warn them against the evils that threatened them, and to many for other reasons that William proposed to discuss elsewhere. William did not at this stage pursue the similarity between the light granted to some dogs and prophecy in humans, simply restating his view of animal knowledge and abilities as lights descending providentially from the creator like being itself: 'Just as, therefore, from the first fountain of being or from the first being, as being, there descends other being, so from the first light of wisdom, as sapiential light, there descend all these lights in accord with the good pleasure of the creator and through his providence for the benefits I mentioned and countless others.'[103]

William proceeded to explore the significance of the descending lights that informed animal behaviour. Immediately he stressed that they did

[103] *De universo*, 1.3.3, pp. 758B–759A: 'et quod mirabilius videtur esse, in canibus non solum olfactus nobilior est, quam in multis aliorum animalium, sed etiam velut quoddam lumen prophetiae, seu divinationis, quibusdam canibus a creatore inditum est naturaliter, ita ut latrones, et homines occultos hoc lumine investigent, dignoscant, et apprehendant. Causa autem in hoc est, quoniam canis creatus est propter custodiam hominum, et rerum ipsarum, quam ipsi sollicitudine sua et amicabilitate quadam, exhibere videntur hominibus, nec non latratibus, et morsibus, quibus arcere nituntur ea, quae videntur eis nocitura hominibus dominis suis, vel rebus eorum evidenter indicant. Quia igitur latrones, et occulti homicidae de his sunt, quae multum nocent hominibus, et rebus eorum, lumen hujusmodi, quasi divinationis cujusdam, datum est canibus, veruntamen paucissimis, vel propter nobilitatem ipsius luminis, vel propter raritatem dispositionis, quae illos receptibiles illius luminis facit. Quemadmodum et quidam dixit de splendore prophetiae, quia tanta bonitas complexionis rarissime invenitur in hominibus, quae receptibilis sit splendoris illius: ideo rarissime invenitur in illis. Tibi vero certum potest esse, splendorem istum non sequi bonitatem complexionis, quin potius datur ab ipso praeter dispositionem, quoniam multis data est propter meritum sanctitatis ipsorum, multis propter alios instruendos, et praemuniendos contra mala, ipsius imminentia, multis ob alias causas, quas audies suo loco, et interdum valde male complexionatis invenies et datum esse, et dari bonum istud. Quemadmodum igitur a primo fonte essendi, sive a primo esse, ut esse, descendit esse aliud: sic a primo lumine sapientiae, ut est lumen sapientiale, descendunt omnia hujusmodi lumina pro beneplacito creatoris, et per providentiam ejusdem, ad utilitates, quas dixi, et alias innumerabiles.' The quotations are from William of Auvergne, *The Providence of God*, pp. 42–3.

not legitimate mistaken belief in auguries by offering some kind of explanation of how they worked. It was not the case that lights descended on some types of birds, giving them forebodings about human events that they indicated to humans by their chattering, flight and other movements.[104] They did, however, explain the different 'weapons' that animals possessed: 'It is also seen in this way that all things that have virtue and strength [...] always descend from the first virtue or strength and power – as virtue and strength and power – through [the creator's] providence and as the necessities and benefits of the recipients require.' Thus, oxen and cows defended themselves from wolves with horns. Wild boars and crocodiles protected themselves with tough skin. Bears and lions had teeth and claws for both attack and defence.[105] Similarly, all instances of beauty, goodness, knowledge, loftiness and sweetness descended from the first beauty, goodness, knowledge, loftiness and sweetness respectively.[106] Despite this multitude of effects, William insisted at some length that there was no question of diversity in the creator, and that the likenesses generated by descent did not undermine the creator's profound difference from all that was created.[107]

[104] *De universo*, 1.3.3, p. 759A: 'Debes in hoc etiam scire, quia stultitia augurium, et opinio tam antiqua de veritate auguriorum, qua opinione multi adhuc errare noscuntur, hanc potest videri habuisse occasionem sui esse, et suae credulitatis, tanquam super corvos, et cornices, aliasque aves, circa quas observantur auguria, descenderent quaedam lumina praesagiorum a lumine antedicto, et quae per haec de eventibus humanis praesagirent aves hujusmodi, garritibus, et volatibus, aliisque corporum suorum motibus hominibus indicarent.' See William of Auvergne, *The Providence of God*, p. 43.

[105] *De universo*, 1.3.3, p. 759A: 'Videtur etiam juxta hanc viam, ut omnia, quae sunt virtutis, et fortitudinis [...] descendant similiter a prima virtute, sive fortitudine, sive potentia, ut est virtus, et fortitudo, et potentia, semper per providentiam ipsius, et prout requirunt necessitates, et utilitates recipientium. Unde in quibusdam sunt arma defensionis, sicut in bobus, et vaccis apparet in cornibus, quia per illa se defendunt a lupis: quaedam vero sunt arma protectionis sicut duritia cutis in apris, et cocodrilis, licet et aliae sint utilitates istorum. In aliis vero dentes, et ungues ad impugnationem pariter, et defensionem sunt, sicut in ursis, et leonibus.' The quotation is from William of Auvergne, *The Providence of God*, pp. 43–4.

[106] *De universo*, 1.3.3, p. 759A: 'Sic etiam de pulchritudinibus dicendum videtur, quoniam omnes descendunt a prima pulchritudine, ut est pulchritudo, et bonitates a prima bonitate, ut est bonitas, similiter scientiae, vel sapientiae, a prima scientia, ut est scientia, et altitudines a prima altitudine, ut est altitudo, et suavitates veri nominis a prima suavitate, ut est suavitas.' See William of Auvergne, *The Providence of God*, p. 44.

[107] *De universo*, 1.3.3, p. 759A. See also William of Auvergne, *The Providence of God*, pp. 44–5.

William stressed that all animals received 'illuminations' of the kind that he had been discussing, though some were smaller and less noble, and others larger. Furthermore, 'the luminosity of the wisdom of the creator' penetrated not only to the least of the animals, but also to the least of seeds. This prompted William to cite Aristotle to the effect that 'the lights that fall upon seeds are like skills', to which William added that 'such lights are not only like arts or skills in operating, but are like commands of the creator, which seeds necessarily have to carry out'. He explained further that seeds did not operate with free will but out of necessity, and he attributed to Aristotle the view that nature generally operated 'in the manner of a servant'.[108] William clearly meant this to apply to animals too, and, although he did not make the point explicitly, he implied a key difference between animals and humans which, as we have seen, he set out elsewhere: animals could only behave according to their nature, using the lights that they had received from the creator; humans, however, had free will.

Having at least implied a clear boundary between humans and animals, William then returned to the nature of the lights that descended on animals and to the comparison with prophecy, at which point hesitation about the boundary returned. Seeking to identify the type of cognition or knowledge that these lights provided, William explained that there were three types of cognition. First, innate knowledge came directly from the creator and existed in the knower from the moment of the knower's creation. Second, infused knowledge also came directly from the creator, but was given by the creator at some point after the knower had been created. Third, there was knowledge that came from things and the images of those things, and it was as

---

[108] *De universo*, 1.3.3, p. 759B: 'Quia vero similes illuminationes eis, quas supra posui, habere videntur omnia alia animalia et quaedam multo minores, minusque nobiles, quaedam etiam majores [...]: apparet tibi ex omnibus his luminibus luminositatem sapientiae creatoris penetrare atque pertingere non solum usque ad extrema animalium, sed usque ad extrema seminum; lumina enim quae cadunt super semina, similia sunt artificiis, ut dixit Aristoteles: attende etiam quod lumina hujusmodi non sunt tantum sicut artes, aut artificia operandi, sed sunt velut imperia creatoris, quae necesse habent implere ipsa semina. Non enim ex libero arbitrio operantur, sed ex necessitate per modum scilicet servientis, quod et Aristoteles aliter alibi generaliter dixit, de natura scilicet, quoniam ipsa operatur per modum servientis.' The quotations are from William of Auvergne, *The Providence of God*, pp. 45–6. For William's debt to Avicenna rather than Aristotle, see William of Auvergne, *The Providence of God*, pp. 41, n. 14; 45, n. 18; 46, n. 19.

diverse as the things and their images. Depending on whether things
were universal or particular, knowledge of them would be universal or
particular. Innate and infused knowledge, however, imitated their
cause. Innate knowledge was knowledge of many genera and species,
while infused knowledge was one in number and entirely indivisible
with regard to all genera, species and individuals. The lights that
descended on animals fell into this latter category and were characterised by unity: like the first wisdom, they did not have the lines or
divisions of books, or any gathering together of parts. Using the first
person, William declared that he said the same about prophetic splendour since it was one, indivisible, and was not made up of many
particular splendours. Again in the first person, William repeated that
he said just this about the lights that descended on animals. He pulled
back from asserting that these lights and human prophecy were identical, adding that they should not be called lights in comparison with
prophetic splendour. Immediately, however, he reasserted their similarity, insisting again that in one fundamental respect they were indeed
comparable, namely in their unity and indivisibility. Moreover, he
noted that if similar lights were found in humans, the ability to find,
identify and catch robbers, or to spin, make thread, weave webs and
hunt, without any instruction or teaching having been given, no one
would fear to call these splendours prophetic.[109] Shifting his emphasis

[109] *De universo*, 1.3.3, pp. 759B–760A: 'De hoc quoque, quod quaerebatur,
cujusmodi cognitiones, vel scientiae essent lumina ista: reminisce debes
eorum, quae alibi audivisti per me, videlicet, quoniam scientiarum, sive
cogitionum, aliae sunt descendentes desuper a luminositate creatoris, et hae
vocantur scientiae inditae, vel infusae, et inditae quidem, quae naturaliter
insunt, et cum his creantur, quibus inditae sunt, et nominantur recte scientiae
naturales, vel innatae. Aliae vero, quae post naturam completam dono creatoris
adveniunt, communiter vocantur infusae. Tertiae vero rebus ipsis adveniunt,
quemadmodum imagines resultantes in speculis ab inspicientium faciebat, et
istae sunt, quae sequuntur numerositatem rerum, et varietatem, atque
diversitatem, utpote causatae ab ipsis. Nec mirum cuiquam videri debet, si
multitudinem, aut varietatem rerum sequantur imagines earum, et verificatur
istud per argumentationem a causa, et a proportione. Cum enim res omnes ad
hujusmodi imagines suas similiter se habeant, sive proportionaliter, consequens
est, ut permutatim, sicut res ad invicem se habent, sic et imagines earum se
habeant ad invicem, et propter hoc, ut est diversitas in rebus ad invicem, sic et
in imaginibus. Propter hoc igitur, sive res hujusmodi universales fuerint, sive
particulares, eodem modo erunt, et scientiae, vel universales, vel particulares.
Scientiae vero aliae, videlicet tam innatae, quam infusae sequentur imitationem
causae suae, et propter hoc una earum est multorum generum, et multarum

back and forth between assertions of similarity and difference, apparently continuing in the deliberately playful mode that he said he used when questioning others about how animals were taught their behaviours, William did not seem to be drawing a very firm boundary between animal behaviour and human prophecy.

The boundary seemed weaker still when he then chose to account for scholarly ways of speaking about animals in terms of academic practice and social context. He explained that we do not usually say that animals or seeds operate by 'that knowledge', by which he presumably meant the lights that he had been discussing, or through any kind of knowledge, for two reasons. What he meant by the first is not entirely clear: 'propter paucitatem nostrae exercitationis in his', which Teske translates, 'on account of the paucity of our experience in them'. Given that he went on to discuss the views of the uneducated, it seems likely that this refers to the learned and to a lack of work or research in this field, as we would put it today. The second reason for not saying that animals and seeds operated by knowledge was that it would entail novelty, something that common and uneducated people always wondered at and very much abhorred. This was why Aristotle had been unwilling to say that there were skills in seeds, referring rather to powers that were like skills. And this was why, more appropriately, in speech that had been adapted to fit, 'we do not say that those lights are knowledge or arts or skills, but rather likenesses of knowledge, arts, and skills'.[110] So, apparently, the only reasons that William had for not

specierum; quaedam vero una numero, et per omnem modum impartibilis est omnium generum, specierum, et individuorum. Hinc est, quod lumina, quae numeravi tibi, et nominavi, sequentur hoc modo unitatem ipsius; nec habent lineationes, aut descriptiones librorum, nec aggregationes partium, quemadmodum nec sapientia prima. Et idem dico de splendore prophetico, quoniam unus est, non divisibilis, neque aggregatus ex particularibus splendoribus, et in illo, et per illum visa est a prophetis tanta rerum, et eventuum multitudo, atque diversitas. Sic dico et de istis luminibus, quamquam nec lumina dicenda sint comparatione splendoris prophetici: in uno tamen ei assimilantur, videlicet in hac unitate, et indivisibilitate. Si tamen invenirentur in hominibus lumina similia, videlicet investigandi latrones, et dignoscendi, atque deprehendendi eos; aut nendi, sive filandi, texendique retia, et venandi; si inquam invenirentur in hominibus praeter eruditionem, et doctrinam, splendores illos propheticos, nemo nominare vereretur.' See William of Auvergne, *The Providence of God*, pp. 46–7.

[110] *De universo*, 1.3.3, p. 760A: 'Sed neque scientia illa, neque per scientias operari animalia, vel semina usualiter dicimus, propter paucitatem nostrae exercitationis in his, et propter novitatem, quam semper mirantur, et

accepting that animals had genuine forms of knowledge, arts and skills were that scholars had not got to grips with the issue and for fear of a negative reaction from the ignorant.

Unsurprisingly, William could not let the matter rest here and he addressed the issue of whether or not animals had knowledge head on, asking whether a spider knew how to spin its web. William began with a distinction: either the spider did what it did knowingly or by chance and without intention. He then made a series of points in favour of the spider acting knowingly. If one held that the spider acted unknowingly, how did it avoid all error in its actions? Moreover, Aristotle said that being able to speak was a sign of knowing, in which case why was being able to do something not a sign of knowing? Furthermore, what sign was there in a woman making thread that she knew how to do this that did not appear in a spider to better and greater effect? The response that the woman did this by art, knowledge or skill ran into Aristotle's statement that what is naturally so is more so, so that natural art is more an art, natural knowledge is more a knowledge, natural skill is more a skill, and knowing naturally is a higher form of knowing. Thus, the spider was more knowing and acted more knowingly than a woman who knew because she had been taught or had found out for herself.[111]

plurimum abhorrent vulgares homines, et imperiti: propter quod Aristoteles dicere noluit, quod artificia essent in seminibus, sed virtutes similes artificiis: propter quod, et convenientius accommodato, aptatoque, sermone non dicimus lumina ista scientias, aut artes, seu artificia, sed magis similitudines scientiarum, et artificum, et artificiorum.' The quotations are from William of Auvergne, *The Providence of God*, p. 47.

[111] *De universo*, 1.3.3, p. 760A–B: 'Si quis autem quaerat, utrum aranea sciat nere, sive filare, et retiacula tendere, et alia facere, quae facit, proponet quaestionem non facile determinabilem imperitis. Aut enim scienter facit aut casu, quod facit, et praeter intentionem. Quod si respondeat quis, quia nescienter facit, quod facit: qualiter igitur declinat errorem omnem in operibus suis? Amplius. Si quemadmodum dicit Aristoteles, quia omnino scientis signum est dicere posse, cur non potius signum scientis erit ficere posse. Amplius. Quod signum est in muliere filante, quod ipsa filare sciat, quod non et melius, et magis appareat in aranea? Si vero dixerit, quia mulier hoc facit arte, vel scientia sive artificio, oblitus videtur hujusmodi homo sermonis, quem dixit Aristoteles, quia quod naturale tale, magis tale: quare naturalis ars, magis ars, et naturalis scientia, magis scientia, et naturale artificium, magis artificium, et naturaliter sciens, magis sciens. Quare et magis sciens est aranea hujusmodi operis, et magis scienter operatur fila, et retia, quam mulier quae per doctrinam alienam, aut per propriam adinventionem hoc scit, vel didicit.' See William of Auvergne, *The Providence of God*, pp. 47–8, and 47, n. 22 and n. 23 for suggested references to Aristotle's *Politics* and *Metaphysics*.

There was another possible response, however: simply that the spider acted by natural instinct ('instinctu naturae'). But this raised even more challenging questions. What was instinct and what was nature? William focused on nature and pointed out that the same question now had to be asked about nature that had previously been asked about the spider: did nature instigate the spider's actions knowingly or unknowingly? William returned to the distinction between being a subject and being in a subject that he had applied to nature earlier in the chapter. If nature acted knowingly, it could not be in a subject because things that existed in a subject could not know or do anything knowingly. William had previously maintained, citing Aristotle, that nature did exist in a subject, but he did not make that point here. Rather, he pointed out that if nature were a subject, other questions arose. Did it act by itself or at the instigation of another? If it acted by itself, what was the benefit and for whom? If the benefit was its own, nature was identical with the spider because the hunting of flies benefitted only the spider. If, however, nature acted at the instigation of another, this other could be the creator, and in this case divine providence would be made more manifest when it was found that the spider acted at the creator's instigation. But if the other were not the creator, the spider must act at the instigation of one or many substances more noble than itself. If there were only one substance, it had to rule all spiders, teaching them the skills they needed to live or instigating their actions, a role either given to it by the creator or innate. Either way, it was clearly apparent that all skills of this kind existed and were exercised by the providence of the creator. Similarly, if there were many substances ruling spiders, their rule also had to be either innate or granted by the creator.[112] William had returned to the

---

[112] *De universo*, 1.3.3, p. 760B: 'Quod si responderit, quia instinctu naturae hoc facit aranea, involvit se difficilioribus quaestionibus, de instinctu scilicet, et natura, quid utrunque istorum sit. Eadem enim restat quaestio de natura, utrum scienter instiget araneam ad ista facienda, aut inscienter. Quod si scienter, non erit hujusmodi natura in subjecto: eis enim, quae in subjecto sunt, nullo modorum congruit scire, vel scienter aliquid facere. Si vero subjectum fuerit natura hujusmodi, sequentur aliae quaestiones de hujusmodi subjecto, an per se hoc faciat, an alieno instinctu. Quod si per se, restat quaestio, qua utilitate, et cujus: si enim sua utilitate hoc facit, non erit hujusmodi subjectum, nisi ipsa aranea; venatio enim muscarum soli araneae, quae illam exercet, utilis esse videtur. [...] Si vero alieno instinctu hoc facit hujusmodi natura, perveniet haec eadem ad creatorem, et fiet per hoc manifestior in rebus hujusmodi providentia divina, cum inventum fuerit,

theme of divine providence that was the point of the chapter, but it was very unclear whether or not he thought that spiders knew what they were doing, although he had presented and not refuted a series of arguments indicating that the spider acted knowingly.

At this point, William resumed his discussion of how language should be used in matters like this. He urged that there should be no contention about words or names with those who philosophised properly. Rather, they should be used without dispute and contention as 'the community of human beings' used them. Although this community was presumably different from the common and uneducated to whom he had referred earlier, the same attitude to language was invoked. Strangeness in words, which common usage repudiated, and novelty were to be avoided in every way by those who philosophised. William acknowledged that there might be exceptions in technical academic language: lack of an appropriate term or necessity might require the invention of new words or formulations. Nevertheless, it was to avoid strangeness and novelty, previously said to be abhorred by the common and uneducated, but now said to be rejected by common usage, that Aristotle had not wished to say that the powers in seeds were arts or skills, but that they were like skills. Now, however, William attributed a further view to Aristotle: he had also said, 'without an intolerable abuse', that these powers 'are certain arts or certain skills of nature'. William further insisted that there should be no contention with what he had said previously about whether spiders acted knowingly because common usage accepted that they knew what they were doing and that they received a tiny light from the luminosity of the wisdom of the creator so that they could acquire sustenance.[113]

---

quod per ejus instinctum et filant araneae, et texunt fila sua, et retia, et venantur. Si autem non pervenerit hoc usque ad creatorem, necesse est, ut veniat hoc ad aliam substantiam nobiliorem, quam sit aranea, et hoc, vel unam, vel multas: quod si fuerit una sola, apparebit esse regitiva omnium aranearum, docens eas hujusmodi vivendi artificia, vel instigans eas ad hoc, ut illa exerceant, quod vel erit ei commissum a creatore, vel erit eidem innatum. Per utranque autem viarum istarum apparet evidenter omnia hujusmodi artificia et esse, et exerceri providentia creatoris. Eodem modo si multae fuerint hujusmodi substantiae regitivae aranearum, non poterit esse dubium, quin regimen hujusmodi sit eis vel innatum, vel commissum a creatore.' See William of Auvergne, *The Providence of God*, p. 48.

[113] *De universo*, 1.3.3, p. 760B: 'Tu ergo attende in his, et similibus, quia non est contendendum recte philosophantibus de vocabulis, aut nominibus, quin potius sine litigio, et contentione utendum his, sicut utitur communitas hominum;

Evidently William had indeed been arguing that the spider acted knowingly, and ultimately he appealed to common usage to support both this assertion and his earlier theory of lights descending to inform animal behaviour.

William continued to discuss his theory of descending lights, to give yet more examples of remarkable animal behaviour, and to stress that all bore witness to the omnipresent providence of the creator. He briefly raised the question of whether or not animals could know universals and particulars, noting that 'because the statements of the philosophers concerning the souls of non-rational animals report that they cannot apprehend universals and because they said that this is proper to rational souls and intelligent substances, it does not seem, according to them, that in the souls of animals there are imaginations or other impressions of universals'.[114] Despite seeming to distance himself from this position by attributing it to others, even though elsewhere he himself contrasted rational humans and non-rational animals, as we have seen, William made it clear that he was not saying that animals knew in the way that humans ordinarily knew. Rather, they knew through lights descending from the creator in the way that humans sometimes knew through prophecy, without universals and particulars. The view that animals lacked rationality was not therefore challenged by his approach. William repeatedly insisted that all depended on divine providence, and his philosophical discussion rather petered out:

> extraneitas autem, quam repudiat usus communis in vocabulis, modis omnibus fugienda est philosophantibus. Similiter et novitas earum, nisi forte defectus, vel necessitas cogat nova vocabula fingere, aut saltem circunlocationibus utendum est eis. Propter hoc igitur Aristoteles noluit dicere virtutes quae sunt in seminibus, artes esse, vel artificia, sed similes artificiis, quamquam absque abusione intolerabili dixisset eas esse quasdam artes, seu quaedam artificia naturae. Neque contendendum est tibi super hoc, quod dixi, videlicet utrum araneae sciant facere, quod faciunt, vel utrum scientiae ibi faciant, quod faciunt: cum usus communis hominum recipiat eas scire operari, et scienter, opera hujusmodi, et tantillum luminis accepisse eas a luminositate sapientiae creatoris ad acquirendum sibi sustentationem vitae, sicut dixi.' The quotations are from William of Auvergne, *The Providence of God*, pp. 48–9.

[114] *De universo*, 1.3.3, p. 761B: 'Quia vero sermones philosophorum de animabus animalium non rationabilium ferunt eas apprehendere universalia non posse, et dixerunt hoc esse proprium animarum rationalium, et substantiarum intelligentium, non videtur secundum eos quod in animabus animalium [...] sint imaginationes, vel aliae impressiones universalium.' The quotation is from William of Auvergne, *The Providence of God*, p. 51.

'On these points, therefore, you see from me some ways of exercising your mind. But if God grants that you see something better on these points, I would rejoice and wish that it would happen to me.'[115]

William's chief concern was to demonstrate the ubiquity of divine providence through consideration of animal behaviour. In doing so, the boundary between animals and humans was very clear in some respects: humans were rational, animals were not; humans had free will, animals did not. But in other respects, and for much of the discussion, the boundary was very faint. Initially he maintained that animals were not said to have true knowledge, arts and skills only because scholars had not got to grips with the matter and to conform to the views of the common and uneducated people. Even then, animals had powers that were *like* knowledge, arts and skills. William went on to put many arguments in favour of animals having knowledge, and then cited usage common to the community of human beings, distinct from the vulgar and uneducated, as legitimating this way of talking about animals. Most important of all, he explained animal behaviour in terms of lights descending from the creator, and if these were not the same thing as prophetic knowledge in humans, in their unity and in the absence of universals and particulars, they worked in exactly the same way. By playfully shifting back and forth between assertions of similarity and difference, William held complex ideas in uncertain balance.

William again likened knowledge in animals to prophecy in humans at the end of an extended analysis of the relationship between God and animals in which he probed the limits of providence by considering whether it extended to hunting. Did God care whether one fish was caught in the fisherman's net rather than another? The same could be asked about hares, goats and other animals that were hunted. And when animals hunted other animals, was it through divine care and providence that a lion caught and ate one wild ass rather than another, or that a cat did the same to one mouse rather than another? The same could be asked about spiders and flies, swallows and little flies, dogs and bones, vultures and dead bodies, birds and seeds. William's response was unequivocal: 'the wisdom of the creator in no way extends to the smallest things less than to the greatest or those in

---

[115] *De universo*, 1.3.3, p. 762A–B: 'Vides igitur per me in his nonnullas vias exercitationis ingenii tui: quod si melius videre dederit tibi Deus in his, gauderem, et hoc ipsum vellem fieri mihi.' The quotation is from William of Auvergne, *The Providence of God*, p. 53.

between, and on the other hand, he knows the uses, although they are very small, of the smallest no less than those of the greatest, although they are the greatest'.[116] William stressed, however, that in this context caring and not caring could be said in two ways. The first referred to an emotional response: not caring about something meant being neither happy if it happened nor upset if it did not. In this way the common people said that the creator did not care about things that neither offended nor pleased him, in other words when he neither punished nor rewarded. Thus, the creator did not care about the number of flies caught by spiders or gulped by swallows. This usage, however, only pertained to the creator metaphorically because he was utterly impassible and immutable. The second sense of caring meant to give heed to or to think about something, and this pertained to 'our noble apprehensive power and to the creator in accord with the excellence of his nobility' for there was nothing 'in created things or their events' about which the creator did not care in this way.[117] In this sense the creator

---

[116] *De universo*, 1.3.10, p. 773A: 'Utrum autem venationes hominum, et animalium, sic in divinam curam cadant, et providentiam [...] quaestionem habet [...]. Hujusmodi sunt, an per curam, et providentiam creatoris cadat iste piscis in rete piscatoris potius, quam alius, et an evadant alii per providentiam creatoris, quasi parcat eisdem a captione, et devoratione. Et eadem est quaestio de leporibus, et capreolis, et aliis retiaculis venatorum. In animalium vero venationibus similis est quaestio de onagris, et leonibus, videlicet an per curam, et providentiam divinam capiatur, aut devoretur potius unus onager a leone uno, quam alius, et unus mus a murilego potius, quam alius. Eadem est quaestio de araneis, et muscis, et hirundinibus, et musculis, et devenient istae quaestiones ad canes, et ossa, ad vultures, et cadavera, ad gallinas et grana, et alias aves, quae granis vescuntur. [...] Dico igitur in hoc, quia sapientia creatoris non minus attingit ullo modorum minima, quam maxima, vel media, vel econverso, nec minus cognoscit utilitates minimorum, licet minimas, quam maximorum, licet maximas.' The quotation is from William of Auvergne, *The Providence of God*, pp. 84–5.

[117] *De universo*, 1.3.10, pp. 773B–774A: 'Debes autem scire, quia quantum pertinet ad id, de quo nunc agitur, curare, aut non curare, per duos modos, aut intentiones dicitur. Et una ex his est pertinens apud nos ad virtutem nostrum motivam internam mobilem, et est secundum hunc modum, non curare, non habere cordi eousque [*sic*] aliquid, ut nec gaudeat, si fiat, nec offendatur, si non fiat, aut econverso, et juxta hunc modum non curare dicitur creator apud vulgus omne id, quo nec offenditur, nec placatur. Hoc autem est dicere, pro quo nec poenam infert, nec remunerationem largitur, et hoc modo nec numerum muscarum, quae ab araneis capiuntur, aut ab hirundinibus glutiuntur [...] curat creator [...], et ad creatorem non pertinet ista intentio, nisi per tropum, quem scis, cum ipse sit in ultimitate impassibilitatis, et immutabilitatis. [...] Secundo modo, vel intentione dicitur

did care about the number of flies caught by spiders and eaten by swallows because 'he sees all things by his fixed and most lucid gaze, along with their uses and ends'.[118]

Expanding on God's purpose, William maintained that the question of why one fish or beast was captured rather than another should be regarded like all things that seemed to happen by chance: a multitude of contributory causes could be found. One fish was caught because it went in one direction to feed or fled the noise made by the fishermen's friends, whereas another fish fed in a different place or at a different time, or the noise of the fishermen did not reach it or it fled elsewhere. William elaborated on the possible reasons why this other fish got away. His point was that 'the wisdom of the creator sees each and every one of these and orders them to the most suitable ends and uses that are perfectly known only to him'.[119] William then attributed one important purpose to God, and that was preservation of the species. If all fish and beasts were caught at the same time, there would be universal destruction of fish and beasts. Even if only some were caught, it might result in the destruction of particular species in a specific piece

curare, attendere, vel cogitare, et hoc modo pertinet ad vim nostram apprehensivam nobilem, et juxta excellentiam nobilitatis suae ad ipsum creatorem; nec est aliquid in rebus creatis, vel earum eventibus, quod per modum istum, et intentionem non curet creator.' The quotations are from William of Auvergne, *The Providence of God*, pp. 85–7.

[118] *De universo*, 1.3.10, p. 774A: 'Per modum igitur istum curat et numerum muscarum, quae capiuntur ab araneis, et muscularum, quae deglutiuntur ab hirundinibus, et omnem ordinem captionis, atque devorationis earum: omnia enim intuetur intuito fixo, ac lucidissimo cum utilitatibus, ac finibus suis.' The quotation is from William of Auvergne, *The Providence of God*, p. 87.

[119] *De universo*, 1.3.11, p. 774B: 'sic cum ibat piscis forsan ad pastum per viam aliquam, contingebat tunc trahi rete per eandem, vel forte fugiebat a clamore, et strepitu, quem faciebant socii trahentium rete. Occurrerunt igitur sibi invicem piscis, et rete, occursus autem causa est evidenter captionis, alius autem piscis eadem hora, vel eadem via non ibat ad pastum, vel forte non pervenit ad eum terror piscantium, ut fugeret, aut forte fugit in profundiores latebras, aut per aliam viam, et ideo non occurrit reti, aut reti illi, et propter hoc non est retentus ab ipso. Causa vero prioritatis captionis suae manifesta est, interdum propinquioritas sua ad rete, vel major natatus velocitas, vel prioritas perventionis terroris ad ipsum. Evasionis autem, id est, non captionis plurimae possunt esse causae, quas per semetipsum videre, tibi facile est, quemadmodum major hora, vel tarditas natatus. [...] et haec omnia universa, et singula intuetur, et attendit sapientia creatoris, et ordinat ad fines, et utilitates convenientissimas, et sibi soli perfecte notissimas.' See William of Auvergne, *The Providence of God*, pp. 88–9; the quotation is from p. 89.

of water or a specific region; for example, when there were few fish in a river or pond, the taking of those few would mean the eradication of that species in that place. It was not therefore a source of wonder 'if by his care and providence the creator and preserver ["conservator"] of natures watches out for particular natures, as he does for them all[,] so that they are not totally destroyed and do not perish, until their use or usefulness has to cease'. William pointed out that earthly princes and lesser lords sometimes banned hunting and fishing on their property, motivated by greed rather than any wish to conserve nature, so it made even more sense for the creator to conserve what he had created to be so very useful.[120] So, God was a conservationist, at least for as long humans needed animals, and he had a strong record: the Old Testament told how he had ordered that types of animals be conserved in Noah's ark.[121] Moreover, this explained why God had given animals their characteristic skills and behaviours: for survival. William proceeded to list a series of God-given skills that permitted various species to avoid predation by either humans or other animals: deer stuck to trodden paths to avoid wolves; wild asses bore great thirst so that they could avoid watering holes until lions had finished drinking; hares ran fast; rabbits had deep holes; swallows and other birds flew at great speed. Survival also meant catching food, however, and William noted that swift flight enabled swallows to catch flies.[122]

---

[120] *De universo*, 1.3.11, p. 774B: 'Ne dubites autem, quia sicut omnes pisces simul capi, omnesque feras, destructio esset universalis in piscibus, et feris, ita quasdam, et quosdam, quandoque capi, et comedi, destructio esset naturae particularis in eisdem quantum ad aquam unam, vel ad regionem, verbi gratia, cum pauci sint aliqui pisces in flumine, vel stago aliquo, paucos illos capi, vel comedi est vastatio atque destructio generis illius in eodem. Non est igitur mirum si creator, et conservator naturarum per curam, et providentiam suam praecavet naturis particularibus, sicut et universalibus, ne ex toto vastentur, et pereant, donec cessare debeat usus, et utilitas earum, de quo in praecedentibus audivisti. Si vero principes terrarum, et minores domini earundem, interdicunt interdum venationes, et piscationes in aquis, et terris jurisdictionis suae, avaritiae suae solummodo per hoc consulere intendentes, non naturae de conservatione providere: quanto magis bonitas creatoris naturarum conservationi, quas tantis utilitatibus creavit, consulere non dedignabitur ne pereant usquequaque?' The quotation is from William of Auvergne, *The Providence of God*, p. 89.

[121] *De universo*, 1.3.11, p. 774B: 'Et notum est tibi ex lege Hebraeorum, qualiter in arca illa famosissima conservare praecipit per bina, et septena animalium genera, contra aquas diluvii.' See William of Auvergne, *The Providence of God*, p. 89.

[122] *De universo*, 1.3.11, p. 775A: 'Quis enim docuit cervas in via calcata parere ad declinandas luporum insidias? Quis docuit eas quod lupi vias calcatas timeant,

But who taught animals these survival skills or gave them the knowledge that they needed? All this brought William back to the source of animal knowledge and behaviour, and he reprised his ideas about lights and prophetic splendour, inviting his reader to consider 'the wonders of the creator in natural things and the radiance of his wisdom, by which all animals are illumined for governing themselves and their life, even if by small lights, although the animals themselves are large'.[123] Furthermore, he demanded that animals be admired when compared with human souls and intellects that had been obscured by original sin and darkened further by subsequent vices. Continuing the comparison of animals and humans, William repeated his point that the knowledge and abilities displayed by animals would undoubtedly be regarded as prophetic in humans if they did the same things without being taught or studying books.[124] In these chapters of the *De universo*, the status of animals did not seem so low after all. There was a sense in which God the conservationist cared about all animals, preserving each species by giving its members the skills and

et declinent? Quis docuit onagros sustinere vehementem sitis ardorem, donec leones ab aquis potatis reversi sint, ne si hora illa, qua leones ad aquam vadunt, vel inde redeunt, leonibus occurrant, ab ipsis devorarentur? Quis eos fecit scire, quod leones eisdem insidientur? Sic et leporibus levitatem pedum, et cuniculis profunda, et pene inaccessibilia aliis receptacula ad conservationem sui esse dedit creator; sic et hirundinibus tantam velocitatem volatus, et multis aliis aviculis, et multi credunt hanc esse causam, quare nulli avi rapaci hirundo unquam praeda fiat. Mihi tamen videtur, quod acquisitio victus ejus tota est per volatum, quoniam per ipsum solummodo venatur musculas volitantes.' See William of Auvergne, *The Providence of God*, pp. 89–90.

[123] *De universo*, 1.3.11, p. 775A: 'Hoc autem incidenter dixi [...] ut erigam, et elevem intellectum tuum et cogitatum tuum ad considerationem mirabilium creatoris in rebus naturalibus, et radiositatis sapientiae suae, qua illuminantur omnia animalia ad regendum se et vitam suam, licet luminibus permodicis, quamquam magna sint.' The quotation is from William of Auvergne, *The Providence of God*, p. 90.

[124] *De universo*, 1.3.11, p. 775A: 'et merito esse debeant in admiratione nostra, et in comparatione obtenebrationis animarum humanarum, et obfuscationis, quam patitur intellectus humanus ex corruptione originali, et superadditis tenebris ex vitiis, et peccatis. Hac quippe comparatione splendorem propheticum reputaremus in animabus humanis eam sagacitatem, sive sensum naturae, seu quodcunque aliud nomen nominari libeat, in canibus virtutem investigandi, et apprehendendi latrones: sic et providentiam formicarum, de qua dixi tibi, si absque doctore, et absque libri inspectione inveniretur in hominibus, sicut et alia innumera hujusmodi lumina, quae non dubitaremus splendores vocare propheticos in hominibus, si absque doctrina, et eruditione invenirentur in eis.' See William of Auvergne, *The Providence of God*, p. 90.

knowledge that they needed for survival. Humans were to admire animals because they lacked the capacity to sin; corruption rather than free will was the distinctive characteristic of humans. While William would not say that the lights received by animals were identical with prophetic knowledge in humans, by insisting that the same knowledge and behaviour in humans would, if not acquired through teaching or study, be regarded as prophetic, he used a formulation that deliberately avoided outright assertion of difference and gave greater weight to similarity.

Another similarity was the capacity to learn by experience and even in some sense to be taught. William attacked the idea that a soul of the world could act unknowingly by arguing that any natural ignorance would have been removed by experience so that it acquired knowledge. In support of this, he pointed out that even brute animals learn by experience, and so surely the soul of the world would do so too: 'For we see in brute animals many instances of natural ignorance are removed by experience and that they are taught in many things as if through a discipline, so that we even see that some of them talk or speak, if such a mimicking of human speech should be called speech.'[125] According to William, animals did not just learn by experience but could actually be taught, although they were taught '*quasi disciplinabiliter*', '*as if* through a discipline'. Moreover, some animals learned to speak, although they could only imitate speech. William presented the capacity of animals to learn as like that of humans, similar but not identical. A boundary was in place, but it was characterised by similarity as much as difference.

William identified another kind of similarity when his efforts to understand processes of cognition in spiritual substances led him to consider how a spider knew that a fly was caught in its web. The spider detected that a fly had fallen into its web when it felt the slightest movement or concussion of a single thread. This movement did not seem, however, to be the sole reason for the spider's knowledge; it was not just that the fly fell into the web, causing movement that stimulated the spider. Rather, the spider was stimulated by a light that was within it, and this caused the spider's apprehension of the fly. William

---

[125] *De universo*, 1.3.28, p. 800B: 'In brutis enim animalibus videmus per assuetudinem naturales ignorantias multas tolli, et ipsa in multis quasi disciplinabiliter erudiri, ita etiam ut quaedam ex illis loqui, sive discere videamus, si loquela dicenda est locutionis humanae talis effigiatio.' The quotation is from William of Auvergne, *The Providence of God*, p. 165.

immediately said that the human intellect worked in the same way. Although he did not name him, he cited the view of Augustine that the human intellect, when stimulated through the senses, generated intelligible forms and intellectual reasons through and in itself. Moreover, Aristotle seemed to agree with this when he said that the intellect did not experience material or corporeal forms as the senses did, because understanding that something was hot did not make us hot, whereas feeling that something was hot did make us hot. William concluded that, given the above, it should not seem impossible or extraordinary that new cognitions or apprehensions should be generated 'occasionally' in spiritual substances, stimulated by things that could be sensed, but going beyond what was experienced by the senses.[126]

In his next chapter, William explained this process more fully, drawing on the Aristotelian notion of *solertia*, the ability to infer something immediately. While the spider's apprehension of the fly's fall or capture was caused 'occasionally' by the movement or the striking of a thread in its web, it was caused 'effectively or efficiently' by an innate light, or by an art naturally placed in the spider, or in the way in which, just as you see reminiscences and recollections proceed out from the treasure of the memory, similarly thoughts and passions proceed out from the habits of the sciences, the virtues and the vices, occasioned by the lightest of stimuli of external things. To illustrate the point, William cited an example of *solertia* taken from Aristotle's *Posterior Analytics*: someone sees a person speaking with a money-changer, and from this sight forms the opinion that this person wishes

---

[126] *De universo*, 2.2.74, pp. 927B–928A: 'Manifestum est intueri volentibus araneas in latibulis, quae sibi ad hoc contexuerunt, casus muscarum in telas suas deprehendere, et hoc levissimo unius fili motu, sive concussione. Motus vero hujusmodi non videtur, cum et unus, et unum sit, signare totam istam rationem, videlicet muscam aliquam in telam hujusmodi cecidisse, sed potius, quasi commotionem facere, seu excitare ipsam araneam, illa vero sic excitata ex lumine, quod apud ipsam est, rationem hujusmodi apprehendere; et sensit hoc idem de vi intellectiva nostra unus ex nobilioribus sapientibus Christianorum, dicens in sermone suo, quia passionibus sensuum, quasi pulsatur, seu excitatur intellectus, ipse vero per semetipsum, et in semetipso format sibi formas intelligibiles, et rationes intellectuales; et in hoc concordare videtur Aristoteles, ubi dicit, quia intellectus non patitur a formis materialibus, seu corporalibus, quemadmodum sensus, intelligentes enim calidum non calefimus, et tamen sentientes calidum calefimus. Jam igitur per ea, quae praecesserunt, nec impossibile, nec mirum tibi videri debet, a rebus sensibilibus, praeter passiones, et impressiones, occasionaliter, quemadmodum dixi, fieri, seu generari novas cognitiones, seu apprehensiones in substantiis abstractis spiritualibus.'

to have money changed by the money-changer; this sight therefore gives the occasion for *solertia*, out of which comes this thought or suspicion. William explained that it was manifest that a sight of this kind could not in any way be a cause in itself of a thought or suspicion of this kind. There was no doubt, however, that it was some sort of occasion for the thought, and that it was some sort of small aid that helped with the generation of the thought. *Solertia* in itself, however, was the cause of the generation of the thought, which came out from it like an overflowing or a stream from its own source.[127] So, this was not a sequence of thoughts expressed as a syllogism, but a sudden grasping of the conclusion.

Focusing first on the spider, William had turned to an example of human thinking to illustrate how the animal thought. The boundary between humans and animals was apparently non-existent, and William now used the human to make what for him was the real point about spiritual substances. If new bits of knowledge or opinions were stimulated in humans by such slight occasions, this must be much more possible in spiritual substances which were much quicker than human souls to form all thoughts and apprehensions. They were necessarily stimulated much more easily than human souls by even smaller occasions in external things, bringing the perfection of their intellect and will to bear upon them. William had to acknowledge that these

[127] *De universo*, 2.2.75, p. 928A: 'Est igitur apprehensio, quam dixi araneae super casu, seu captione, muscae occasionaliter ex motu seu concussione fili in tela ipsius, effective vero, sive efficienter, est ex innato lumine, sive ex arte, sive artificio naturaliter indito ipsi, vel per modum, quo procedere vides ex thesauro memoriae reminiscentias, et recordationes in effectu, similiter ex habitibus scientiarum, et virtutum, atque vitiorum cogitationes, et passiones, levissimis excitationibus rerum obviantium, quemadmodum se habet in exemplo, quod de solertia posuit Aristoteles, videlicet de eo, qui videt aliquem loquentem cum cambitore, sive campsore, et ex hoc viso incidit ei opinio quod velit ab illo mutuari pecuniam, dat igitur occasionem iste aspectus solertiae, ut ex ea exeat ista cogitatio, sive suspicio. Manifestum autem est aspectum hujusmodi nullo modorum per se causam posse esse hujusmodi opinionis, sive suspicionis, dubium vero non est, quin aliqua occasio sit, et quin aliquod adminiculum praestet generationi illius, solertia vero per se causa est generationis illius, et ex ea exit tanquam inundatio, vel rivus ex proprio fonte.' See Aristotle, *Posterior Analytics*, trans. Hugh Tredennick (Cambridge, Mass., 1960, reprinted 1966), I.34, pp. 170–3 where the example and an explanation of the meaning of *solertia* is given, though Aristotle's original example was of a rich man, not a money-changer. See Marrone, *William of Auvergne and Robert Grosseteste*, pp. 62–3; Moody, 'William of Auvergne', p. 76.

occasions were presented to human souls through sense organs which spiritual substances lacked, but it was impossible that the perfection of spiritual substances should dull their *solertia*, or any other noble habit.[128] This prompted him to return to examples that he had previously given which concerned the sense of nature, an internal sense rather than an external one. It was by the sense of nature that a dog tracked and apprehended a robber. As William had said, these and other such cases seemed to involve something like prophetic splendour, and not the customary passions of the sense organs. Now, William added that they arose from the lightest occasions.[129]

William had begun with the spider feeling a thread of its web being struck and a human seeing someone talk to a money-changer. These sense-based experiences rooted in bodies had led to the deployment of *solertia* by both spider and human, so that they both immediately inferred further knowledge. Insisting that spiritual substances must, in their superior condition, have the same ability, indeed to a higher degree, William took the senses out of the picture, and returned to the possibility of knowing without them, to the sense of nature used by the tracker dog, continuing, however, to emphasise knowledge stimulated by occasions. But if the senses were not involved, what were these occasions? William thought it not improbable that the robber, the prostitute and all others who were vehemently inimical to human

---

[128] *De universo*, 2.2.75, p. 928A–B: 'Quod si in nobis per adeo exiguas, et exiles occasiones, sive excitationes generantur novae scientiae particulares, sive opiniones, aut alterius modi apprehensiones, quanto longe minoribus in substantiis abstractis hoc fieri possibile est? Praesertim cum incomparabiliter promptiores, et expeditiores sint ad omnes cogitatus, et apprehensiones, quam animae nostrae; sicut apparere tibi potest in ipso exemplo solertiae, qui quanto fortior, et major est, tanto facilius, et expeditius, ac per modum omnem occasione minori ab ea exeunt solertes cogitationes, et cogitatus. Quapropter necesse est minoribus adminiculis rerum exteriorum particularium incomparabiliter facilius excitari ad haec, quae dixi, istas substantias, quam animas nostras, necesse insuper est adminicula, quae praestantur animabus nostris per passiones, quae fiunt in organis sensuum nostrorum, suppleat perfectio virtutis intellectivae, et etiam imperativae in substantiis, de quibus agitur: non enim possibile est, ut perfectio soporet eis solertiam, vel alium nobilem habitum.'

[129] *De universo*, 2.2.75, p. 928B: 'quod si reminisce velis exemplorum, quae in praecedentibus posui tibi, videlicet de sensu naturae, quo canis investigat, et deprehendit latronem, et de aliis hujusmodi, quae multum assimilantur propheticis splendoribus, videbis non ex consuetis passionibus organorum sensibilium ista fieri, sicut praedixi, sed levissimis pene occasionibus'.

nature could not be anywhere, even for a short time, without leaving some signs or impressions of their malice, and that through these signs the sense of nature apprehended things that were noxious or inimical to it. William held this view especially because many things that were good or friendly to human nature manifestly left indications of their existence or presence in the places where they had been. Thus, after the presence of saints and the most blessed angels, a brightness was sometimes left and felt in the places where they had appeared, sometimes a fragrance or odour of sweetness, and sometimes a sense of sanctity and reverence or the venerable. Similarly, horrific and foul places resulted from the presence of malign spirits. Those who went near them were left perpetually disfigured, and it was even worse for those who were vexed or possessed by them. If, however, such evident signs, detectable to the senses, were left by the presence of both those that were friendly and those that were hostile to human nature, William thought there would be little wonder if they imprinted small signs, undetectable to the senses, in the places where they had been, for it was obvious that the smaller and lighter the impressions, the more easily they could be left compared with bigger ones that were more detectable to the senses.[130]

In the last part of the chapter, William returned to animals, referring to other examples that he had previously discussed, reviewing them in light of his analysis of occasions. He considered both the possibility

---

[130] *De universo*, 2.2.75, p. 928B: 'Quod si quis dixerit, quia et latro, et meretrix, et omnia alia, quae vehementer inimica sunt naturae humanae, non possunt esse alicubi, etiam ad modicum, quin relinquant signa aliqua, vel impressiones malitiae suae, et per haec signa, scilicet sensus naturae deprehendit hujusmodi noxia, et inimica illi, non videtur mihi hoc improbabile. Praesertim cum de multum bonis, et naturae humanae amicis relinqui manifestum sit indicia existentiae suae, sive presentiae in locis, in quibus fuerint: quemadmodum de praesentia sanctorum, ac beatissimorum angelorum, interdum fulgor, interdum fragrantia, sive odor suavitatis, interdum etiam sanctitas, et reverentia quaedam, seu venerabilitas in locis, in quibus apparent, et relinquitur, et sentitur: sic ex praesentia malignorum spirituum loca horrifica, et foetida. Ipsi etiam, qui vel ad modicum appropinquaverunt eis in maleficis operibus, horrore aspectus, sive vultus, ab eis perpetuo horribiles relinquuntur; multo autem amplius, si ab eis aliquando vel vexati fuerint, vel arrepti; si autem tam evidentia signa, et sensibilia, ex utraque praesentia relinquuntur, hoc est amicorum, et inimicorum naturae, quid mirum, si minima, et insensibilia ab eis in locis, in quibus fuerint, imprimuntur? Manifestum enim est minores, et leviores impressiones tanto facilius, et levius imprimi, quam majores, et sensibiliores, quanto eisdem leviores fuerint, ac minores.'

that animals read signs without the use of senses and the possibility
that their senses were superior to those of humans. He began with the
power of divination attributed to vultures. Their ability to foresee the
imminent slaughter of humans and a multitude of dead bodies of
humans and horses had to be explained in one of two ways. Either
they foresaw by an innate light within themselves in ways that William
had already presented, or they were stimulated by some external sign
impressed in the air or in another part of the inferior world. Developing the second possibility, William noted that great events were cus-
tomarily preceded by signs: comets when kingship changed,
monstrous births, fiery dragons flying through the air when a king
was about to be overthrown, fiery swords in the air when human
conflict was about to occur below. The hedgehog that foresaw powerful winds in Constantinople, however, did not foresee this in any sign
that could be apprehended by humans by their senses or in any other
way. Just as the dog apprehended things by smell which humans could
not smell at all, and the lynx saw things that were not apprehensible to
humans, similarly there was no doubt that many future things were
apprehensible to some animals by means of hidden signs that humans
could not detect. This was the case with the dog that sensed hares and
partridges in advance, which the most experienced bird-catchers and
hunters could not.[131]

---

[131] *De universo*, 2.2.75, p. 929A: 'Juxta hunc modum poteris negociari circa
divinationem, quae imponit vulturibus, de qua et dixi tibi. Non enim possunt
praevidere imminentem stragem hominum, sive multitudinem cadaverum
occidendorum hominum, aut equorum, nisi altero duorum modorum, quos
dicam tibi, videlicet aut in ipso innato sibi lumine juxta modos, quos prius
audivisti, aut aliquo signo forinseco excitati in aere, vel in alia parte mundi
inferioris, impresso. In magnis enim eventibus fieri consuevit, ut signa aliqua
eos praecedant, sicut saepe audivisti de apparitionibus stellarum, quae comatae
vel cometae dicuntur, et solent fieri in mutationibus regnorum, similiter et in
partubus, seu in foetibus monstruosis, atque prodigiosis, quales sunt partus
mularum, et hominum, sive aliorum animalium, duo capita, aut aliam
monstruositatem habentium. Sic apparuerunt nonnunquam et dracones ignei
volantes per aera imminente dejectione alicujus regis de regno suo per alium,
sive ab alio; sic et gladii ignei apparuerunt in aere imminente strage hominum
sub aere illo habitantium. Eodem modo se habet et de aliis terroribus
manifestis. Eritius vero qui praevidit in urbe Constantinopolitana ventum
magnum futurum, atque fortissimum, non praevidit hoc in aliquo signo
sensibili, aut aliter nobis deprehensibili. Quemadmodum enim canis olfactu
aliquid deprehendit de odorabilibus, in quod non potest olfactus noster, et
lynx aliquid visu suo, quod non est apprehensibile nostro, similiter se habere

William thus began by arguing that both humans and spiders deployed *solertia* in response to occasions that they detected by the external senses. Both humans and some animals could therefore instantly infer new knowledge, a rational operation described by Aristotle. Indeed, William used humans as an example to illustrate how the spider thought: the animal was the thinker and the human the explanatory device. William's main concern, however, was to understand spiritual substances, and his key point was they must have the same ability to infer knowledge in response to 'occasional' stimuli, but to a higher degree. Because spiritual substances did not have sense organs, William discussed signs that were not detectable by the senses as well as those that were. In both cases he thought that some animals were able to read signs that humans could not apprehend at all. In the first part of his analysis, William attributed *solertia* to some animals as well as to humans, and indeed spiritual substances. In the latter part, in which *solertia* was not explicitly discussed, he found animals to be superior to humans in their ability to detect signs, whether by the senses or not.

Animals and humans also turned out to be much the same when William analysed the power of the will. He stated that, by the vehemence of its affection, the will (*vis motiva*) aided the apprehensive power (*vis apprehensiva*) both in human souls and in the souls of other animals. As a consequence, holy men ('viri', so men rather than humans) saw and spoke much more deeply and clearly in matters pertaining to the honour and glory of the creator and to the promotion of the reward of future happiness, than many who were deemed great scholars by humans and who pursued sacred doctrine by study. Similarly, William stressed the way in which the will strengthened the female imagination.[132] Seeking the cause, William explained that the

non dubites, et de occultis signis multis rerum futurarum, multa apprehensibilia esse aliqualibus animalibus, quae nobis non sunt, sicut apparet in cane leporario, et exploratore perdicum, qui praesentit tam lepores, quam perdices, quod non possunt exercitatissimi, vel aucupes, vel venatores.' For the hedgehog in Constantinople, see Aristotle, *On Marvellous Things Heard*, 8, in Aristotle, *Minor Works*, trans. W. S. Hett (Cambridge, Mass., 1936, reprinted 1963), pp. 242–3.

[132] *De universo*, 2.2.70, p. 922B: 'Debes igitur scire in omnibus his, et hujusmodi, quia vis motiva et in animabus nostris, et aliorum animalium, vehementia suae affectionis incredibiliter adjuvat vim apprehensivam: neque enim vane dictum est, ubi intenderit ingenium ibi valet, propter quod et viri sanctissimi in eis quae

apprehensive power was subject to the will as its ruler, for the will governed not only its motion, but those things that aided its motion, such as foreknowledge, deliberation, and the opening and raising of the eyes. William noted that in some cases the power of the imagination could seem very similar to prophetic splendour that could shape the imagination, and indeed one type of prophecy was imaginative in that it worked in the imagination so that it received prophetic knowledge without exterior senses. William emphasised, however, that the cause here was natural luminosity (*luminositas naturalis*) that multiplied within the soul as it escaped the blockage constituted by the senses. He explained what he meant with a series of analogies based in the physical world. In one analogy, this was like water rushing past an obstruction by which its flow was held back. In another, he noted that people with feeble, crippled feet and legs had much stronger hands and arms, and those who were disabled in one hand and arm were restored in the other hand and arm, and the same applied to feet and legs. Taking this idea that a weakness should be compensated for by a strength, William insisted that it must be obvious that what little was obtained by exterior sight was supplemented by the imaginative power or a common interior sense. And this supplement was either the product of the abundance of natural light or derived from the addition of a divine gift that was similar to prophetic splendour. Despite the similarity to prophecy, William stressed that many wonderful apprehensions were made by the sense of nature, by which he meant natural light rather than the senses. He explained that nature abhorred whatever was greatly inimical to it, either greatly saddening or greatly pleasing, without any apprehension being involved, so whoever experienced this could, without the senses, detect the presence or proximity of that which was vehemently saddening or pleasing. And here again, William illustrated his point with reference to women. A story was told about a woman who was struck with terror

pertinent ad creatoris honorem, et gloriam, et ad promerendam futurae foelicitatis remunerationem, longe profundius, et clarius vident, et enunciant, quam multi, qui nomen magnorum doctorum obtinent apud homines, sacraeque doctrinae studiis insistendo senuerunt [...]: sic non immerito aestimandum est imaginationem mulieris.' For William's view of the will as the dominant power in the human soul, see Moody, 'William of Auvergne', pp. 86–7; Roland J. Teske, 'The will as king over the powers of the soul: uses and sources of an image in the thirteenth century', *Vivarium* 32 (1994), pp. 62–71.

when her son was killed even though she could apprehend nothing about his killing. William recalled that he had himself seen a woman who so dreaded her husband that she fell ill whenever he entered the house even though she was otherwise entirely ignorant of his presence. And prostitutes, William explained, could suffocate their children before they were born.[133]

William then turned to animals. It was just the same with dogs tracking and catching robbers. Because the duty to protect humans

[133] *De universo*, 2.2.70, p. 923A–B: 'Quod si quaerat aliquis, quid causae est, quod virtus motiva ita adjuvat apprehensivam? Respondeo, quia sic posset forsitan quaerere, qua de causa apprehensiva adjuvat motivam, manifestum tamen est, quia vis apprehensiva subest virtuti motivae tanquam imperanti: imperat enim vis motiva non tantum motum, sed etiam ea, quae adjuvant motum, ut praecogitationem, deliberationem, apertionem oculorum, et elevationem [...] verisimile est virtutem imaginativam accedere aliquatenus ad splendorem propheticum, de quo certum est exercitatis in eo, quod descendere habet virtutem super imaginativam, et quaedam species prophetiae imaginativa est, quoniam sit in virtute illa, et secundum ipsam, et adjuvatur virtus imaginativa ad recipiendum hujusmodi splendorem privationibus sensuum exteriorum [...]. Causa autem in hoc est, quoniam luminositas naturalis, seu natura animarum nostrarum ex obturatione sensuum multiplicatur interius, tanquam aqua currens ex obice, vel per obicem retinentem, seu prohibentem fluxum illius, [...] et debes scire in hoc, quia non sit solum per hujusmodi retentionem, vel privationes, confortatio, seu multiplicatio virtutum apprehensivarum, sed etiam motivarum, propter quod qui debiles habent pedes, et tibias, manus plerumque fortissimas habent, et brachia, et qui debilitatis incommodum habent in altera manuum, vel brachiorum, eis in altera restauratur, et de pedibus, et tibiis similiter se habet. Manifestum igitur tibi esse debet ex his, quia quod minus habebat in visu exteriori, suppletum est ei in ipsa virtute imaginativa, vel in sensu communi interiori: et quia suppletio ista fuit ei vel ex multitudine dicti nativi luminis, vel ex superadditione divini muneris similis prophetico splendori, nihilominus tamen sciendum est tibi sensu naturae multas apprehensiones mirabiles fieri [...]. Quae enim vehementer inimica sunt naturae, hoc est, vehementer contristantia ipsam, vel vehementer delectantia ipsam, horret, et refugit natura absque ulla apprehensione ipsorum, et ex hujusmodi horrore convincit, et conjecturatur ipse, qui hoc patitur, praesentiam seu, propinquitatem rei hujusmodi: et eodem modo se habet de vehementer delectantibus, et sicut narratur, ita fuit in muliere, quae ita pavebat, et horrebat, interfectorem filii sui, cum nihil de interfectione ejus apprehendisset. [...] Memini etiam me vidisse mulierem, quae adeo exhorrebat maritum proprium, ut quoties intrabat domum, in qua ille erat, morbo caduco arriperetur, licet alias omnino eum ignoraret esse. Similiter se habet de meretrice, et fornicatore, meretrix enim non parum inimica est humanae naturae, meretricium enim nobilissimos fructus humanae naturae, antequam nascantur, suffocat, et praeextinguit, hoc est, filios, et filias.' On William's reforming work with and other writings about prostitutes, see Biller, *Measure of Multitude*, pp. 74–8.

and their property had been imposed on them by natural law, or by God the creator, they, or rather a few individuals amongst them, were also given the cunning (*astutia*) to track and catch robbers. To explain how it was with dogs, William presented humans as an analogy: the power of reason was given to all humans by the creator so that they could direct and arrange their lives and customs, but prophetic splendour was given to a very few to the same end. Returning to dogs, the reason for alluding to prophecy in humans became clear when William explained that no external apprehension was involved when dogs tracked and caught robbers. Rather than following a scent or anything else that could be sensed, the dog perceived the harm of the robbery by a sense of nature or a natural light. And in the same way it perceived the person who did the harm and the road by which that person carried away the stolen goods. This ability was not necessarily limited to dogs because William remarked that some humans said that they tracked and caught robbers in the same way. Animals were still William's main concern, however, because he went on to discuss vultures. Much the same process was in operation in vultures if one believed those who said that vultures knew in advance where to find the slaughter of humans and horses, and therefore imminent battles in which such slaughter would occur. Because the diet of vultures consisted mostly of the bodies of humans and horses, this kind of foresight was given to them to assist their nutritive power. In just the same way and for the same reason the spider was given the skill to spin and the cunning to trap flies. It also seemed more likely, as Aristotle claimed, that the hedgehog gave an indication of coming winds in Constantinople by blocking the entrance to its little cave when that entrance was open to winds that only came later. It could not know in advance about these winds, before they actually came, in any other way than by the aforementioned sense of nature that was given to it to assist its power of self-preservation. In just the same way and for the same purpose humans were given many skills, such as spinning, weaving, sewing, and such like. William here ignored his own point made elsewhere that humans were taught their skills.[134]

---

[134] *De universo*, 2.2.70, p. 923B: 'Quemadmodum apparet de cane investigante, et deprehendente latrones, cum enim impositum sit ei tanquam a lege naturae, vel institutoris ipsius, et conditoris Dei altissimi, velut officium custodiendi homines, et res eorum, additur ei, licet in paucis individuis, astutia haec investigandi scilicet, et deprehendendi latrones. Astutia enim haec adjutrix est efficacissima

William clearly held that humans and animals were the same in that they could know and act without the use of their physical senses but rather by virtue of what he variously called natural light and the sense of nature. When he discussed specific examples, however, he chose primarily to focus on women and animals. It is tempting to speculate that this was because he thought men could achieve more by sense-based reasoning, but at no point did he say this. Once again, the way in which animals knew was likened to prophecy, though on this occasion it was clearly presented as something different which both humans and animals could deploy. Animals and humans, especially female humans, were not entirely different.

It would seem that rationality did not make humans so very different or superior with regard to the power of the will, and William had an explanation. The rational soul was naturally more powerful and commanding than the soul of any inferior, irrational animal with regard to their respective bodies, but the will of the rational soul was impeded by

ipsius ad implendum sive exequendum hujusmodi officium. Quemadmodum vides, quod ratio, seu virtus ratiocinativa, data est a creatore generi humano in omnibus individuis suis propter gubernationem, et compositionem vitae suae, et morum. Et nihilominus superadditus est splendor propheticus, licet in paucissimis, atque rarissimis, additus inquam eis propter eandem causam, quae est compositio, et decoratio vitae, nec sit ista investigatio, aut deprehensio latronum per apprehensionem aliquam, quae a foris sit. Neque enim latro, neque latrocinium odoris alicujus vestigio, vel cujuslibet alterius sensibilis, investigabilia sunt, sed sicut praedixi, velut sensus naturae aut aliud lumen est, quo sentit nocumentum latrocinii canis investigator. Et eodem sensu sentit et ipsum, qui nocumentum intulit, et viam, per quam rem furtive subreptam asportavit. Et dicunt nonnullos ex hominibus astutia simili praeditos, videlicet investigandi, et deprehendendi latrones, et via simul simillima ad hoc eos uti. Juxta hunc modum se habet res in vulturibus, si creditur hominibus, qui dicunt eos praesentire strages hominum, et equorum, et propter hoc praelia imminentia, in quibus facienda est strages hujusmodi. Cum enim in vulturibus maxima pars victus sit in cadaveribus hominum, et jumentorum, data est eis ista, ut ita dicatur, praevidentia in adjutorium virtutis ipsorum nutritivae, quemadmodum araneae in adjutorium virtutis ejusdem data est nendi, sive filandi quaedam peritia, et insidiandi muscis astutia. Juxta hoc melius videtur, et magis verisimile est, Eritium, de quo narrat Aristoteles, quod dedit indicium ventorum imminentium apud Constantinopolim per hoc, quod ingressum speluncellae suae obstruxit ex ea parte, qua patebit ventis, qui postmodum secuti sunt, vel eos praesentire, antequam essent, vel alio modo sentire non potuisse, quam sensu, quem praedixi naturae, qui datus fuit ei in adjutorium virtutis suae conservativae, quemadmodum hominibus data sunt artificia, et artes multae in simile adjutorium, quales sunt ars, seu artificium nendi, texendi, filandi, suendi, seminandi, et aliorum hujusmodi.'

the corruption of the fall, just as its body was made subject to innumerable sufferings and death by the same corruption.[135] William even
suggested that one might ask whether the human soul had been more
powerful with regard to the movement of its body than the souls of
birds that flew, and whether it could make its body fly and move fast
before it had been impeded by corruption. He replied that this was very
likely because at that time it was not prevented from moving its body
by any difficulty, nor could its body resist its command with any
slowness or heaviness since the body was utterly subject and obedient
to it by natural law, and the body was free from all the sufferings by
which it was now oppressed. It followed that if, at that time, the soul
commanded its body to fly or run faster, the body would fulfil this kind
of command without any rebellion or resistance. Not all irrational
souls were equally powerful, however. Some had greater command
over their bodies than others, as did swallows and other birds in
comparison with those that walked or crawled. Everyone could see
that worms responded more weakly to command in their bodily movements than dogs and tigers. The soul's power of command over the
body was limited, however, so that animals' speed of movement was
not simply what they desired, otherwise a hare would never escape a
pursuing dog by speed of movement, nor would a partridge ever escape
a hawk.[136] Once again William recognised that a balance between
species was necessary to ensure that all survived.

[135] *De universo*, 2.2.71, p. 925B: 'Anima vero rationalis potentior est, et
imperiosior naturaliter, quam anima cujuscunque inferioris animalis
irrationalis in corpus proprium: impedita autem est virtus ejus motiva per
corruptionem originalem, quemadmodum et ipsum corpus passionibus
innumeris, et morti factum est obnoxium, per eandem corruptionem.' For
William's view in his *De anima* that the sin of the first humans resulted in
rationality being 'put to sleep and buried' and 'a brutality and a perversity far
worse than brutality' entering the soul, see Roland J. Teske, 'William of
Auvergne on the various states of our nature', *Traditio* 58 (2003),
pp. 201–18 at 212.

[136] *De universo*, 2.2.72, pp. 925B–926A: 'Quod si quaerat, an anima humana
potentior esset in motus proprii corporis, quam animae volatilium, et intendo,
an posset in motum volatus, vel aeque nobilem, aut velocem, antequam
impedimentum istius corruptionis haberet. Respondeo, quia verisimile est,
quod sic; nulla enim difficultate prohibebatur movere corpus suum eo
tempore, nec ipsum corpus tarditate aliqua, vel gravitate resistere poterat tunc
imperio illius, cum esset ei jure naturali subditissimum, et obedientissimum,
atque ab omnibus passionibus, quibus nunc premitur, et aggravatur, immune,
atque liberum; quare si eo tempore imperaret ei cursum, vel volatum, velocius

Although William often seemed to lose sight of his argument, the whole point of this discussion was to understand the powers of spiritual substances, including the human soul. He now sought to demonstrate that they could move bodies by the power of their will, and to this end, he cited examples of animals which could do this. If animals had this power, then it was beyond doubt that hierarchically superior spiritual substances possessed it too.

William stated that the less tightly spiritual substances were bound to bodies, the more powerful their wills were, and so perfect freedom from bodies liberated them and established appropriate dominance over bodies. The most obvious proof was the most omnipotent power of the creator: just as the creator had ultimate freedom and distance from bodies, so the creator had ultimate power of command and strength over their movement. Separation and natural freedom from bodies did not in any way impede the power of spiritual substances to move bodies. If this were not the case, then the creator would be the least able to move bodies, indeed his ultimate distance from bodies would make him powerless to move not only any bodies, but even himself.[137] William suggested, however, that in all spiritual substances except God, this power was limited by distance between the spiritual

absque ulla rebellione, et resistentia, hujusmodi imperium adimpleret: nec dubitari debet etiam de animabus irrationabilibus, quin quaedam earum fortioris imperiositatis sint super corpora sua quibusdam aliis, sicut hirundines, et alia volatilia gressibilibus, et naturalia serpentibus. Quis enim non videat climacas, et vermes longe debilioris esse imperii in corpora sua, quantum ad motum, quam canes, aut tigrides, aut aspiolos? Scito tamen imperiositatem istam limitatam esse, ut non sit velocitas motus eorum pro desiderio ipsorum, alioquin nec lepus velocitate motus canem unquam effugeret insequentem, nec perdix accipitrem, et ad hunc modum se habet de multis aliis.'

[137] *De universo*, 2.2.73, p. 926A: 'dico, quia sicut paucitas alligationis spiritualium substantiarum ad corpora auget virtutem motivam in eis, sive fortificat; sic perfecta absolutio, et libertas ab eisdem, et illas liberat, et absolvit, et in complemento congruentis sibi fortitudinis constituit. Cujus indicium evidentissimum est virtus omnipotentissima creatoris. Quae sicut est in ultimitate libertatis, et elongationis a corporibus, ita est et in ultimitate imperiositatis, et fortitudinis super motus eorum. Separatio igitur, et libertas naturalis a corporibus nullo modorum impedit, aut retardat potentiam substantiarum hujusmodi, nec prohibet apud eas esse potentiam, seu virtutem motivam corporum, nec prohibet eam esse apud hujusmodi substantias. Alioquin cum maxima sit hujusmodi libertas, et separatio apud creatorem, maxime prohiberet illum ab hujusmodi potentia, vel virtute. Quapropter in ultimitate elongationis esset creator elongatus ab ea, et in ultimitate

substance and the body it was to move. Rather surprisingly, perhaps, he illustrated his point by turning to the material world. It was just like the power of a magnet which attracted and repelled iron, but not from further than a mile. It was also like the torpedo ray that only had an effect on a body if it was touched by a part of the body or by some instrument, like a stick, that was held, and then only as long as it was held, though it did not matter how long or short the stick was. William stressed the effect of both contact and distance by returning to the magnet. A needle that touched a magnet was magnetised. A second needle that touched the first needle was magnetised by the power of the magnet. A third needle that touched the second needle was magnetised in its turn, and so on. The magnetic power diminished, however, as successive needles became more distant from the magnet, until the power entirely disappeared. Resuming his discussion of the torpedo ray, William noted that its soul brought about the opposite of strong and rapid movement by immobilising its victim's body, and this solely by its will. It did not therefore seem improbable that noble spiritual substances should bring about incomparably more powerfully the strongest and noblest movements in bodies. This was reinforced when one considered the sucking fish. If the soul of the sucking fish, by its will alone, restrained the most immense ship, however fast it was running through the sea, propelled by the winds, how could it not be likely that spiritual substances should bring about, solely by their will, the strongest and fastest motions in bodies? William stressed that it was by their will alone, since neither the ray nor the sucking fish used any kind of instrument. There were powers in their souls through which they brought about this kind of effect without the use of their bodies or any instruments. It was possible, however, that animals of this kind felt contact or injury through their bodies from things that touched them or from ships which sailed over them, and that they were driven by this to anger or some other passion through which their effects were achieved. It was through the most vehement anger that the basilisk killed a human with its gaze, for example.[138]

prohibitionis prohibitus ab eadem, esset igitur non solum impotens movere quaecunque corpora, sed et impotentissimus ad id ipsum.'
[138] *De universo*, 2.2.73, p. 926A–B: 'Fortassis autem virtus haec in omnibus aliis spiritualibus substantiis limitata est etiam secundum notam longitudinem: quemadmodum virtus lapidis magnetis in attrahendo, et repellendo, ad se, et a se ferrum; non enim attrahit ipsum a longe per miliare unum, nec repellit illud

The relationship between passions and the will was evident in both animals and humans. William invited his reader to consider the lion that broke the hip-bone of a bull or a strong ox, which four oxen would hardly be strong enough to do, and it would be apparent that this was achieved by strength of will, stemming from vehement anger, a burning appetite or hunger, because a lion did not seem to have greater strength than a bull or an ox. In humans, the power of the will was even more obvious if one considered its workings in the enraged, the possessed and the melancholic. It was manifest that the insane were much stronger in an insane fury than they were previously when sane.

a se per longitudinem miliaris [...]. Et manifestum est in animali, quod torpedo vocatur, quia tropidum efficit membrum tangentis, quod utique non efficit nisi tangat membrum illud, vel instrumentum, quo tangitur, et hoc solummodo quandiu instrumentum illud tenetur, vel tangitur a tenente ipsum, et intendo quia quandiu tenet manu virgam, vel baculum quis, quo, vel qua, tangit torpedinem, tandiu torpet manus ejusdem, nec refert, quantum ad operationem hujusmodi, quam longa, vel brevis sit virga, qua tangitur. Simile ex parte aliqua est illud, quod accidit ex adhaerentia, qua sibi invicem adhaerent acus, cum prima earum tetigerit magnetem, vel adamantem, quod inde indubitanter est, quia secunda sentit in prima virtutem lapidis illius, et tertia in secunda, et quarta in tertia, et ad hunc modum de aliis; fortassis autem minuitur, et debilitatur virtus haec, qua transfundi videtur in acus sic ordinatas per elongationem ab ipso lapide, donec omnino deficiat. Notae quippe longitudinis esse videtur operatio hujus virtutis per omnem modum: sicut igitur anima antedicti animalis, hoc est, torpedinis in membro fortissimi, ac velocissimi motus, operatur contrarium ejus, hoc est, immobilitatem corporis, et hoc solo imperio, vel desiderio, quomodo improbabile hoc videnti videri potest, ut substantiae tam nobiles incomparabiliter fortius operentur motus fortissimos, ac nobilissimos in corpora antedicta, si echeneidis anima similiter solo imperio, vel desiderio, retinet navem ingentissimam, quantocunque ventorum impetu per mare currentem, quomodo non potius verisimile est substantias hujusmodi motus fortissimos, ac velocissimos, solo desiderio, vel imperio, in antedicta corpora operari, solo imperio, vel desiderio dico, quoniam neque torpedo, neque echeneis instrumentum ad hoc vel adhibent, vel movent, propter perficiendas hujusmodi operationes. Quare in animabus earum sunt principia, et virtutes, ex quibus exeunt hujusmodi operationes absque ullo corporis, vel instrumenti alterius adjumento, nisi forte quis dicat, quia hujusmodi animalia per corpora sua sentient attactum, vel laesionem a tangentibus, vel navibus, quae super ea feruntur, ex quibus commotae sive ad iram, sive ad aliam passionem, operantur per hujusmodi passiones antedictas operationes, quemadmodum dixi tibi de basilisco, quod per iram vehementissimam, qua exardescit in hominem, quem intuetur, interficit illum.' On torpedo rays in ancient and medieval thought, see Stanley Finger and Marco Piccolino, *The Shocking History of Electric Fishes: From Ancient Epochs to the Birth of Modern Neurophysiology* (Oxford, 2011).

They could now break the strongest chains which they could not when sane. It was now extremely difficult to tie them up, whereas it had been much less difficult before their insane fury. Since their bodies were not made stronger in any way by this sort of illness, it was apparent that their strength, with their insanity, came from part of their souls through vehemence or some such passion. The melancholic could keep going all day without rest or weariness, which the sane could not. Overall, it was clear that the will and the passions generated both strength and movement.[139] William's purpose was to show that spiritual substances moved bodies by the power of their will. This had to be the case because, lower down the hierarchy of being, humans and some animals had this power. Along the way he therefore also demonstrated that in this regard humans and some animals were the same.

William also pointed to similarities between humans and animals when human corruption, rather than being contrasted with animal incapacity to sin, was likened to their general qualities, now characterised negatively. William invited his reader to compare the state of the first man, before he sinned, and the state of corruption today. Before the fall, the first man was in a truly human state, and he was truly a man. After the fall, human status was largely brutish, indeed it persisted as entirely brutish unless its brutishness was reduced through

---

[139] *De universo*, 2.2.73, p. 927A: 'Considera in leone vim imperativam motus, quo abrumpit a tauro, vel bove fortissimo, totam coxam ipsius, quod quatuor boves vix facere sufficerent, et apparebit tibi hujusmodi abruptionem fieri per fortitudinem virtutis imperativae, quae vel est ira ipsa vehemens leonis, vel ardens appetitus, sive fames ejusdem; non enim fortiores nervos habere videtur leo, quam taurus, vel bos. Quod igitur nervi taurini, sive bovini cedunt leoninis, debetur fortitudini imperativae virtutis, quam dixi, fiet quoque fortitudo hujusmodi virtutis tibi manifestior, cum consideraveris eam, et ejus operationes in furiosis, et arreptitiis, et melancholicis. Manifestum enim est freneticos longe fortiores esse in ipso furore suo frenetico, quam prius essent in sanitate sua, et hoc declaratur ex vinculis fortissimis, quae tunc dirumpunt, quae cum sani erant, dirumpere non valebant, similiter ex eo, quod tanta difficultate ligantur, qui ante furorem freneticum longe minus difficile ligarentur; cum igitur corpora eorum per hujusmodi morbum nullo modorum fortiora effecta sint, apparet evidenter istas, ut ita dicatur, fortitudines provenire freneticis, et aliis insanientibus, a parte animarum per vehementiam, sicilicet hujusmodi passionum. Videbis enim melancholicos tota die absque quiete, et lassitudine, obambulantes quod nullo modorum sanati facere sufficiunt. Haec igitur omnia aggregata consideratione confer apud temetipsum, et fiet tibi lucidum de vehementia virtutum imperativarum influere fortitudines obedientiarum, sive executionum motus, de vehementia, quam virtuti imperativae superaddunt hujusmodi passiones.'

erudition or the help of others. This was clearly apparent in children who grew up separate from humans and did not know how to walk, talk, or anything else that pertained to the nobility of human perfection. The first man, however, was not at all brutish, having nothing at all of brutish foolishness, rashness or haste. Rather he was rational and modest in his state, and attentive to and engaged with spiritual goods, and distant from lower matters, from the carnal and the temporal. As a result, the first man did not know the nudity of his own body.[140] Here William presented a hard boundary between the truly human and animals: true humans were noble in their perfection, rational and modest. That, however, was a thing of the past; fallen humans were like animals in that they were not always rational and virtuous. A blurred boundary between humans and animals was a consequence of the fall.

The boundary seemed to disappear entirely when William discussed the relationship between the power of souls and the size of bodies in both humans and animals. He wished to counter the argument that the human soul was infinite because each human soul filled its whole body, moving and governing its body however big that body was, even if it was infinite in size, a view he dismissed as erroneous and based on foolish reasoning. First, the human soul did not fill those parts of the human body that were not alive, and these included the four humours, the brain, the marrow and perhaps more. Furthermore, the bodies of giants had been the largest in human nature, and it was probable that human nature was not receptive to greater magnitude because such size

---

[140] *De universo*, 2.2.59, pp. 903B–904A: 'Si enim consideraveris statum primi hominis, antequam peccasset, etiam in puritate, et nobilitate solarum perfectionum naturalium, et statum praesentis hujus corruptionis, cum qua nascimur, invenies, quia status ille fuit vere humanus, et veri hominis; hic autem status est ex magna parte brutalis, et etiam totaliter brutalis persisteret, nisi eruditione, et aliis [...] adjutoriis a sua brutalitate aliquatenus recederet. Quod evidenter apparet in parvulis seorsum ab hominibus nutritis, qui nec ambulare, nec loqui, nec aliud, quod ad humanae perfectionis nobilitatem pertineat, facere norunt. Primus vero homo nihil omnino brutalitatis habuit, hoc est, nihil omnino brutalis desipientiae, aut temeritatis, sive praecipitationis habuit, sed rationalis, et modestus erat in statu illo, et erectus ad bona spiritualia, et suspensus ad illa, et aversus ab infimis suis, hoc est, a carnalibus, et temporalibus; propter quod nec ipsam nuditatem corporis sui cogitabat, vel cognoscebat.' For William's views on the states of human nature before and after the fall, see Teske, 'William of Auvergne on the various states of our nature', pp. 201–18.

had not been found either before or after, and it did not appear that it would be found in the future. Magnitude therefore seemed to be naturally limited in human bodies, and this limitation seemed to be one of forms rather than materials because much more bodily material and food was to be found than needed by the bodies of giants. The limitation therefore lay with souls that were not sufficient to move or govern larger bodies. William said that one could manifestly see that the power of human souls was limited with regard to the movement and rule of human bodies because each soul could only move and govern one body, and even that made it faint and weary. William then suggested that the size of the heavens might be limited for the same reason. Moreover, William said that it seemed entirely possible that the size of the tiniest animals was limited, and they were restricted to such smallness, by their form, in other words by their souls. Such multitudes of these kinds of animals were generated, there were so many bodies and such an abundance of material of these kinds of animals, that their small size could not stem from a defect in or lack of material, so it had to stem from their form, that is from their souls. As examples, William cited multitudes and armies of fleas and small mice. He concluded that their smallness was dictated by their souls, which were not sufficient to move and govern larger bodies.[141] Animals and humans were therefore

---

[141] *De universo*, 2.2.67, p. 918A–B: 'Quod si quis voluerit per hanc viam astruere similem infinitatem de animabus nostris, quia cum unaquaeque anima humana totum corpus suum impleat, et quantumcunque majus esset illud, nihilominus impleret, moveret, et regeret, etiamsi infinitum quantitate esset. Dico, quia opinio hujusmodi hominis erronea est, et ratiocinatio imbecillis. Primum, quoniam ea, quae non vivunt in corporibus humanis, non implet anima humana. Et de his sunt quatuor humores, cerebrum, medullae, et forsitan aliqua alia. Deinde corpora gigantium in natura humana maxima fuerunt, et verisimile est naturam humanam non esse receptibilem majoris magnitudinis, cum nec ante, nec post, tanta magnitudo inventa sit in eis, neque appareat posse in posterum inveniri. Quare limitata videtur naturaliter in humanis corporibus magnitudo, et potius a parte formarum, quam a parte materiarum videtur ista limitatio esse in hominibus, cum et materiae corporum, et alimenta longe majora inveniantur, quam requirant corpora gigantaea. A parte igitur animarum, quae majora, vel movere, vel regere non sufficerent, est ista limitatio. Manifeste etiam vides, quia limitata est virtus animarum nostrarum circa motum, et regimen corporum humanorum, cum unaquaeque earum non sufficiat movere, vel regere, nisi unum et ex motu etiam illius, et regimine adveniunt ei lassitudo, et taedium. [...] In minimis quoque animalibus, quorum tanta multitudo generator, non immerito videri potest a parte formae, hoc est, a parte animarum ipsorum limitata esse quantitas eorum, et ad tantam parvitatem redacta, sive restricta, cum tanta corpora, tantaque

exactly the same in that the limited power of their souls dictated the limits to their physical size.

William argued for a physical compatibility between humans and animals when he discussed incubi and succubi. His view was that humans and demons could not genuinely have sexual intercourse with each other, so there could not be true generation of offspring, and demons could not be true fathers or mothers. It was, however, possible to entertain the opinion that they could procure generation.[142] These spirits knew the nature of the seed of men, women and other animals better than all doctors and physicians, and so they could speed up generation and affect the size, strength, colour and beauty of fetuses.[143] Moreover, the seed of some animals could combine with human seed to result in generation. William gave what he called a well-known example. In Saxony a bear seized the wife of a knight and lived with her in his cave for years. She bore him sons. When she was

abundantia inveniatur materiae hujusmodi animalium; non est igitur ex defectu, seu paucitate materiae hujusmodi animalium diminutio quantitatis in eis, quare est a parte formae, sive animarum ipsorum. Abundat quippe, et subabundat materia eorum, cum innumerabiles multitudines ex eis tam saepe generari videamus; quis enim numerare sufficiat pulicum, et muscularum, multitudines, et agmina, et aliorum similium: inde igitur apparet esse parvitas quantitatis in eis, hoc est, a parte animarum, quae non sufficiunt movere, et regere corpora majora.'

[142] *De universo*, 2.3.25, p. 1071A–B: 'Manifestum igitur ex omnibus his veri nominis generationem, et rectae rationis concubitum, sive commixtionem non esse possibilem inter hujusmodi spiritus, et veros viros, verasque mulieres, et propter hoc nec veram generationem, qua vel veri patres, vel verae matres possint, vel debeant nominari. [...] Dico igitur, quia nec vere generare, nec veri patres esse possunt propter dictas causas, generationem tamen posse eos procurare opinabile est.' See Jacques Berlioz, 'Pouvoirs et contrôle de la croyance: la question de la procréation démonique chez Guillaume d'Auvergne (vers 1180–1249)', *Razo, Cahiers du Centre d'études médiévales de Nice* 9 (1989), pp. 5–27 at 16–21; Maaike van der Lugt, *Le ver, le démon et la Vierge: Les théories médiévales de la génération extraordinaire: Une étude sur les rapports entre théologie, philosophie naturelle et médecine* (Paris, 2004), pp. 252–63; van der Lugt, '"Abominable mixtures": the "Liber Vaccae" in the medieval west', pp. 262–3; Thomas B. de Mayo, *The Demonology of William of Auvergne: By Fire and Sword* (Lewiston, N.Y., 2007), pp. 169–73.

[143] *De universo*, 2.3.25, p. 1071B: 'Dubitari siquidem non potest super omnes medicos, et phisicos hujusmodi spiritus nosse naturam tam virilis seminis, quam muliebris, similiter et aliorum animalium, atque differentias eorum ad invicem, similiter et adjutoria, quibus adjuvari possunt ipsa semina ad accelerationem generationis, ad majoritatem, et fortitudinem foetuum, et ad alias multas dispositiones, sicut ad colores, et pulchritudines foetuum.'

rescued and restored to her husband, they lived with her and became knights. They were true humans, but something of the bear's nature showed a bit in their faces, and they took their name from their father, Ursini. William explained that the bear was similar to humans in two respects. Bears copulated like married humans, by which William presumably meant face to face with the man on top of the woman. When skinned, the whole shape of their body appeared similar to that of humans, because of which many people refused to eat their flesh, as if they would be eating human flesh. It was not therefore surprising if the seed of bears was so similar to human seed that it was even suited to join with it to bring about generation. Demons knew about this similarity and could take advantage of it; taking seed from animals that were similar to humans in this way and inserting it into women whom they deceived with imaginary sex was one of the means by which they could procure generation as incubi.[144] With regard to seed and generation there was therefore no boundary at all between humans and some animals.

In the *De universo*, William of Auvergne noted a host of differences between humans and animals. Most importantly, humans possessed reason and free will, while animals had neither. Humans were more noble and perfect, and they were entitled to use animals as they saw fit.

---

[144] *De universo*, 2.3.25, p. 1071B: 'De seminibus autem quorundam animalium qui cum humano semine convenienter se applicent ad generationem, uno exemplo notissimo faciam te scire. Scito igitur, quia in provincia Saxoniae ursus quidam rapuit uxorem cujusdam militis, et detulit in speluncam, in qua inhabitabat, ibique habuit eam diebus multis, et annis, genuitque ibidem filios ex ea, qui postmodum recuperata muliere illa, et restituta viro suo, vixerunt cum eadem muliere, et facti sunt postmodum milites. Et cum essent veri homines, de natura ursina hoc apparebat in eis, quod vultus eorum in similitudinem ursinorum vultuum aliquantulum declinabant, cognominationem autem acceperunt a patre, scilicet urso, a quo geniti fuerant, et vocati sunt ursini. Tu autem scis, quia ursus in duobus assimilatur hominibus, videlicet in hoc, quod coeunt, sicut conjugati, et cum decoriati sunt, tota figura corporis similis apparet hominibus, propter quod et multi esum carnium suarum abhorruerunt, videlicet tanquam esum carnium humanarum. Non igitur mirum est, si semen ursinum etiam tanta similitudine humano semini appropinquet, ut ei etiam ad generationem convenienti conjunctione applicetur. Cui autem intelligenti non est notum, hujusmodi spiritus facile esse subito exhibere, et adhibere mulieribus, quas sic ludificant, semina animalium, quae cognoverunt ad generationem convenientia.' On ancient Roman ideas about how bears copulate, and on medieval concern about eating bears, see Franco Morenzoni, 'Le monde animal dans le *De universo creaturarum* de Guillaume d'Auvergne', *Micrologus* 8 (2000), pp. 197–216 at 212–14.

Animals lacked the capacity to sin and were sometimes hostile to humans. The human body was superior to the animal body, although animals sometimes had better senses and greater physical abilities. Animals had no future beyond the Last Judgment. All of this suggested a strong boundary between humans and animals, but William also noted significant similarities and ways in which animals were the same as humans. Most tellingly, some animals knew and thought in very similar ways to humans: they knew by means of a light that in humans would be regarded as straightforwardly prophetic, though William avoided coming to a definite conclusion by playfully switching between assertions of similarity and difference; *solertia* allowed them to make immediate inferences; they learned by experience. The power of their wills was similar to that of humans, and in some cases gave them remarkable abilities that no human possessed. Humans had become much more like animals after the fall. Human and animal bodies were restricted in size by the power of their souls, and the seed of some animals could be combined with human seed to generate offspring. These similarities were most likely to receive attention when William discussed providence or when he analysed animals in order to work out the nature of higher beings on the grounds that if something of lower standing in the hierarchy of being had a power or quality, beings higher up must also possess that same power or quality, though to a greater degree and perhaps with other powers in addition. This last approach meant that William treated animals as a profoundly valuable learning resource, one predicated on the existence of meaningful similarities across the boundaries that structured the hierarchy.[145]

---

[145] For comment on the permeability of this boundary in the *De universo*, see Morenzoni, 'Le monde animal', pp. 215–16.

2 | *The Summa Halensis and Bonaventure*

Alexander of Hales and Bonaventure, who said that he had been taught by Alexander, were crucial figures in the development of the study of theology in the Franciscan order. Alexander was born at Hales in Shropshire around 1185. He studied and taught first the arts and then theology in Paris. He was one of the secular masters who departed from Paris in 1229 when William of Auvergne lost control of the university after student riots. He taught many Franciscans and entered the order himself in 1236. By then he had produced much of his theological work, which included being the first to use Peter Lombard's *Sentences* as the basis for lectures in theology, something which subsequently became a standard part of becoming a master of theology. Before his death in 1245, he had probably designed the structure for a wide-ranging theological summa and begun its composition. It was, however, very much a collective endeavour with work continuing long after his death, leading roles being taken by Jean of La Rochelle, an anonymous compiler and William of Melitona. It is variously referred to as the *Summa universae theologiae*, the *Summa fratris Alexandri*, the Halesian Summa and the Summa Halensis.[1] Animals are brought into discussion at various points. The Summa is sometimes sparse on argument, with weight simply being attached to quotations from authorities, so analysis of the Summa necessarily focuses on these quotations.

Bonaventure was born, the son of a doctor, in central Italy, in the town of Bagnoregio, between 1217 and 1221. Although Bonaventure never met Francis of Assisi, he believed that he had been cured of a childhood illness when his mother called upon Francis to come to his aid. As he put it in the prologue to one of two lives of Francis that he

---

[1] On the nature and dating of the Summa Halensis, see Hubert Philipp Weber, 'Alexander of Hales's theology in his authentic texts (Commentary on the *Sentences* of Peter Lombard, various disputed questions)', in Michael J. P. Robson (ed.), *The English Province of the Franciscans (1224–c.1350)* (Leiden, 2017), pp. 273–93, esp. 273–5, 289–93.

later wrote, 'I recognize that God saved my life through him, and I realize that I have experienced his power in my very person.'[2] Bonaventure was probably educated by Franciscans in his hometown before going to Paris to study the arts in the mid 1230s. He entered the Franciscan order in 1243 when he began his studies in theology. From 1253 he was in effect a regent master of theology, although as a result of the conflicts between the secular masters and the friars he did not formally receive the title until the pope insisted that it be granted in 1257. In that year he was elected minister general of the Franciscans, which plunged him into the thick of the controversy that was splitting the order. As the order had developed, it had become difficult to adhere strictly and literally to the ideals of poverty that Francis had espoused. The order could not hope to carry out its preaching mission on an international scale if it did not have buildings, books, and other material resources. Compromises had therefore been made, but some members of the order regarded these compromises as a betrayal of Francis. Some of them had also taken up the prophecies of Joachim of Fiore, identifying themselves as the new religious order that would come to the fore in the last age before the end of the world. Bonaventure's predecessor as minister general, John of Parma, was amongst them, and he was forced to resign by Pope Alexander IV. Bonaventure's formidable task was therefore to hold the order together by persuading as many as possible that the institutionalisation of the order was consistent with a legitimate interpretation of the ideals of Francis, while dealing forcefully with those who continued to dissent. As minister general, Bonaventure was based in Paris but travelled widely. He remained involved in university affairs, preaching on many occasions to university audiences. In 1273 Pope Gregory X made him a cardinal. He died in July 1274 while participating in the Council of Lyons.[3] He produced his *Commentary on the Sentences* in the early 1250s and revised it subsequently.[4] He too had much to say about animals.

---

[2] Bonaventure, *The Life of St Francis (Legenda Maior)* in Bonaventure, *The Soul's Journey into God; The Tree of Life; The Life of St Francis*, trans. E. Cousins (New York, 1978), p. 182.

[3] For the life of Bonaventure, see Ewart H. Cousins, *Bonaventure and the Coincidence of Opposites* (Chicago, 1978), pp. 29–43; Christopher M. Cullen, *Bonaventure* (Oxford, 2006), pp. 3–14; Zachary Hayes, *Bonaventure: Mystical Writings* (New York, 1999), pp. 16–18.

[4] Cullen, *Bonaventure*, p. 11.

The Summa Halensis

The tendency throughout the Summa Halensis was to present a very hard, clear, impermeable boundary between humans and animals. This was very much the case when it considered 'whether it befitted the dignity of the human body to have an upright figure'.[5] The Summa began its response by quoting Ecclesiastes 7:30, 'God made man right [rectum]', explaining that this was true with regard to the disposition of the body and the habitus of the mind. In light of this authority, the Summa declared that uprightness was natural to the human body with regard to three states, the state of innocence, the state of grace and the state of glory.[6]

The vestige of innocence was represented in the uprightness of the human body with regard to three things, power in presiding, wisdom in speaking and goodness in loving, because power, wisdom and goodness had characterised the human condition before the fall.[7] Concerning power, the Summa quoted Gregory of Nyssa:

man's form is upright, and extends aloft towards heaven, and looks upwards: and these are marks of sovereignty which show his royal dignity. For the fact that man alone among existing things is such as this, while all others bow their bodies downwards, clearly points to the difference of

---

[5] Alexander of Hales, *Doctoris Irrefragabilis Alexandri de Hales Ordinis Minorum Summa Theologica* (Quaracchi, 5 vols., 1924–48), Bk 2, P1, In4, Tr2, Q1, M3, C2; vol. 2, pp. 581–4: 'Quaeritur ergo utrum competat corporis humani dignitati habere figuram erectam.' Henceforth SH. With slight adaptation, the citation is intended to conform to the standard proposed by the excellent project entitled *Authority and Innovation in Early Franciscan Thought (c.1220–45)* led by Lydia Schumacher; the above citation refers to book 2, part 1, inquiry 4, tractate 2, question 1, membrum 3, chapter 2, followed by the volume and page references to the edition.

[6] SH, Bk 2, P1, In4, Tr2, Q1, M3, C2; vol. 2, p. 581: '"Deus fecit hominem rectum", ut *Eccle.* 7, 30 habetur, et quoad dispositionem corporis et quoad habitum mentis. Unde concedo quod naturalis rectitudo dignitas est corporis humani et attestatur ista dignitas homini secundum triplicem statum, innocentiae, gratiae, gloriae.'

[7] SH, Bk 2, P1, In4, Tr2, Q1, M3, C2; vol. 2, pp. 581–2: 'Vestigium ergo innocentiae quoad tria repraesentatur in hac rectitudine: quoad potentiam in praesidendo, sapientiam in loquendo, bonitatem in diligendo. Haec tria, scilicet potentia, sapientia et bonitas, erant conditionis hominis quantum ad statum innocentiae, antequam cecidit in infirmitatem potentiae et tenebras ignorantiae et malitiam concupiscentiae.'

dignity between those which stoop beneath his sway and that power which rises above them.[8]

Concerning wisdom, the Summa pointed out that only man was a rational and mortal animal. If his body were bent and not erect, he could not have the use of speech and would not therefore be the most excellent sign of divine wisdom. Gregory of Nyssa had demonstrated this to be the case when showing that only man had 'manus ad loquendum'. The argument, according to the Summa, was that if man had a bent body, he would not have hands because all bent animals had forelimbs that ended in feet; and, according to both Gregory and Aristotle, if man did not have hands, he would not have the use of speech to communicate with others, and so he could not display wisdom.[9] Although this might seem to indicate that gesture was fundamental to rational communication, what it really meant was revealed in the quotation from Gregory that followed:

if man were destitute of hands, the various parts of his face would certainly have been arranged like those of the quadrupeds, to suit the purpose of his feeding: so that its form would have been lengthened out and pointed towards the nostrils, and his lips would have projected from his mouth, lumpy, and stiff, and thick, fitted for taking up the grass, and his tongue would either have lain between his teeth, of a kind to match his lips, fleshy,

---

[8] SH, Bk 2, P1, In4, Tr2, Q1, M3, C2; vol. 2, p. 582, quoting Gregory of Nyssa, *De imagine*, 8: 'rectus est hominis habitus et ad caelum sese sustollens sursumque respiciens; principalia haec dona certissimum est esse approbantia regiam potestatem: quod enim solus ita formatus est ceterorumque omnium prona sunt corpora et in deorsum proclivius inclinata, manifesta differentia eius honoris ostenditur, dum constet illa esse huius subiecta potentiae, hunc autem supereminentis existere dignitatis.' See 'Le "De imagine" de Grégoire de Nysse traduit par Jean Scot Érigène', ed. M. Cappuyns, *Recherches de théologie ancienne et médiévale* 32 (1965), 205–62 at 216. I have quoted a translation from the Greek: Gregory of Nyssa, *Dogmatic Treatises*, ed. and trans. Philip Schaff (Grand Rapids, Mich., 1892), *On the Making of Man*, 8, p. 536.

[9] SH, Bk 2, P1, In4, Tr2, Q1, M3, C2; vol. 2, p. 582: 'Solus homo est animal rationale mortale; sed si corpus eius esset inclinatum et non erectum, non posset habere usum sermonis et ita non esset excellentissimum signum sapientiae divinae. Et quod ita sit, patet per Gregorium Nyssenum, cap. 9, ostendentem quod solus homo habet manus ad loquendum. Unde potest confici ratio secundum consequentias huiusmodi: si enim homo haberet corpus inclinatum, non haberet manus, quia in omnibus animantibus inclinatis anteriora membra corporis pedes sunt et, secundum Gregorium eumdem et secundum Philosophum, si non haberet manus, non haberet usum sermonis in communicatione ad alterum, et tunc non ita manifestaretur in ipso sapientia, et inde ut prius.'

and hard, and rough, assisting his teeth to deal with what came under his grinder, or it would have been moist and hanging out at the side like that of dogs and other carnivorous beasts, projecting through the gaps in his jagged row of teeth. If, then, our body had no hands, how could articulate sound have been implanted in it, seeing that the form of the parts of the mouth would not have had the configuration proper for the use of speech, [. . .] but now, as the hand is made part of the body, the mouth is at leisure for the service of the reason.[10]

So, hands were necessary not for gestures, but so that man could have the kind of mouth required for speaking rather than one needed for feeding without the aid of hands. Concerning goodness, the Summa argued that the weight of the body naturally tended downwards, but the human body was the organ of the spirit and therefore spiritual in some way, so that it tended upwards, and here Cassiodorus was cited in support.[11] Humans therefore differed from other animals because of their dignity and dominance, their ability to use reason and to speak, and spiritual qualities that were apparent even in their bodies.

The vestige of grace appeared in man's uprightness in two ways, with regard to casting off carnal delight, and with regard to following

---

[10] SH, Bk 2, P1, In4, Tr2, Q1, M3, C2; vol. 2, p. 582, quoting Gregory of Nyssa, *De imagine*, 9: 'Si homo sine manibus extitisset, percipiendorum ciborum necessitate membra vultus eius ad instar quadrupedum formarentur, ita quod oblonga facies tenuaretur simul et emineret in naribus, oris etiam labia callosa et grassiora essent atque firmissima et ad carpendas herbas competenter aptata, et lingua grandiori corpore durior esset et asperior, quae cooperaretur dentibus ad ea quae mandenda perciperet, liquidior existens. Si ergo manus non adessent corpori, quo modo ei vox articulata figuraretur? cum talis eius oris formatio ad usum sermonis minime conveniret; nunc autem sunt manus accomodatae corpori, ut os ad ministerium verbi liberum permaneret.' See 'Le "De imagine" de Grégoire de Nysse', p. 218; Gregory of Nyssa, *Dogmatic Treatises*, p. 536. For similar use of Gregory of Nyssa, see William of Saint Thierry, *De natura corporis et animae*, 2; *De natura corporis et animae*, ed. and trans. Michel Lemoine (Paris, 1988), pp. 148–55; *The Nature of the Body and the Soul*, in *Three Treatises on Man: A Cistercian Anthropology*, ed. Bernard McGinn (Kalamazoo, Mich., 1977), pp. 131–2. On William's discussion of the human hand, see Peggy McCracken, *In the Skin of a Beast: Sovereignty and Animality in Medieval France* (Chicago, 2017), pp. 82–3; Karl Steel, *How to make a Human: Animals and Violence in the Middle Ages* (Columbus, Ohio, 2011), pp. 48–9.
[11] SH, Bk 2, P1, In4, Tr2, Q1, M3, C2; vol. 2, p. 582: 'ipsa autem corpora naturali suo pondere tendant deorsum, ipsum autem corpus humanum, quod est organum spiritus et ita quodam modo spirituale, quodam naturali affectu tendit sursum'.

the spirit.[12] Regarding the former, other animals were bent downwards and looked at their stomachs, and this signified the carnal desire
that they pursued, but man was not like this, and a quotation from
Basil emphasised the point.[13] The pursuit of the spirit was explained by
a passage from one of Bernard of Clairvaux's sermons on the Song of
Songs, presented without comment:

God indeed gave man an upright stance of body, perhaps in order that this
corporeal uprightness, exterior and of little account, might prompt the
inward man, made to the image of God, to cherish his spiritual uprightness;
that the beauty of the body of clay might rebuke the deformity of the mind.
What is more unbecoming than to bear a warped mind in an upright body? It
is wrong and shameful that this body shaped from the dust of the earth
should have its eyes raised on high, scanning the heavens at its pleasure and
thrilled by the sight of sun and moon and stars, while, on the contrary, the
heavenly and spiritual creature lives with its eyes, its inward vision and
affections centered on the earth beneath; the mind that should be feasting
on dainties is wallowing in the mire, rolling in the dung like a pig.[14]

Bernard's point was that the spirit might be inspired or shamed by the
upright body into looking upwards to God. According to the Summa,
therefore, grace enabled humans, unlike animals, to escape carnality
and seek spiritual goals.

The vestige of glory was displayed in the body's uprightness with
regard to contemplation of the terrestrial and the celestial. The

[12] SH, Bk 2, P1, In4, Tr2, Q1, M3, C2; vol. 2, p. 582: 'Vestigium gratiae imitandae
apparet in hac erectione, et hoc quoad duo: primum est quoad carnalem
delectationem abiciendam, secundum quoad spiritualem sectandam.'
[13] SH, Bk 2, P1, In4, Tr2, Q1, M3, C2; vol. 2, p. 582: 'Primum patet sic: animantia
cetera prona sunt et in ventrem suum reciprocatur eorum visus: in quo
designatur voluptas carnalis quam appetunt; homo vero non.'
[14] SH, Bk 2, P1, In4, Tr2, Q1, M3, C2; vol. 2, p. 582: 'Corporis staturam dedit
Deus homini rectam, forsan ut illa corporea exterioris viliorisque rectitudo
figmenti hominem illum, qui ad imaginem Dei factus est spiritualis, suae
servandae rectitudinis admoneret et decor limi deformitatem argueret animi.
Quid enim indecentius quam curvum recto corpore gerere animum? Perversa
res est et foeda luteum vas, quod est corpus de terra, oculos habere sursum,
caelos libere suspicere caelorumque luminaribus oblectare aspectus, spiritualem
vero caelestemque creaturam suos e contrario oculos, id est internos sensus,
atque affectus trahere in terram deorsum, et quae debuit nutriri "in croceis",
haerere luto tamquam unum de suibus amplexarique "stercora".' Bernard of
Clairvaux, *On the Song of Songs II*, trans. Kilian Walsh (Kalamazoo, Mich.,
1976), sermon 24, pp. 46–7.

terrestrial was contemplated so that man could contemplate his own beauty.[15] A passage from Ambrose emphasised the point:

But something must be said on the subject of the human body. Who can deny that it excels all things in grace and beauty? Although it seems in substance to be one and the same with all earthly things, certain wild animals have superiority in strength and size. Yet the form of the human body, by reason of its erectness and stature, is such that it lacks massive hugeness as well as abject lowliness.[16]

The celestial was contemplated so that man's soul should always be found there, and a string of supporting authorities expressed the idea that humans had a lofty potential that animals did not. Bernard, *Sermons on the Song of Songs*, 24:

'Blush, my soul, that you have exchanged the divine for a bestial likeness; blush that despite your heavenly origin you now wallow in filth.' And it continues, 'Therefore to pursue and enjoy the worldly warps the soul, while, on the contrary, to meditate on or desire the things that are above constitutes its uprightness.'[17]

Ovid's *Metamorphoses*:

[Prometheus] gave to man an uplifted face and bade him stand erect and turn his eyes to heaven.[18]

---

[15] SH, Bk 2, P1, In4, Tr2, Q1, M3, C2; vol. 2, p. 582: 'Similiter vestigium gloriae proponitur ei in hac rectitudine quoad contemplationem duplicem, scilicet terrestrium et caelestium. Inter terrestria, ut contempletur se ipsum pulcherrimum.'

[16] SH, Bk 2, P1, In4, Tr2, Q1, M3, C2; vol. 2, p. 583: 'Iam aliqua dicenda sunt de corpore hominis, quod praestantius ceteris decoris gratia esse quis abnuat? Nam si una atque eadem omnium terrenorum corporum videatur esse substantia, fortitudo quoque et proceritas quibusdam maior in bestiis, forma tamen humani corporis est venustior, status erectus et mediocris, ut neque enormis proceritas sit neque vilis et abiecta pusillitas.' Ambrose, *Hexameron, Paradise, and Cain and Abel*, trans. John J. Savage (New York, 1961), p. 268.

[17] SH, Bk 2, P1, In4, Tr2, Q1, M3, C2; vol. 2, p. 583: '"Erubesce, anima, divinam pecorina commutasse similitudinem: erubesce volutari in coeno, quae es de caelo"; et sequitur: "Quaerere et sapere quae sunt super terram, curvitas est animae, et de regione meditari et desiderare quae sursum sunt, rectitudo."' Bernard of Clairvaux, *On the Song of Songs II*, sermon 24, p. 47.

[18] SH, Bk 2, P1, In4, Tr2, Q1, M3, C2; vol. 2, p. 583: 'Os homini sublime dedit caelumque videre iussit et erectos ad sidera tollere vultus.' Ovid, *Metamorphoses*, trans. Frank Justus Miller (Cambridge, Mass., 2 vols., third edition 1977, reprinted 1984), Book 1, lines 85–6; vol. 1, p. 9. On the use of this

Augustine, *De diversis questionibus*:

The human body is unique among the bodies of land animals in not being stretched out prone on its stomach. However, although it could see [in that position], the body stands erect in order to look upon the heavens [...] it is such that it is more adapted for viewing the heavens; the human body can rightly be regarded as created more in the image and likeness of God than the other bodies of animals.[19]

The Summa thus took these authorities to demonstrate that humans excelled animals because their bodies were more beautiful and they could contemplate the heavens.

In this part of the Summa Halensis, the uprightness of the human body bore great symbolic significance, and it expressed a clear divide between humans and animals in a host of ways. Humans had more dignity and authority than animals, they alone were rational and possessed the power of speech, only they could eschew bodily desires, their bodies were more beautiful, and they had spiritual qualities by which they were oriented heavenwards.

The Summa expanded on what was meant by the power of presiding that it had presented as a vestige of innocence in the upright human body when it considered 'whether Adam had dominion over the animals'.[20] It stated baldly that before the fall the first man had dominion, and this was fitting on the part of both man and animals. Before sin had been committed, it was fitting that the first man should have dominion over the other creatures of the sensible world because, having been made in the image of the God, he excelled them all. Being perfectly obedient to his creator according to reason, and not turning away from that obedience with any unsettled or irrational behaviour, it was just that he should enjoy undisturbed power and authority over all

---

image in Ovid's *Metamorphoses* by other medieval scholars, see Steel, *How to make a Human*, pp. 44–7.

[19] SH, Bk 2, P1, In4, Tr2, Q1, M3, C2; vol. 2, p. 582: '"Corpus hominis solum inter animalium terrenorum corpora non pronum in arvum prostratum est, cum sit visibile, et ad intuendum caelum erectum." Et infra: "Tale est ut ad contemplandum caelum sit aptius; magis in hoc ad imaginem et similitudinem Dei quam cetera corpora animalium merito videri potest."' Augustine, *Eighty-Three Different Questions*, trans. David L. Mosher, The Fathers of the Church: A New Translation 70 (Washington, D.C., 1982), Question 51, section 3, pp. 86–7 (the Summa has reordered some of the material).

[20] SH, Bk 2, P1, In4, Tr3, Q5, C2; vol. 2, pp. 780–3: 'Utrum Adam dominabatur animalibus'.

things that lacked reason. The penalty for the first sin, however, was
that man lost this dominion, but this did not entail the complete
disappearance of human dominion because, on the part of animals, it
remained fitting that they should be subject to man's dominion and
disposition because they were fashioned for the sake of man.[21] What
this meant for the relationship between humans and animals after the
fall was explained in the reply to one of the objections. It was pointed
out that many types of animal were completely untamable and could
not be dominated; they could not be subdued by human company or
by training. If Adam did not have dominion over some animals, he did
not have dominion over all animals.[22] In reply the Summa asserted,
though without prejudice to a better opinion, that before the first sin
animals in paradise were subject to the rule of man and lived peacefully
with each other and obediently to man. But once man turned away
from obedience to his superior through sin, it was just that what was
subject to man in the natural order should turn against him through
disobedience. Man did not, however, lose his natural power of dominion, namely the governing power of reason, but as his power was
weakened and diminished by sin, so, as man fell, creatures that lacked
reason degenerated and became less suited to obeying the authority of
reason, less tame and more ferocious. This was evident when one
considered that before there was sin, animals did not live by eating
other animals but fed peacefully on herbs and fruit, as Bede had
established in his gloss on Genesis.[23] Animal behaviour therefore

---

[21] SH, Bk 2, P1, In4, Tr3, Q5, C2; vol. 2, p. 781: 'Respondeo quod primus homo
ante lapsum habuit dominium, et hoc congruebat congruentia sumpta ex parte
hominis et congruentia sumpta ex parte animalium. Congruebat enim quod ante
peccatum haberet potestativam dominationem ceterarum creaturarum huius
mundi sensibilis secundum eam partem qua, factus ad imaginem Dei, omnibus
ceteris praecellebat. Iustum namque erat ut, secundum rationem suo Creatori
perfecte obediens et ab eius obedientia nusquam aliquo perturbato et irrationali
motu divertens, omnia ratione carentia sub suo contineret potestativo et
imperturbato atque pacato imperio. [...] Quod autem nunc hominibus nocent,
poena primi peccati est: dominium autem illud amisit propter peccatum. [...]
Alia autem est congruentia ex parte animalium. Congruebat enim ut animalia,
quae propter hominem condita erant, eius dominio et dispositioni subderentur.'
[22] SH, Bk 2, P1, In4, Tr3, Q5, C2; vol. 2, p. 780: 'Item, omnino indomabili nullus
potest dominari; sed multa genera animalium erant huiusmodi: multa enim sunt
quae nulla frequentia hominum vel studio possunt domari; ergo non
dominabatur cuilibet, et ita non dominabatur omni animali.'
[23] SH, Bk 2, P1, In4, Tr3, Q5, C2; vol. 2, pp. 781–2: 'Ad illud quod obicitur
quod "plura sunt animalia indomabilia" etc.: dicendum, sine praeiudicio

changed when humans fell: some ceased to be vegetarians and became hostile to humans. Consequently, human dominion became less effective, though it did not disappear. The boundary between humans and animals was strong, the fall notwithstanding. Humans, made in the image of God and endowed with the power of reason, dominated other animals that had been created for their sake and become hostile and disobedient after the fall.

The distinctively human power of speech received further treatment when the Summa assessed the role of the serpent in tempting Eve and enquired 'whether the sound emitted through the serpent was formed by the devil and expressed through the serpent, or both formed and expressed by the serpent'.[24] The Summa was clear that the sound was produced by the power of the devil. The sensible soul in animals that possessed a heart and vocal instruments could produce a voice, but reason was needed to generate words with meaning. The human tongue was therefore different because it had the potential to produce speech perfectly whereas the tongue of the serpent and other brutes had it imperfectly. The Summa concluded that no new power was given to the serpent when it spoke, but rather the potential that it possessed imperfectly was used by the devil with divine permission.[25] Humans

---

melioris sententiae, quod animalia in illo statu erant in paradiso sub hominis imperio concorditer ad invicem et obedienter ad hominem viventia. Homine autem per peccatum recedente et declinante a sui superioris obedientia, iustum erat ut ordine naturali sibi subiecta sentiret adversum se per inobedientiam contumacia, per quam iustitiam et caro facta est rebellans spiritui et quae exterius ratione carent, repugnantia ipsi homini. Non tamen amisit homo naturalem potestatem dominii, id est rationis imperativam potestatem, sed sicut potestas eius est infirmata et per peccatum vitiata, ita ipsa quoque ratione carentia, labente homine, sunt deteriorata et ad obediendum imperanti rationi minus habilia et minoris mansuetudinis et maioris crudelitatis. – Quod patet per hoc quod ante peccatum animalia animalium esu non vivebant; unde *Gen.* 1, 29: "Ecce dedi vobis omnem herbam" etc. Ibi dicit *Glossa* Bedae: "Patet quod ante peccatum hominis terra nihil noxium protulit, non herbam venenatam, non arborem sterilem; omnibus enim herba et ligna data sunt, hominibus et volatilibus et animantibus terrae, in escam." Unde patet quod tunc animalia animalium esu non vivebant, sed concorditer herbis et fructibus vescebantur.'

[24] SH, Bk 2, P2, In2, Tr2, S2, Q2, C6; vol. 3, p. 201: 'quaeritur utrum sonus emissus per serpentem fuerit formatus a diabolo et expressus per serpentem vel a serpente formatus et expressus'. (Here and hereafter 'S' refers to 'section'.)

[25] SH, Bk 2, P2, In2, Tr2, S2, Q2, C6; vol. 3, p. 201: 'Ad quod dicendum quod non fuit ex virtute animae sensibilis in ipso serpente tamquam a sufficienti principio, sed fuit a virtute diaboli. De se enim habet anima sensibilis in animalibus habentibus cor et instrumenta vocalia, quod possit formare vocem; sed ipsa

were therefore entirely different from animals because they were rational and consequently possessed the power of speech whereas irrational animals could not produce words with meaning.

Another consequence of animal irrationality was discussed when the Summa considered 'whether irrational creatures should be cursed'.[26] It explained that creatures lacking reason should not be cursed in themselves, but only by reason of a rational creature that sinned. Sometimes the curse had figurative meaning, sometimes an irrational creature was cursed because of the sin that was perpetrated in it, sometimes it was to punish a rational creature that had sinned, and sometimes it was because a rational creature was moving to an irrational evil. Always the curse related to a rational creature.[27] Although the Summa did not spell it out, the point was that only rational creatures could sin, and irrational animals ought not to be cursed directly because they were incapable of sin and could never therefore deserve the curse.

Rationality as the defining characteristic of humans was again critical when the Summa considered whether simple fornication was prohibited by the commandment not to commit adultery.[28] The opening objection put forward the argument that no natural act was prohibited by the ten commandments; only wicked acts were prohibited, and virtuous acts commanded. Fornication, however, was a natural act, as was evident from Romans 1:26, 'they have changed the natural use into that use which is against nature', upon which the Gloss commented, 'the natural use is a man with a woman', from which it

discretio vocis litteratae cum significatione est a motore rationali. In hoc autem differt lingua hominis quod habet possibilitatem perfecte ad hoc, sed lingua serpentis et aliorum brutorum imperfecte. Unde non fuit nova potestas data linguae serpentis in ista formatione vocis litteratae, sed possibilitas, quam habuit imperfecte, redacta fuit ad actum per diabolum ex permissione divina.'

[26] SH, Bk 2, P2, In3, Tr3, S2, Q10, C3; vol. 3, p. 459: 'Utrum sit maledicendum creaturae irrationali'.

[27] SH, Bk 2, P2, In3, Tr3, S2, Q10, C3; vol. 3, p. 459: 'Ad quod dicendum quod ipsi creaturae non habenti rationem non est maledicendum propter se, sed ratione rationalis creaturae peccantis. Maledicitur autem ei aliquando in figura, [...] aliquando ratione peccati in ea perpetrati [...]. Aliquando vero fit maledictio creaturae irrationali in poenam creaturae rationalis peccantis [...]. Aliquando vero fertur maledictio ratione creaturae rationalis moventis irrationalem ad aliquod malum [...]. Universaliter ergo in relatione ad creaturam rationalem fertur debita maledictio.'

[28] SH, Bk 3, P2, In3, Tr2, S1, Q2, Tit6, C5; vol. 4, pp. 548–9: 'utrum fornicatio simplex hic prohibeatur'. (Here and hereafter 'Tit' refers to 'title'.)

followed that fornication was not banned in the decalogue.[29] In response, the Summa accepted that the argument was valid for the genus of animals: natural law taught that, for all animals, sex between male and female was natural. The nature of the human species, however, which was rational, meant that sex was only natural between husband and wife, so fornication was not a natural act.[30] The hard boundary between rational humans and irrational animals, between species and genus, was thus held to generate a particular moral requirement for proper sexual conduct that applied only to humans.

Another of the ten commandments came under scrutiny when the Summa considered whether the killing of animals or only of humans was prohibited by the precept 'you shall not kill'.[31] The arguments in favour of the precept being applicable to animals were introduced as the objections of heretics, so the solution was not hard to anticipate, and the opposing objection was simply a quotation from Augustine's *City of God* referring to the Manicheans:

On this basis some try to extend this commandment even to wild and domestic animals and maintain that it is wrong to kill any of them. Why not then extend it also to plants and to anything fixed and fed by roots in the earth? For things of this kind, though they have no feeling, are said to live, and therefore can also die [...]. Thus the Apostle [...] says: 'That which thou sowest is not quickened except it die' [1 Corinthians 15:36], and we find in a psalm, 'He killed their vines with hail' [Psalms 78:47]. Do we from this conclude, when we hear 'Thou shalt not kill', that it is wrong to pull up a shrub? Are we so completely deranged that we assent to the Manichean error?[32]

---

[29] SH, Bk 3, P2, In3, Tr2, S1, Q2, Tit6, C5; vol. 4, p. 548: 'Nullus actus naturalis prohibetur lege Decalogi, sed solum actus vitiosus prohibetur et virtuosus praecipitur; sed fornicatio est actus naturalis, *Rom.* 1, 26: "Mutaverunt naturalem usum in eum qui est contra naturam", *Glossa*: "Naturalis usus est viri cum muliere". Ergo non prohibetur in Decalogo.'

[30] SH, Bk 3, P2, In3, Tr2, S1, Q2, Tit6, C5; vol. 4, p. 549: 'Ad illud ergo quod obicitur quod "naturalis usus est viri cum muliere", patet responsio ex praedictis, quia a natura generis verum est, "secundum quam est ius, quod natura docuit omnia animalia, ut masculus cum femina"; a natura speciei, quae est rationalis, non erit naturalis usus nisi sit viri cum muliere sua. Unde fornicatio non est naturalis actus hoc modo.'

[31] SH, Bk 3, P2, In3, Tr2, S1, Q2, Tit5, M1, C1; vol. 4, p. 521: 'Utrum hic prohibeatur occisio animalis vel solius hominis'.

[32] SH, Bk 3, P2, In3, Tr2, S1, Q2, Tit5, M1, C1; vol. 4, p. 521: 'Contra: a. Augustinus, in I libro *De civitate Dei*, loquens de hoc praecepto "non occides", dicit: "Quidam hoc praeceptum in bestias ac pecora conantur extendere, ut ex hoc nullum etiam illorum liceat occidere. Cur ergo non et

The 'solutio' was the passage from Augustine, *City of God*, book 1, chapter 20 immediately following the one quoted in the argument against:

Hence, putting aside these ravings, if when we read, 'Thou shalt not kill', we do not understand this phrase to apply to bushes, because they have no sensation, nor to the unreasoning animals that fly, swim, walk or crawl, because they are not partners with us in the faculty of reason, the privilege not being given them to share it in common with us – and therefore by the altogether righteous ordinance of the Creator both their life and death are a matter subordinate to our needs – the remaining possibility is to understand this commandment, 'Thou shalt not kill', as meaning man alone, that is, 'neither another nor thyself', for in fact he who kills himself kills what is no other than a man.[33]

Lack of reason was thus presented as the key difference that separated animals from humans, one that meant that animals could not be in community with humans. Furthermore, the creator had subjected animals to human use, so that humans could kill them or not, as suited their needs. The replies to the opening objections expanded on the dominion that humans had been granted over animals from the creation, though no such dominion over humans had been instituted. Since a lord could do as he wished with his property, humans could kill or preserve animals as they chose, without any offence, from the very first, but they could not do the same to other humans. Moreover,

---

herbas et quidquid humo radicitus alitur et figitur? Nam et hoc genus rerum, quamvis non sentiat, dicitur vivere, ac per hoc potest et mori; unde Apostolus: 'Insipiens tu, quod seminas, non vivificatur nisi prius moriatur'; et in *Psalmo* scriptum est: 'Occidit vites eorum in grandine.' Num igitur ob hoc, cum audimus 'non occides', virgultum vellere nefas dicimus et Manichaeorum errori insanissime acquiescimus?"' Augustine, *The City of God against the Pagans*, trans. George E. McCracken (Cambridge, Mass., 7 vols., 1957, reprinted 1966), book 1, chapter 20; vol. 1, p. 93.

[33] SH, Bk 3, P2, In3, Tr2, S1, Q2, Tit5, M1, C1; vol. 4, p. 521: 'Iis deliramentis remotis, cum audimus "non occides", si propterea non accipimus hoc dictum esse de frutetis, quia nullus eis sensus est, nec de irrationabilibus animantibus, volatilibus, ambulantibus, natatilibus, reptilibus, quia nulla nobis ratione sociantur, quam non eis datum est nobiscum habere communem – unde iustissima ordinatione Creatoris vita et mors eorum nostris usibus subditur – restat ergo ut de homine intelligamus quod dictum est "non occides"; nec alterum; ergo nec te: neque enim qui se occidit, aliud quam hominem occidit.' Augustine, *City of God*, book 1, chapter 20; vol. 1, pp. 93–5.

this dominion had not been removed from humans by sin, except insofar as it was sinful to kill animals that belonged to another. According to natural law, all animals were given to humans for their use, and sensible life was ordered to the sustaining of humans, although after sin this was a divine concession. The commandment not to kill prohibited all disordered killing, but the killing of an animal by its master was not disordered.[34]

The Summa Halensis thus insisted that there were clear differences between humans and animals. It consistently stressed that humans were rational while animals were not, presenting many other differences as a consequence of this fundamental contrast, most notably possession of the power of speech. Humans also enjoyed greater dignity, and exercised dominion over animals which they could use as they saw fit. Humans had the capacity to sin and were required to conduct sexual relations within marriage, but their bodies were more beautiful, their corporeal desires could be suppressed, and they had spiritual qualities and aspirations that no animal possessed.

Despite this overwhelming emphasis on a strong and unbreachable boundary between humans and animals, there were some occasions when similarities were emphasised. This was very much the case when the Summa asked 'whether Adam's body was animal'.[35] The Summa's response was that the noun 'animal' was sometimes used in a general sense and sometimes in a special sense, for when a genus was divided into two such that one species had its own name and the other did not, the one that did not have its own name retained the name of the genus. Thus, when 'animal' was divided into rational and irrational, rational animal had its own name, the species 'homo'. The irrational, however,

---

[34] SH, Bk 3, P2, In3, Tr2, S1, Q2, Tit5, M1, C1; vol. 4, p. 521: 'a prima institutione factus est homo dominus brutorum, […] sed non est factus dominus hominis. Unde, cum domini sit facere de re sua quod vult, ex prima institutione potest homo bruta occidere vel servare, si vult, sine offensa, non sic hominem. Hoc autem dominium non est ablatum homini per peccatum, nisi quantum facta est appropriatio; unde qui occidit bovem alterius non peccat in eo quod est occidere, sed in eo quod damnificat proximum in re propria, et ideo peccat contra illud praeceptum "non furaberis". […] secundum legem naturalem omnia bruta data homini in usum, et vita sensibilis ordinata est ad sustentationem hominis et ex concessione divina post peccatum. […] cum dicitur "non occides", prohibetur omne occidere inordinatum; occidi autem brutum a domino suae vitae non est inordinatum.'

[35] SH, Bk 2, P1, In4, Tr2, S2, Q1, Tit1, M4, C1; vol. 2, pp. 589–95: 'Utrum corpus Adae erat animale'.

did not have its own name, so members of this species were called by the name of the genus, 'animal'. The noun 'animal' could thus be used in one way as the name of the genus common to both rational and irrational animals, and in another way as the name of brutes. Similarly, the adjective 'animal' had two senses. If it derived from the genus of humans and brutes, it applied to humans of every state, whether of innocence, sin, grace or glory. If, however, it derived from the species of brutes and was used of a human ('homo animalis'), it meant similar to a brute.[36] This got the Summa into the whole question of similarity.

A human could be said to be similar to a brute in two ways, according to the body or according to the soul. If a human were likened to a brute according to the body, it meant that we are animals now because we need food like brutes, just as Adam had been an animal because he had needed food in paradise.[37] If a human were likened to a brute according to the soul, this too could be said in two ways. The following passage survives in something of a muddle. The Summa only referenced Augustine, *Eighty-Three Different Questions*, question 67, but first it quoted Peter Lombard's commentary on 1 Corinthians 2:14, 'dicitur enim homo animalis vel vita vel animi sensu', indicating that a person was called animal either by his life or 'by the sense of the soul', though the meaning of 'animi sensu' is not obvious. With regard to his life, Augustine, *Eighty-Three Different Questions*, question 67 was indeed quoted, though the same passage was to be found both in Peter Lombard's commentary and the *glossa ordinaria*:

[36] SH, Bk 2, P1, In4, Tr2, S2, Q1, Tit1, M4, C1; vol. 2, p. 590: 'Ad hoc dicendum quod hoc nomen "animal" quandoque sumitur generalius, quandoque specialius. Quandoque enim dividitur genus in duo, quorum unum habet nomen proprium, aliud non habet; illud autem dividentium, quod non habet nomen proprium, retinet nomen generis, sicut patet cum dicimus animal dividi in rationale et irrationale: animal rationale habet nomen proprium, quia huius speciei "homo"; irrationale vero non, et ideo irrationalia nomine generis nominantur et dicuntur "animalia". Cum ergo animal dupliciter dicatur, uno modo est nomen generis communis ad rationalia et irrationalia, alio vero modo est nomen brutorum. Similiter "animale" derivatum ab eo quod est "animal", dicitur dupliciter. Nam, si derivetur ab "animali" quod est genus ad hominem et bruta, tunc convenit homini secundum omnem statum, sive innocentiae sive culpae sive gratiae sive gloriae; si vero derivetur ab "animali" quod est nomen brutorum, tunc dicitur homo animalis, id est similis brutis.'

[37] SH, Bk 2, P1, In4, Tr2, S2, Q1, Tit1, M4, C1; vol. 2, p. 590: 'sed hoc dupliciter, quia vel similis brutis secundum corpus vel secundum animam. Si primo modo, sic dicimur animales nunc et Adam similiter tunc in paradiso, quia cibis indigemus ut bruta et cibis indigebat Adam secundum corpus.'

he was called animal when 'he is carried along by the dissolute lascivi-
ousness of his own soul, which the spirit neither governs nor restrains
within the limits of the natural order, for even the spirit itself does not
submit itself to the rule of God', so in this case, the Summa explained,
'animal' meant the same as 'carnal'. With regard to 'the sense of his
soul', Peter Lombard's commentary was quoted once more, though
again the passage was also in the *glossa ordinaria*: he was said to be
animal when he judged about God according to corporeal imagination,
the letter of the Law, or by philosophical reason. 1 Corinthians 2:14
was then invoked: 'But the sensual man perceiveth not these things that
are of the Spirit of God. For it is foolishness to him: and he cannot
understand.' The Summa's question was specifically about Adam
rather than humans in general, however, and it explained that these
last two ways of likening the human to a brute, both according to the
soul, did not apply to Adam in paradise, and the question was not
about them. It therefore concluded that Adam's body was only animal
in the sense of needing food, a position that Peter Lombard had also
taken in his *Sentences*.[38]

[38] SH, Bk 2, P1, In4, Tr2, S2, Q1, Tit1, M4, C1; vol. 2, p. 590: 'Si vero animalis
dicatur homo secundum animam, scilicet similis bruto, hoc dicitur adhuc
dupliciter, secundum Augustinum, in libro *83 Quaestionum*: dicitur enim
homo animalis vel vita vel animi sensu. Vita animalis dicitur, quando "fertur
dissoluta lascivia animae suae, quam intra naturalis ordinis metas spiritus rector
non continet, eo quod ipse se Deo regendum non subicit", et sic animalis idem
est quod carnalis. Animi vero sensu dicitur animalis, qui de Deo iuxta corporum
phantasiam vel Legis litteram vel rationem philosophicam iudicat, et de tali
dicitur illud *I Cor.* 2, 14: "Animalis homo" etc. Iis duobus modis ultimis non
erat Adam animalis in paradiso nec de iis modis est quaestio, quia hic
intendimus de animalitate quantum ad corpus secundum quod dicitur animale,
id est egens alimoniis, et sic intendit Augustinus et alii loquentes de materia ista.
Concedimus ergo quod corpus Adae erat animale, id est indigens alimoniis, sicut
determinat Magister, II *Sententiarum*, 19 dist., cap. [2]: Solent plura quaeri etc.
Dicit enim ibi: "In primo statu fuit corpus hominis animale, id est egens
alimoniis ciborum."' Peter Lombard, *In Epistolam I ad Corinthios*, *Patrologia
cursus completus, series Latina*, ed. J.-P. Migne, 221 vols. (1844–61), vol. 191,
col. 1552: 'Homo autem dicitur animal, vel vita, vel animi sensu. Vita animalis
dicitur quae fertur dissoluta lascivia animae suae quam intra naturalis ordinis
metas spiritus rector non continet, eo quod ipse Deo se regendum non subjicit.
Animi vero sensu dicitur animalis, qui de Deo juxta corporum phantasiam, vel
legis litteram, vel rationem philosophicam judicat.' Augustine, *Eighty-Three
Different Questions*, Question 67, 5, pp. 153–4; *Biblia latina cum glossa
ordinaria* (Strasbourg, 1480–81); *Biblia latina cum glossa ordinaria: Facsimile
Reprint of the Editio Princeps, Adolph Rusch of Strasburg, 1480/81*, ed. with
introduction, Karlfried Froehlich and Margaret T. Gibson (Turnhout, 4 vols.,

Although the focus of the question was on Adam's body, the various usages of the term 'animal' were painstakingly set out, and the Summa explained the sense in which humans were animals. It explored when humans were in effect the same as animals (when they needed food) and when they could be said to be like animals. The notion that humans were animal-like when judging about God according to corporeal imagination, the letter of the Law, or by philosophical reason surely connects with polemical strategies in other kinds of texts that condemned non-Christians and Christians unduly influenced by them. In general, being 'like' animals meant keeping the boundary between humans and brute animals even when they seemed the same. The boundary between humans and animals was therefore sustained, but similarities were brought very much to the fore.

The same preoccupation with similarities can be seen when the Summa Halensis considered 'Why temptation was made through the medium of the serpent'.[39] The Summa presented a list of points, attributing a variety of characteristics to different animals, all tending to suggest that another animal might have been more suitable. Each point was then considered in turn, the purpose being to explain why the serpent was used.

Taking the first two points together, it was suggested that the devil could have assumed an airy body that was like a human body, and that this would have been a more fitting way to tempt a human. Moreover, many other animals were agreeable to humans and in harmony with them, such as the dove and other types of animal, and it would have been more suitable to tempt a human with one of these.[40] The

---

1992), vol. 4, p. 310: 'Animalis homo. Dicitur vita qui fertur dissoluta lascivia animae suae quam intra naturalis ordinis metas spiritus rector non continet eo quod ipse deo regendum se non subiicit. Animi vero sensu dicitur animalis qui deo iuxta corporum fantasiam vel legis litteram vel rationem phisicam iudicat.' Peter Lombard, *Sententiae in IV libris distinctae*, Spicilegium Bonaventurianum 4 and 5 (Grottaferrata, 1971 and 1981), Liber 2, Distinctio 19, Cap. 2; vol. 1, p. 422.

[39] SH, Bk 2, P2, In2, Tr2, S2, Q2, C5; vol. 3, pp. 199–201: 'Quare tentatio facta fuerit mediante serpente'.

[40] SH, Bk 2, P2, In2, Tr2, S2, Q2, C5; vol. 3, p. 199: 'Videtur enim, cum diabolus habuerit posse assumendi corpus aereum in similitudine corporis humani, quod in illo corpore convenientius debuerit tentasse hominem. Item, multa sunt alia animalia praetendentia delectabile homini, ut columba et alia genera animalium, quae consona sunt homini; videtur ergo quod per huiusmodi genera animalium magis congrueret tentasse hominem ad seductionem.'

Summa's response was that although other animals were more in harmony with human nature, temptation through the serpent had been permitted. Here similarity between humans and animals was simply accepted as an unproblematic reality. Then, however, the Summa claimed that the serpent was in a crucial way similar to humans before sin. It stated that the serpent had a maidenly countenance so that it could more easily deceive through similarity, 'for similarity is the mother of falsity'.[41] Peter Comestor had introduced the idea of the serpent having a maidenly countenance into scholarly debates in his *Historia Scholastica*. He said that it came from Bede, and the Summa followed him in this, though nothing like this has been found in Bede's authentic works. The Summa immediately took a very hostile attitude to similarity as 'the mother of falsity', using a phrase to be found in Augustine's *Soliloquies*, though Peter Comestor had not distrusted similarity in this way, explaining that a serpent with a maidenly countenance had been chosen 'quia similia similibus applaudunt', 'because like favours like', a decidedly more neutral assessment.[42] Returning to the Summa, it continued by noting that the serpent had a slippery and sweet motion, so that it suited the motion of interior temptation, which was slippery and light.[43]

Third, it was noted that there were many kinds of animals, such as birds, that had an instrument more suited to producing a voice similar

---

[41] SH, Bk 2, P2, In2, Tr2, S2, Q2, C5; vol. 3, p. 200: 'Ad primum et secundum dicendum quod, licet animalia alia sint magis consona naturae hominis, per serpentem tamen permissus est tentare; serpens enim ille, sicut dicit Beda, vultum habuit virgineum, ut per simile facilius deciperet: similitudo enim mater est falsitatis.'

[42] Peter Comestor, *Scolastica Historica*, ed. Agneta Sylwan, Corpus Christianorum Continuatio Mediaeualis CXCI (Turnhout, 2005), 1.22, p. 40. Augustine, *Soliloquies and Immortality of the Soul*, with introduction, translation and commentary by Gerard Watson (Warminster, 1990), *Soliloquies*, 2.10, p. 84: 'Similitudo igitur rerum, quod ad oculos pertinet, mater est falsitatis.' See Nona C. Flores, '"Effigies amicitiae ... veritas inimicitiae": antifeminism in the iconography of the woman-headed serpent in medieval art and literature', in Nona C. Flores (ed.), *Animals in the Middle Ages: A Book of Essays* (New York, 1996), pp. 167–95 at 167–8; Henry Ansgar Kelly, 'The metamorphoses of the Eden serpent during the middle ages and renaissance', *Viator* 2 (1971), pp. 301–29 at 308–9 (308 for translation of Peter Comestor); McCracken, *In the Skin of a Beast*, pp. 103–4.

[43] SH, Bk 2, P2, In2, Tr2, S2, Q2, C5; vol. 3, p. 200: 'Praeterea, serpens habet quemdam lubricum motum et suavem; unde convenit motui tentationis interioris, qui est lubricus et levis.'

to speech. Since temptation began through speech, it would have been more fittingly done through flying animals of this kind.[44] The Summa accepted that many animals had an instrument for producing a voice similar to speech, and similarity was again unproblematic here, but explained that it was not necessary for the first temptation to be made through them. A more suitable organ was not required because the devil spoke through the serpent, and the devil had the power to produce a voice similar to speech, or even speech.[45]

Fourth, it was also pointed out that some animals, such as monkeys, were very similar in figure to humans, and it would therefore have been more appropriate for temptation to have been made through something that was close in this way.[46] In response, the Summa did not challenge the view that some animals were very like humans, preferring to argue that before the fall the serpent had been in fact very similar to humans. Although *now* the serpent did not have a countenance that was maidenly and like that of a human, indeed *now* had a terrible countenance, it had not looked that way *then*. The devil had therefore tempted more fittingly through the serpent than through an animal that now resembled the human in figure. At this point the Summa changed tack, abandoning the argument about similarity and preferring to stress the symbolism of the serpent's form of motion, as it had done briefly when relating the slipperiness of the serpent's movement to that of interior temptation. It was especially appropriate for the devil to tempt through the serpent because it prefigured the way in which man, who was created upright, would bend emotionally so that he would be joined to the earthly. The animal which most inclined to

---

[44] SH, Bk 2, P2, In2, Tr2, S2, Q2, C5; vol. 3, p. 200: 'Item, sunt multa genera animalium, ut avium, quae convenientius habent organum ad formandum vocem similem locutioni; cum ergo per illam partem inciperet tentatio, convenientius fieret per huiusmodi animalia volatilia.'

[45] SH, Bk 2, P2, In2, Tr2, S2, Q2, C5; vol. 3, p. 200: 'Ad tertium vero dicendum quod, licet sint multa animalia quae habent organum ad formandum vocem similem locutioni, non tamen per illa oportuit fieri tentationem primam. Non enim requiritur convenientia organi maior, cum diabolus per ipsum serpentem loqueretur, qui potestatem habebat formandi vocem similem locutioni vel etiam locutionem.'

[46] SH, Bk 2, P2, In2, Tr2, S2, Q2, C5; vol. 3, p. 200: 'Praeterea, sunt quaedam animalia, quae assimilantur in figura ipsi homini, ut simia; convenientius ergo per quod vicinum erat fieret tentatio.'

the earth was the reptile, and thus it was called a serpent because it crawled ('serpit').[47]

Fifth, it was noted that according to Genesis 3:1, 'the serpent was more subtle than any of the beasts', and in the Septuagint it was 'the most prudent of beasts'. It seemed, however, that in the genus of animals bees and ants were held to be more prudent, along with many other kinds of animals about which one could read in Avicenna's *De naturis animalium*.[48] To this, the Summa replied that the serpent was not said to be more subtle or the most prudent because of its own nature but because of the devil's operation in it.[49]

A sixth and final point, supposing that the devil would surely not have chosen to tempt through the serpent, queried whether he had possessed the power to tempt through another kind of animal.[50] The Summa's reply was that the devil had not enjoyed the power to choose the animal he wished, but had to accept the one that was granted to him.[51]

This discussion showed awareness of many types of similarity between different animals and humans. It sought to accommodate them within conventional parameters of difference, but the similarities were deemed real and meaningful. Sometimes they were dangerous, misleading, the mother of falsity. Not always though: in many respects

---

[47] SH, Bk 2, P2, In2, Tr2, S2, Q2, C5; vol. 3, p. 200: 'Ad quartum vero dicendum quod, licet modo non habeat serpens vultum virgineum vel similem homini et nunc habeat vultum terribilem, tunc tamen non habuit; unde potuit congruentius tentare quam per animal quod assimilatur nunc homini in figura, et hoc maxime ut praesignaret quod hominem, qui rectus erat creatus a principio, sicut dicitur *Eccle.* 7, 30, intenderet incurvare per affectum ut coniungeretur terrenis. Inter vero animantia illud, quod plus incumbit terrae, est reptile, et ideo serpens dicitur quia serpit.'

[48] SH, Bk 2, P2, In2, Tr2, S2, Q2, C5; vol. 3, p. 200: 'Item, occasione huius quaeritur de hoc quod dicitur *Gen.* 3,1, quod "serpens erat callidior cunctis animalibus", et secundum litteram Septuaginta dicitur "prudentissimus bestiarum". Videtur enim quod in genere animalium apes prudentiores dicantur et formicae similiter et multa etiam genera animalium, de quibus legitur in libro *De naturis animalium*.'

[49] SH, Bk 2, P2, In2, Tr2, S2, Q2, C5; vol. 3, p. 200: 'Ad quintum vero dicendum quod serpens non dicitur "callidior" vel "prudentissimus" ratione naturae suae, sed ratione operationis diaboli in ipso.'

[50] SH, Bk 2, P2, In2, Tr2, S2, Q2, C5; vol. 3, p. 200: 'Praeterea, numquid elegit diabolus serpentem ad tentandum per ipsum, an potestatem habuit per aliud genus animalis tentare?'

[51] SH, Bk 2, P2, In2, Tr2, S2, Q2, C5; vol. 3, pp. 200–1: 'Ad sextum dicendum quod non fuit in optione diaboli eligere animal quod vellet, sed quod ei concessum fuit.'

it was fine for some animals to be in harmony with humans or to be able to produce a voice similar to speech.

Overall, the Summa Halensis most frequently stressed clear difference and a strong boundary between humans and animals. Similarities were recognised, however, especially in relation to the corporeal. The Summa was not consistent in its approach to these similarities: sometimes they were simply natural features posing no moral or intellectual challenges, whereas on other occasions they were dangerously deceptive and symbolic of human sin.

Bonaventure

Bonaventure's *Commentary on the Sentences* was relentless in its emphasis on the fundamental differences separating humans and animals. This was readily apparent in his treatment of the nature of animal souls. He considered, for example, 'whether the souls of irrational beings were produced out of something'.[52] Having explored and rejected a range of possible answers, he concluded that the souls of brute animals were produced out of something seminally but not materially. By this, he meant that animal souls were not produced out of nothing, but from potential in matter, from what he elsewhere called seminal reasons, a concept he took from Augustine.[53] He

---

[52] Bonaventure, *Commentaria in Quatuor Libros Sententiarum Magistris Petri Lombardi*, Bk 2, D. 15, A. 1, Q. 1; *Doctoris Seraphici S. Bonaventurae Opera Omnia* (Quaracchi, 10 vols., 1882–1902), vol. 2, pp. 372–7: 'Utrum animae irrationalium sint productae ex aliquo'. Henceforth *Comm. in Sent.*

[53] *Comm. in Sent.*, Bk 2, D. 15, A. 1, Q. 1; vol. 2, p. 374: 'Et ideo est quartus modus dicendi quod animae, quae sunt pure sensibiles, productae sunt ex aliquo seminaliter sed non materialiter. Seminaliter, inquam, quia formae sunt generabiles et corruptibiles per naturam ; et ideo, sicut aliae formae naturales non ex nihilo producuntur, sed est alia potentia activa in materia, ex qua fiunt tamquam ex seminario; sic etiam intelligendum est in animabus sensibilibus, quae sunt formae tantum, cuiusmodi sunt in brutis animalibus. Et ideo concedendum est animas sensibiles sive animas brutorum esse ex aliquo, non, inquam, materialiter sed seminaliter; quia, cum anima sensibilis sit forma, non habet materiam partem sui, sed solum fit ex potentia materiae activa, quae ab agente excitatur; et sic proficit, quousque fiat anima, sicut globus proficiendo fit rosa.' For extended analysis of how Bonaventure understood animal souls to be produced from seminal reasons, see Etienne Gilson, *La Philosophie de Saint Bonaventure* (Paris, 1924), pp. 285–90. For his theory of seminal reasons more generally, see Cullen, *Bonaventure*, pp. 47–8; Anton Charles Pegis, *St. Thomas and the Problem of the Soul in the Thirteenth Century* (Toronto, 1934),

considered this response to be more reasonable and more secure than the others because it fitted with the views of both Augustine and Aristotle.[54] Taking the irrationality of animals for granted, Bonaventure thus emphasised how animal souls were different from human souls in the way they were made.

This difference was again evident when Bonaventure considered 'whether Adam's soul was produced out of matter'.[55] He argued that the rational soul, that is to say the human soul, had spiritual matter while the soul of a brute animal did not. He recognised that there were other views: some said that no soul, rational or brute, had matter, while others said that both the rational and the brute soul were composed of matter and form. Bonaventure held, however, to a third position. The rational soul had matter and form because it 'naturally subsists by itself, and acts and undergoes, moves and is moved', because, in the technical language of the schools, 'it is a *hoc aliquid*', a 'this something'. This was not the case with the soul of a brute animal 'since it is founded in the body'. The matter of the human soul, however, was 'above the condition of extension and above the condition of privation and corruption, and therefore it is called spiritual matter.'[56] Human and brute animal souls were therefore fundamentally different in nature.

pp. 44–50 (at 44–5 Pegis succinctly describes 'the doctrine of seminal reasons' as involving a 'conception of matter as in some sense pregnant with all things to be produced in the course of time').

[54] *Comm. in Sent.*, Bk 2, D. 15, A. 1, Q. 1; vol. 2, p. 375: 'Haec autem positio rationabilior est et firmior, quia concordant in hoc tam Augustinus quam Philosophus.'

[55] *Comm. in Sent.*, Bk 2, D. 17, A. 1, Q. 2, vol. 2, pp. 413–16: 'Utrum anima Adae fuerit producta ex materia'. See Richard C. Dales, *The Problem of the Rational Soul in the Thirteenth Century* (Leiden, 1995), pp. 99–107 for Bonaventure's analysis of the rational soul, and pp. 101–2 for this question.

[56] *Comm. in Sent.*, Bk 2, D. 17, A. 1, Q. 2, vol. 2, pp. 414–15: 'Ad praedictorum intelligentiam est notandum quod circa hoc diversi diversa opinati sunt. Quidam enim dixerunt nullam animam, nec rationalem nec brutalem, habere materiam, quia spiritus sunt simplices; animam tamen rationalem dixerunt habere compositionem ex quo est et quod est, quia ipsa est hoc aliquid et nata est per se et in se subsistere. Sed cum planum sit animam rationalem posse pati et agere et mutari ab una proprietate in aliam et in se ipsa subsistere, non videtur quod illud sufficiat dicere quod in ea sit tantum compositio ex quo est et quod est nisi addatur esse in ea compositio materiae et formae. Ideo fuerunt et alii, qui dixerunt non solum animam rationalem sed etiam brutalem ex materia et forma compositam esse, cum utraque sit motor corporis sufficiens. Sed quia anima brutalis propriam operationem non habet nec est nata per se subsistere, non

Another essential difference, according to Bonaventure, was that human souls were immortal while brute animal souls were not. After establishing that the human soul was immortal, Bonaventure considered whether any soul, even that of a brute animal, was immortal 'from the first condition', that is, when first created.[57] Bonaventure noted that some wished to say that the souls of brute animals were immortal because the same souls animated the bodies of animals and humans, and these souls passed from body to body depending on the sins that they committed. He dismissed this view as heretical and derogatory to humans precisely because it treated humans and beasts as equal. Those who defended it were 'bestial humans' because they believed that their souls had either been the souls of animals or would be in the future.[58] Others wanted to say that while the souls of brute animals could not live on after their bodies had died, they could keep going unless an impediment arose from their bodies. According to this view, an impediment to their continuation was introduced into the bodies of brute animals because of human sin, for if Adam had not sinned, no brute animal would have died. Animals were thus rendered subject to death by the sin of humans whom they were made to serve.

videtur quod habeat materiam intra se. Et ideo est tertius modus dicendi, tenens medium inter utrumque, scilicet quod anima rationalis, cum sit hoc aliquid et per se nata subsistere et agere et pati, movere et moveri, quod habet intra se fundamentum suae existentiae et principium materiale a quo habet existere, et formale a quo habet esse. De brutali autem non oportet illud dicere, cum ipsa fundetur in corpore. Cum igitur principium, a quo est fixa existentia creaturae in se, sit principium materiale, concedendum est animam humanam materiam habere. Illa autem materia sublevata est supra esse extensionis et supra esse privationis et corruptionis, et ideo dicitur materia spiritualis.' Translations from Dales, *The Problem of the Rational Soul*, p. 101.
[57] *Comm. in Sent.*, Bk 2, D. 19, A. 1, Q. 2; vol. 2, pp. 461–4: 'Utrum quaevis anima, etiam brutalis, ex prima conditione fuerit immortalis'. For his discussion of the immortality of the human soul, see *Comm. in Sent.*, Bk 2, D. 19, A. 1, Q. 1, pp. 457–61: 'Utrum anima humana per naturam sit immortalis'.
[58] *Comm. in Sent.*, Bk 2, D. 19, A. 1, Q. 2; vol. 2, p. 462: 'Ad praedictorum intelligentiam est notandum quod aliqui dicere voluerunt brutorum animas esse immortales pro eo quod eaedem animae sunt quae vivificant corpora brutorum et corpora hominum, cum merito peccatorum suorum de corpore ad corpus circumeundo pertranseant. Et haec positio quorumdam philosophorum et haereticorum fuit, sicut dictum est supra, et iam improbata est supra tamquam haeretica; et prorsus abicienda est ista positio tamquam vilis et derogans dignitati creaturae rationalis, dum ponit homines et bestias esse pares, in hoc enim indicat quod sui inventores et defensores sunt homines bestiales, dum animas suas credunt vel bestiarum fuisse vel futuras esse.'

Bonaventure pointed out that this ran counter to the views of Augustine, who had said that animals killed each other for food even before
the fall. Nor was it reasonable that a sheep should be killed because a
human sinned since the human neither shared the sin with nor transferred it to the sheep. It was also impossible to imagine where on earth
all the animals would have lived considering the vast number that
would have been born between the beginning and the end of the world
if none of them had died.[59]

Bonaventure was very clear that only the rational soul was immortal. This was apparent from the end for which creatures were made, as
a result of which either perpetuity or corruptibility was granted to
them, according to their need. While all creatures were made for the
sake of God, only the rational creature was made to delight in God, to
be beatified in God, and in the image of God. Other creatures, which
only possessed vestiges of the divine, were made for the manifestation
of divine goodness or the service of the rational creature.[60] Bonaventure developed his argument first with regard to the principal end of

[59] *Comm. in Sent.*, Bk 2, D. 19, A. 1, Q. 2; vol. 2, pp. 462–3: 'Fuerunt et alii qui
dicere voluerunt quod animae brutorum nec sunt adeo immortales, sicut animae
rationales ut possint post corpora vivere, nec sunt adeo corruptibiles sicut aliae
formae quae habent contrarietatem; sed, quantum est de sui natura, natae sunt
continue durare, nisi impedimentum suae durationis habeant ex corpore sine
quo non possunt subsistere. Huiusmodi autem impedimentum durationis
introductum esse dicunt in corpora brutorum propter peccatum hominum. Si
enim Adam non peccasset, nullum animal brutum decederet. Unde sicut merito
peccati humani quae ad eius obsequium facta sunt, deteriorata fuerunt, sic et
bruta animalia facta sunt morti obnoxia. Sed istud prima fronte obviat ei quod
dicit Augustinus, Super Genesim ad litteram, libro III, quod si homo non
peccasset, nihilominus essent animalia viventia de rapina, quae ad suam vitam
servandam alia interficerent animalia. Repugnat etiam rationi, cum nulla ratio
dicat congruum esse ovem interfici propter hoc quod homo peccavit, cum nullo
modo ei in peccato communicaverit nec peccatum suum in ovem transfuderit.
Repugnat etiam imaginationi sensibili. Ubi enim essent tot animalia, quae
multiplicata essent super terram ab initio mundi usque in finem, si nulla essent
mortua?'
[60] *Comm. in Sent.*, Bk 2, D. 19, A. 1, Q. 2; vol. 2, p. 463: 'Et ideo dicendum est
tertio modo quod nulla alia anima, nisi rationalis, immortalis est. Et ratio huius
apparet, si aspiciamus ad finem propter quem creaturae factae sunt, ex quo fine
ponitur in rebus perpetuitas vel corruptibilitas secundum earum exigentiam.
Cum autem omnes creaturae factae sint propter Deum, iuxta illud: Universa
propter semetipsum operatus est Dominus, sola creatura rationalis facta est ad
fruendum Deo et ut beatificetur in ipso, quae sola est ad imaginem. Aliae vero
creaturae, quae solum tenent rationem vestigii, factae sunt vel ad
manifestationem divinae bonitatis vel ad obsequium creaturae rationalis.'

irrational creatures. Manifestation of the divine exemplar and the goodness of God was to be found in the production of the universe which was an exemplum completely representing the exemplar. Because it was a complete representation, it had to have complete and perpetual duration. The universe, however, had being in two ways, passing and permanent. Passing being could not be perpetual because it was necessary that it should sometimes be at rest. Permanent being, however, was perpetual, and those parts that pertained to the permanent being of the universe, such as the stars and the elements, possessed perpetuity. Those which pertained to its passing being, which depended on generation and corruption, such as minerals, plants and brute animals, had to have limited rather than perpetual being. They decorated the universe with their passing, with their aging and renewal, with their death and coming to life. It was therefore clear that, insofar as they were made to represent divine goodness and wisdom, brute animals were naturally corruptible with regard to both body and soul.[61]

Another argument was based on the subsidiary end of irrational creatures, according to which creatures only possessing vestiges of the divine were made for the sake of the rational creature, namely the human. Some were made for the sake of humans in this life and in heaven, others only for this life, and others only for heaven. Those which were made for the sake of humans in both this life and in heaven

[61] *Comm. in Sent.*, Bk 2, D. 19, A. 1, Q. 2; vol. 2, p. 463: 'Manifestatio autem divini exemplaris et bonitatis Dei est in productione universi, quod est quoddam exemplatum complete repraesentans illud exemplar, et propter repraesentationis completionem completam debet habere et perpetuam durationem. Universum autem dupliciter habet esse, videlicet decurrens et permanens. Esse decurrens non potest esse perpetuum, quia necesse est quod aliquando sit quietum. Esse vero permanens est perpetuum. Illae igitur partes, quae respiciunt universum quantum ad esse permanens, sicut sunt orbes caelorum et elementorum, perpetuitatem habent. Illae vero quae respiciunt quantum ad esse decurrens, utpote quae consistunt in generatione et corruptione, qualia sunt mineralia, plantae et animalia bruta, non debent habere esse perpetuum, sed terminatum, quae quasi quodam transitu suo et quadam inveteratione et innovatione, morte et vivificatione decorant universum. Et sic patet quod bruta animalia quantum ad corpus et animam corruptibilia sunt per naturam, in quantum facta sunt ad repraesentandum divinam bonitatem et sapientiam. Et haec ratio sumta est a fine principali.' For Bonaventure's distinction between permanent and passing existence, despite dismissive comments on this passage, see John H. Wright, *The Order of the Universe in the Theology of St Thomas Aquinas* (Rome, 1957), pp. 20–21.

had to be perpetual because the state of heaven was perpetual, and such were the things that were integral to the dwelling-place of humans, like the sky and the four elements. Those which were made for the sake of humans in this life alone had to be corruptible because this state was transitory and came to an end, and such were brute animals, which were made to supply the bodily needs of humans in this life.[62]

The responses to two of the opening objections are also illuminating. One objection cited Wisdom 1:13: 'God made not death, neither hath he pleasure in the destruction of the living.' It followed that death had only been introduced because of sin, and if humans had not sinned, they would not have become subject to death, and nor would brute animals. This, however, could not have been the case unless brute animals had been originally immortal.[63] Against this, Bonaventure explained that the passage in Wisdom referred to the death of eternal damnation or the temporal death of a creature for which death was a punishment. This could only apply to an animal capable of reason which alone was born to be blessed or wretched, to be rewarded or punished, to which alone was given the power to discriminate between good and evil, true and false. Thus, although brute animals suffered when they were killed or injured, they were not punished, nor were they capable of wretchedness because a creature could only be wretched if it knew or ought to know that it was wretched when it experienced evil.[64]

---

[62] *Comm. in Sent.*, Bk 2, D. 19, A. 1, Q. 2; vol. 2, p. 463: 'Est etiam alia ratio sumta a fine non principali, in quantum scilicet creaturae, in quibus est sola ratio vestigii, factae sunt propter creaturam rationalem, scilicet hominem. Quaedam enim factae sunt propter hominem secundum omnem statum, sive viae sive patriae; quaedam solum secundum statum viae et quaedam solum secundum statum patriae. Et illa quae facta sunt propter hominem secundum omnem statum, sive viae sive patriae, cum status patriae sit perpetuus, debent esse perpetua; et talia sunt quae integrant hominis habitaculum, sicut caelum et quatuor elementa. Illa vero, quae facta sunt propter hominem secundum statum viae, cum ille status sit pertransitorius et habeat finem, debent esse corruptibilia; talia autem sunt animalia bruta, quae facta sunt ad supplendam corporis indigentiam secundum eum statum in quo indiget cibis et alimoniis.'

[63] *Comm. in Sent.*, Bk 2, D. 19, A. 1, Q. 2; vol. 2, p. 461: 'Item, Sapientiae primo: "Deus mortem non fecit nec delectatur in perditione vivorum"; igitur mors non est introducta nisi propter peccatum: ergo si homo non peccasset, nec moreretur ipse nec moreretur brutum animal. Sed hoc non esset nisi animae brutorum essent immortales: ergo etc.'

[64] *Comm. in Sent.*, Bk 2, D. 19, A. 1, Q. 2; vol. 2, p. 463: 'Ad illud quod obicitur de libro Sapientiae, dicendum quod loquitur vel de morte damnationis aeternae vel de morte temporali in eo cui mors est poena. Tale autem, est solum animal

According to the third of the opening objections, given that Peter's soul was immortal, it could be supposed that all rational souls were immortal, there being no greater reason for one rational soul to be immortal than another. On the same principle, if one sensible soul were immortal, all must be. The human sensible soul, however, was immortal because the rational soul never came into existence without it. Since humans and brute animals both had sensible souls, the sensible souls of brutes must be naturally immortal too.[65] Bonaventure countered that the sensible soul was very different in humans and animals. In the human it was a power of the rational soul whereas in the animal it was a form which was substantiated in transmutable matter, and because it depended on this matter for its being, it was corrupted when this matter was corrupted.[66]

Bonaventure again drew a hard boundary. Only humans possessed reason. Humans were made in God's image and could relate to God in ways that were not at all open to animals that bore only traces of the divine. Humans could make moral judgments while animals could not. Humans could be rewarded and punished, and be wretched, in ways that animals could not. Animals were made to serve humans. Human souls were immortal, while brute animal souls were not. Even the sensible souls of brute animals were fundamentally different from the sensible souls of humans.

rationis capax, quod, sicut solum natum est esse beatum, solum natum est esse miserum, sic solum natum est praemiari, solum natum est puniri, quia solum ipsum est cui data est vis discretiva inter bonum et malum, verum et falsum. Unde etsi bestia doleat cum occiditur vel laeditur, non tamen punitur; non enim est capax miseriae; solus enim ille est miser qui vel scit se esse miserum vel scire debet, cum malum habet.'

[65] *Comm. in Sent.*, Bk 2, D. 19, A. 1, Q. 2; vol. 2, pp. 461–2: 'Probato quod anima Petri sit immortalis, probatur quod omnis anima sit immortalis per hypothesim, quia non est maior ratio de una quam de alia, loquendo de animabus rationalibus: ergo pari ratione, loquendo de animabus sensibilibus, si una anima sensibilis est immortalis, ergo et omnes. Sed anima sensibilis humana est immortalis, quia nunquam est rationalis sine sensibili: ergo cum in hac communicet homo cum brutis, anima sensibilis brutorum animalium per naturam est immortalis.'

[66] *Comm. in Sent.*, Bk 2, D. 19, A. 1, Q. 2; vol. 2, p. 463: 'Ad illud quod obicitur, quod anima sensibilis hominis est immortalis, dicendam quod non est simile. Sensibile enim in homine nominat potentiam, scilicet animae rationalis, sicut infra patebit; sensibile vero in brutis nominat formam, quae substantificatur in materia transmutabili; ei quia pendet ex illa quantum ad esse, corrumpitur, illa corrupta.'

A similarly strong boundary emerged when Bonaventure posed a series of questions relating to creation. He considered 'whether all sensible creatures were made for the sake of humans'.[67] He began his response by noting that the end to which things were ordered could be understood in two ways. There was the principal and ultimate end, but there could also be an intermediate end. With regard to the former, the end of all creatures, both rational and irrational, was God because God had made all things for himself, for the praise of his goodness. With regard to an intermediate end, however, all sensible animals were made for the sake of humans. In support of this last point, Bonaventure cited both Aristotle's *Physics* and Genesis 1:26: 'Let us make man to our image and likeness: and let him have dominion over the fishes of the sea, and the fowls of the air, and the beasts, and the whole earth, and every creeping creature that moveth upon the earth.' He further explained that because humans were capable of reason, they had free will and were born to dominate animals. Moreover, because humans were born to strive immediately towards God through similitude, all irrational creatures were ordered to humans so that they were led to their ultimate end through human mediation. Matters were complicated by the fall, however. Animals were ordered to humans in one way according to the state of innocence and in another way according to the state of fallen nature. According to the state of innocence, they were ordered to humans for four reasons: first, to show human authority, which they showed when they obeyed humans in all things; second, to decorate the human dwelling-place which was made very beautiful by the multiplying of animals and not just by trees; third, to rouse the senses of humans so that they saw the many forms of the creator's wisdom in the diversity of the animals; and, fourth, to move the affection of humans so that they were roused to love God when they saw animals behaving correctly according to their nature and loving that for which they were naturally made. It was for these reasons that God made not only beasts of burden, but also wild beasts; they were all useful to humans in the above ways. According to the state of fallen nature, animals were still ordered to the use of humans, but wild

---

[67] *Comm. in Sent.*, Bk 2, D. 15, A. 2, Q. 1; vol. 2, pp. 382–4: 'Utrum omnia sensibilia facta sint propter hominem'. See Gilson, *Philosophie de Saint Bonaventure*, p. 300.

animals in different ways from beasts of burden and cattle.[68] There had
to be a difference because, as Bonaventure explained in his reply to one
of the opening objections, before the fall no animal had harmed
humans, indeed all had been gentle towards them, whereas after the
fall some animals attacked humans.[69] After the fall, therefore, beasts of
burden and cattle were made for humans for four reasons: to relieve
human need with regard to food, clothing, obedience and solace. As
examples of pets that provided solace, Bonaventure mentioned some
types of bird and puppies. Wild beasts that were harmful to humans
also existed to serve humans in four ways; as Augustine explained,

---

[68] *Comm. in Sent.*, Bk 2, D. 15, A. 2, Q. 1; vol. 2, pp. 382–3: 'Ad praedictorum
intelligentiam est notandum quod finis, ad quem res ordinantur, duplex est.
Quidam enim est finis principalis et ultimus, quidam vero est finis sub fine. Si
primo modo loquamur de fine, sic omnium creaturarum tam rationalium quam
irrationalium finis est Deus, quia omnia propter semetipsum creavit Altissimus;
omnia enim fecit ad laudem suae bonitatis. Si autem loquamur de fine non
principali, qui est finis quodam modo et finis sub fine, sic omnia sensibilia
animalia facta sunt propter hominem. Et hoc insinuat Philosophus, cum
dicit: "Sumus finis nos quodam modo omnium eorum quae sunt." Insinuat
etiam Scriptura multo excellentius, cum dicit: "Faciamus hominem ad
imaginem et similitudinem nostram, et praesit piscibus maris" etc. Quia enim
homo rationis capax est, ideo habet libertatem arbitrii et natus est piscibus
dominari; quia vero per similitudinem natus est in Deum immediate tendere,
ideo omnes creaturae irrationales ad ipsum ordinantur, ut mediante ipso in
finem ultimum perducantur. Et sic concedendae sunt rationes ostendentes
animalia propter hominem facta esse. Ad dissolutionem autem rationum quae
inducuntur in contrarium, notandum est quod aliter ordinantur animalia ad
hominem secundum statum innocentiae, aliter secundum statum naturae lapsae.
Secundum statum innocentiae ordinantur ad hominem secundum rationem
quadruplicem. Prima ratio est ad manifestandum eius imperium, quod
manifestarent dum ei per omnia obedirent. Secundo, ad decorandum hominis
habitaculum; perpulcrum enim erat habitationem hominis animalium
multiplicatione, non solum arborum, decorari. Tertio, ad excitandum hominis
sensum, ut in ipsorum animalium naturis diversis videret homo multiformitatem
sapientiae Conditoris. Quarto, ad movendum eius affectum, ut, dum homo
videret animalia secundum rectitudinem suae naturae currere et amare illud ad
quod naturaliter facta sunt, ex hoc excitaretur ad amandum Deum. Et propter
has rationes non solummodo fecit Deus iumenta, sed etiam bestias et pecora;
omnia enim faciunt ad hominis utilitatem secundum rationes praedictas.
Secundum statum naturae lapsae ordinantur ista animalia ad utilitatem
hominis, sed aliter bestiae et aliter iumenta et pecora.'

[69] *Comm. in Sent.*, Bk 2, D. 15, A. 2, Q. 1; vol. 2, p. 383: 'Ad illud quod obicitur de
bestiis, quae sunt contra hominem, dicendum quod homine stante, nulla
animalia ipsum offenderent, sed omnia sibi mansueta essent [. . .]. Quod autem
noceant vel offendant, hoc est propter peccatum hominis, non propter novam
potentiam eis datam, sed propter dignitatis praesidendam ab homine amissam.'

'they punish [man] for his sins, exercise his virtue, try him for his own good, or without knowing it teach him some lesson'.[70] Bonaventure thus held that all animals existed for the sake of humans, though the fall had changed the behaviour of some animals and consequently the ways in which they helped humans. He envisaged a hard boundary between humans and animals: humans had reason, free will and dominion while animals did not; animals existed for the sake of humans and unwittingly provided both material and spiritual benefits.

Bonaventure developed these ideas further when he considered the temporal order, or sequence, in which God had produced sensible things.[71] According to Genesis, animals of the air and water had been made on one day, the fifth, then land animals and humans on another day, the sixth. Bonaventure explained that this sequence had to be considered in two ways: regarding what happened on different days and regarding the order in which things were done on the same day. Things were produced on different days because they were made from different matter and served different ends. Thus, animals of the air and water were made on the same day because they were produced from water to adorn that which was transparent in nature. Animals of the earth, however, not only rational but also irrational, humans and land animals in other words, were made from earth to adorn the earth, so they were made on a different day from animals of the air and water.[72]

[70] *Comm. in Sent.*, Bk 2, D. 15, A. 2, Q. 1; vol. 2, p. 383: 'Iumenta enim et pecora ordinantur ad relevandam hominis indigentiam quantum ad cibum et quantum ad vestimentum et quantum ad obsequium, sicut sunt equi et asini etc., et quantum ad solatium, sicut sunt quaedam aves et catuli et similia: et sic facta sunt propter hominem ratione quadruplici. Similiter bestiae sive animalia noxia ordinantur ad hominem secundum quadruplicem rationem et utilitatem, quam ponit Augustinus, Super Genesim ad litteram, libro III. Dicit enim quod aut poenaliter laedunt aut salubriter exercent aut utiliter probant aut ignoranter docent.' Augustine, *De Genesi ad litteram libri duodecim*, book 3, chapter 17; Augustine, *The Literal Meaning of Genesis*, trans. John Hammond Taylor (New York, 2 vols., 1982), vol. 1, p. 93.
[71] *Comm. in Sent.*, Bk 2, D. 15, A. 2, Q. 2; vol. 2, pp. 384–6: 'Quo ordine ex parte temporis Deus produxerit res sensibiles.' See Gilson, *Philosophie de Saint Bonaventure*, pp. 300–1.
[72] *Comm. in Sent.*, Bk 2, D. 15, A. 2, Q. 2; vol. 2, pp. 384–5: 'Dicendum quod in productione sensibilium duplex attenditur ordo, unus scilicet secundum distinctionem diei a die, alius scilicet secundum ordinem eorum quae eodem die producta sunt. Primus autem ordo attenditur secundum exigentiam finis et materiae. Et quia volatilia et natatilia ex aquis producta sunt, prout aqua communiter accipitur ad humorem et vaporem, et sunt ad ornatum naturae

The sequence in which things were made on the same day had to do with degrees of perfection in nature: the imperfect should be made before the perfect so that the less complete led to the more complete. Thus, on the fifth day animals of the water had been produced first because they were less perfect than animals of the air, and on the sixth day irrational animals were produced before humans.[73] Bonaventure explained that there were many reasons why humans were produced after all the other creatures, and he offered three here. The first was the multitude of parts in the human body. It was the most complete of all bodies and more ordered, and therefore had to be produced last. The second reason was the distance between the soul and the body. Because the soul was very different from the body, and not only as form from matter, but also as spiritual from corporeal, and as perpetual from corruptible, there had to be a great temporal distance between the production of the material beginnings of humans and the joining of their parts. By that distance in time would be understood the distance between the constituent principles. The third reason was the perfection of the union as a whole. Because of the dignity and ordered nature of humans, they were the end of all corporeal beings. They were therefore produced last so that all that had gone before was thereby finished and completed, as an end completes that which is ordered to it. Thus, Bonaventure concluded, 'divine wisdom observed the most fitting order in the production of sensible things'.[74] Bonaventure continued

perspicuae; ideo sacra Scriptura dicit ea facta esse uno die. Quia vero gressibilia non solum rationalia, sed etiam irrationalia ad ornamentum terrae spectant et ex eadem materia sunt producta, scilicet terra, ideo non in eodem die sed alio a praedictis facta sunt.'

[73] *Comm. in Sent.*, Bk 2, D. 15, A. 2, Q. 2; vol. 2, p. 385: 'Secundus autem ordo, qui est inter ea quae producta sunt eodem die, attenditur secundum praecellentiam perfectionis naturae; prius enim producitur quod imperfectum est, et deinde quod perfectum, quia is est ordo, ut a minus completo perveniatur ad magis completum. Et ideo Scriptura prius dicit esse producta natatilia die quinto, quae sunt minus perfecta quam volatilia; et similiter in sexto die prius dicit esse producta irrationalia quam hominem.'

[74] *Comm. in Sent.*, Bk 2, D. 15, A. 2, Q. 2; vol. 2, p. 385: 'Quamvis multiplex assignari possit ratio, quare homo post creaturas caeteras est productus, occurrit autem triplex ratio ad praesens, quare post omnia productus est homo: scilicet propter partium corporis multitudinem, propter animae et corporis distantiam et propter totius coniuncti perfectionem. Propter partium corporis multitudinem debuit homo ultimo produci. Cum enim corpus eius sit completissimum inter caetera corpora, et quanto aliquid compositius tanto posterius, post omnia producendus erat. Propter animae et corporis distantiam debuit fieri post

to maintain a hard boundary between humans and animals. There was a hierarchy amongst sensible beings, and humans were at the top. Humans were more perfect, their bodies were different, and the difference between their bodies and their souls was greater. They were the end of all others.

The question about the sequence of creation was immediately followed by one about the order of the production of animals with regard to God's rest, and specifically whether God rested from all work after he produced the animals.[75] This question was posed at least in part because it did not seem that God had ceased to create animals after the sixth day. Some animals were produced through putrefaction, with their own species and natures, and they were not produced during the six days of creation. Similarly, other animals were produced through mixing of different species, like the mule born of a horse and an ass, and they were not made during the six days of creation, neither as individuals nor in species.[76] The core of Bonaventure's response was that after six days God had created a universe that was perfect because all principles and species were fully in existence. An entirely different sort of perfection, however, involved the subsequent production of things through time and in succession, and in this respect God's work

caetera. Quia enim distat anima a corpore, et non solum sicut forma a materia, sed etiam sicut spirituale a corporali et sicut perpetuum a corruptibili; ideo magna distantia temporis debuit intervenire inter productionem hominis quantum ad materiale principium et coniunctionem suarum partium, ut per distantiam temporis intelligeretur distantia principiorum constituentium. Propter totius compositi perfectionem post caetera debuit homo produci. Quia enim homo sua dignitate et complemento finis est omnium corporalium; ideo post omnia erat producendus, ut sua productione finiret et compleret omnia praecedentia, tamquam finis complet quod ad ipsum ordinari habet. Et sic patet quod divina sapientia in productione sensibilium conservavit ordinem convenientissimum.'

[75] *Comm. in Sent.*, Bk 2, D. 15, A. 2, Q. 3; vol. 2, pp. 386–8: 'quaeritur de ordine productionis animalium ad quietem. Et quaeritur, utrum Deus, postquam animalia produxit, ab omni opere quieverit.'

[76] *Comm. in Sent.*, Bk 2, D. 15, A. 2, Q. 3; vol. 2, p. 386: 'Item, animalia quaedam producuntur per putrefactionem; sed constat quod illa non sunt producta in sex diebus, sicut dicit Augustinus, III Super Genesim ad litteram, et huiusmodi habent species proprias et naturas: ergo videtur quod post sextum diem non cessaverit a productione novarum specierum in genere animalium. Item, quaedam animalia generantur per commixtionem, sicut mulus ex equa et asino; haec autem in sex diebus non fuerunt facta, nec in esse individuali nec in sua specie: ergo post sextum diem non cessavit a rerum productione, non solum quantum ad individua sed etiam quantum ad species et genera.'

continued.[77] When Bonaventure explained how this was true even with regard to animals produced through putrefaction or by the mixing of different species, the sharp divide between humans and animals was manifest. Animals produced through putrefaction or by the mixing of species had been created in their principles as seminal reasons during the six days of creation. They therefore existed as potential in matter from the first making of the universe. Their species did not come into actual existence at that point because they were in some way degenerate and were produced through a sort of degeneration, although they were not superfluous, contributing nonetheless to the adornment of the universe.[78] This explanation was part of a broader understanding of the universe according to which everything produced in succession after the six days of creation fell into one of three categories. First, some were produced during the first days in kind but not in seminal reason. Rational souls were like this because they were always produced through creation, even after the six days, and seminal reason was not therefore involved. They were, however,

---

[77] *Comm. in Sent.*, Bk 2, D. 15, A. 2, Q. 3; vol. 2, p. 387: 'duplex est perfectio universi: una et praecipua secundum esse permanens, alia est secundum ipsius esse decurrens. Prima attenditur in completa existentia principiorum et completo numero specierum, quae quidem species naturam generis participant secundum rectam et ordinatam intentionem naturae. Secunda vero perfectio consistit in productione eorum quae per tempora decurrunt et sibi consequenter succedunt, ex cuius successionis ordinatione resultat quaedam unitatis pulcritudo et perfectio. Quoniam igitur secundum primam perfectionem Deus universum in sex diebus ad esse produxit, scilicet quantum ad completam existentiam principiorum et quantum ad completum numerum specierum, ideo dicitur requievisse ab omni opere quod patrarat. Quia vero continue operatur ad rerum successionem per propagationem et individuorum multiplicationem, ideo dicitur operari usque modo.'

[78] *Comm. in Sent.*, Bk 2, D. 15, A. 2, Q. 3; vol. 2, p. 387: 'Ad illud quod obiicitur de productione eorum quae sunt per putrefactionem et commixtionem, quod sunt novae species, dicendum quod tam illa quae generantur per putrefactionem quam illa quae generantur per diversarum specierum commixtionem, producta sunt in suis principiis et rationibus seminalibus, quamvis non sint producta in simili secundum formam. Principia enim eorum sunt de primaria constitutione universi, utpote species completae et rationes seminales; sed illarum specierum actualis existentia ad primariam constitutionem universi non spectat, quia species illae quodam modo sunt degenerantes et quasi per quamdam degenerationem produci habent, sicut vermes producuntur ex humano corpore per corruptionem aliquam, quae quidem facit corpus humanum a propria forma degenerare. Et ideo non oportuit haec produci in se nec in suo simili ad primariam constitutionem universi; nec tamen sunt superflua, quia universum, quantum ad bene esse, aliquo modo decorant.'

produced in kind when the soul of Adam was produced, after which no new species was produced, only new individuals. Second, others were produced in the first days in seminal reasons, but not in kind. This was the case with animals generated through putrefaction or by the mixing of different species. Third, still others were produced both in seminal reason and in kind, as was the case with plants and brute animals. Everything fitted into one of these categories, and so God rested from all work after the six days of creation in that he produced nothing that had not already been made either in kind or in seminal reason.[79] In the way that both species and individuals were made, therefore, animals and humans were fundamentally distinct.

The same was true when Bonaventure considered whether being in the image of God was a property that befitted humans and no others.[80] He explained that just as being rational or intellectual was not a straightforwardly defining property of humans because it was shared with angels, although it defined humans in relation to corporeal things, so being in the image of God was a property that defined humans with respect to brute animals, but not with respect to angels because both humans and angels were in the image of God.[81] While there was here no boundary at all between angels and humans because they shared the same properties, there was a very hard boundary between humans and

---

[79] *Comm. in Sent.*, Bk 2, D. 15, A. 2, Q. 3; vol. 2, pp. 387–8: 'Unde breviter nota quod eorum quae successione producuntur, quaedam fuerunt in prima dierum distinctione producta in simili, sed non in ratione seminali, utpote animae rationales, quae scilicet producuntur per creationem et ideo non habent rationem seminalem; in simili tamen productae sunt, quando producta fuit anima Adae, post cuius productionem non producitur nova species, quamvis producantur nova individua. Quaedam sunt quae productae sunt in primis diebus quantum ad rationem seminalem, sed non in simili, sicut ea quae generantur per putrefactionem et per diversarum specierum commixtionem. Quaedam sunt quae producta sunt et in ratione seminali et in simili, sicut plantae et bruta animalia, quae producuntur per propagationem. Et ad haec tria rerum genera possunt reduci omnia quae fiunt; et propterea non dicitur Deus producere aliqua de novo [...] sed dicitur ab omni opere requievisse, quia nihil producit quod prius non fuerit vel in simili specie vel in ratione seminali, quae tunc erant de primaria constitutione universi.'

[80] *Comm. in Sent.*, Bk 2, D. 16, A. 1, Q. 3; vol. 2, pp. 398–9: 'Utrum esse imaginem conveniat homini proprie, ita quod nulli alii'.

[81] *Comm. in Sent.*, Bk 2, D. 16, A. 1, Q. 3; vol. 2, p. 399: 'Dicendum est igitur quod sicut esse rationale vel intellectuale non est proprium homini simpliciter, quia convenit in hoc cum angelo, sed est proprium respectu rerum corporalium, sic esse imaginem proprie convenit homini respectu brutorum, non tamen respectu angelorum, immo communiter convenit hominibus et angelis.'

animals: humans possessed reason and were made in the image of God, whereas animals lacked both qualities.

When Bonaventure considered 'whether it was appropriate that temptation should have been by means of the serpent', he raised an issue that had been treated in the Summa Halensis, but he placed much less emphasis on similarities between humans and animals.[82] He first made the general point that the mode of temptation depended not only on the devil's choice but also on divine permission. The devil had not been allowed to tempt in any way he wished or could, but in the way that God permitted. Divine wisdom, which ordered and governed everything, had permitted the devil to tempt the human in the likeness of a brute animal, and not any animal, specifically that of the serpent. Conformity with due order was therefore assured.[83]

Bonaventure went on to explain why it had been fitting for the devil to tempt in the likeness of a brute animal, and then in the likeness specifically of a serpent. First, this was so with respect to the nature of the deed. Because humans were born to be inclined to good at that time, especially with regard to that which was sensible and animal in them, it was fitting that they should be tempted in the likeness of a brute animal.[84] Furthermore, the temptation was made by a suggestion which entered the heart in the manner of a serpent and there spread the

---

[82] *Comm. in Sent.*, Bk 2, D. 21, A. 1, Q. 2; vol. 2, pp. 494–5: 'Utrum tentatio per serpentem fuerit conveniens'.

[83] *Comm. in Sent.*, Bk 2, D. 21, A. 1, Q. 2; vol. 2, p. 494: 'Ad praedictorum intelligentiam est notandum quod modus ille tentandi non tantum fuit ex diabolica electione, sicut dicit Augustinus, sed etiam ex divina permissione. Non enim licuit diabolo tentare omni modo quo vellet et posset, sed eo modo quo Dominus permitteret. Concessit autem divina Sapientia, quae omnia ordinat et gubernat, et permisit quod diabolus tentaret hominem in effigie animalis bruti, et non cuiuscumque, sed serpentis: sic enim exigebat congruentia ordinis.'

[84] *Comm. in Sent.*, Bk 2, D. 21, A. 1, Q. 2; vol. 2, p. 494: 'Quod enim homo tentaretur a diabolo in effigie bruti animalis, congruum erat tum respectu operis, tum respectu finis intenti, tum etiam respectu divini indicii. Respectu operis, quia homo natus est inclinari ad bonum ut nunc, maxime ex parte sensibili et brutali; et ideo congruum erat ipsum tentari in effigie animalis bruti.' On the meaning of 'ut nunc' and its complex resonances, see Paolo Fait, 'Fragments of Aristotle's modal syllogistic in the late medieval theory of consequences: the case of *consequentia ut nunc*', in Sten Ebbesen and Russell L. Friedman (eds.), *Medieval Analyses in Language and Cognition: Acts of the Symposium 'The Copenhagen School of Medieval Philosophy' January 10–13, 1996* (Copenhagen, 1999), pp. 139–61; John A. Oesterle, 'The significance of the universal *ut nunc*', *The Thomist* 24 (1961), pp. 163–74.

venom of sin leading to the spiritual death of humans. So that the
exterior likeness should correspond to what was happening within, it
was therefore fitting that humans should be tempted by the devil in the
likeness of a serpent which crept and spread poison that killed
humans.[85]

Second, the mode of temptation had been fitting with respect to the
intended outcome. Because the temptation was meant to make humans
similar to brute animals in their adherence to changeable good, with
contempt for the unchangeable, it was again fitting that they should be
tempted by the appearance of a brute animal.[86] Moreover, the devil
had intended to turn the face, head and superior mind of humans
downwards, casting them down entirely in order to lead them to evil
with the offer of a pleasurable reward. It was therefore appropriate
that the devil had been permitted to tempt as a serpent which adhered
to the earth with its whole body as it moved.[87]

Third, the manner of temptation was fitting with respect to divine
judgment. Since God, being just and faithful, would not allow humans
to be tempted beyond their capacities, the devil was allowed to present
temptation in such a way that it could be apprehended by humans. The
devil had not therefore been allowed to tempt humans in an entirely
similar form, and so not with human appearance or likeness, but rather
with that of a brute animal.[88] Moreover, according to divine justice,

---

[85] *Comm. in Sent.*, Bk 2, D. 21, A. 1, Q. 2; vol. 2, p. 495: 'Quia enim tentatio fiebat
per suggestionis ingressum, quae intrat ad cor ad modum serpentis et ibi virus
peccati diffundit, ex quo homo habet spiritualiter mori, ideo, ut exterior effigies
operi responderet interiori, congruum fuit hominem a diabolo tentari in effigie
serpentis, cuius est serpere et venenum diffundere et diffundendo hominem
interimere.'

[86] *Comm. in Sent.*, Bk 2, D. 21, A. 1, Q. 2; vol. 2, pp. 494–5: 'Respectu finis intenti
similiter congruum erat, quia ad hoc ordinabatur tentatio ut homo efficeretur
similis animali bruto, cum, contempto bono incommutabili, adhaereret bono
commutabili et ibi quiesceret; et ideo ad hoc insinuandum in specie animalis
bruti debuit tentari.'

[87] *Comm. in Sent.*, Bk 2, D. 21, A. 1, Q. 2; vol. 2, p. 495: 'Quia enim intendebat
diabolus faciem hominis et caput et superiorem mentem convertere deorsum et
totum prosternere, et sic prosternendo ad malum finem deducere, proponendo
sibi praemium aliquod delectabile, ideo permissus est tentare in serpente, qui
secundum totum suum corpus habet terrae in suo incessu adhaerere.'

[88] *Comm. in Sent.*, Bk 2, D. 21, A. 1, Q. 2; vol. 2, p. 495: 'Respectu divini iudicii
etiam congruum fuit, quoniam Dominus iustus et fidelis non permittit hominem
tentari ultra quam possit. Et ideo sic patitur diabolum in tentatione latere ut
nihilominus possit ab homine deprehendi, et ideo non passus est quod diabolus

enmity had to arise between the tempted and the tempter, and so temptation had been fittingly made through the serpent because after the fall humans greatly feared it while it laid in wait to harm humans with its cunning.[89] This justification of the devil's snakelike appearance was qualified somewhat in the reply to one of the opening objections, however. It had been argued that temptation was more effective when the tempter was more affable, so the devil should have assumed human appearance because speech was to be expected of a human whereas a talking animal was more likely to cause terror than to persuade.[90] Bonaventure agreed that the devil would have been more affable in human likeness, and it was for this reason that divine providence had allowed the devil to assume the body of a serpent with the face of a virgin. The devil was thus concealed in one part but readily apprehended in another.[91]

Unlike the Summa Halensis, explaining and justifying the use of the serpent to tempt humans did not lead Bonaventure to think much about similarity between humans and animals. He did not go beyond recognition that there was something sensible and animal within the human, that the devil sought to make humans more like animals, and that the serpent was given the face of a virgin. Rather, Bonaventure stressed that the serpent was a tool that God permitted the devil to use in dealing with humanity, one that became hostile to humans, and bore complex symbolic meaning in its body.

hominem tentaret omnino in specie consimili, et per hoc non in specie vel effigie humana, sed potius brutali.'

[89] *Comm. in Sent.*, Bk 2, D. 21, A. 1, Q. 2; vol. 2, p. 495: 'Congruum etiam erat respectu divini iudicii. Quia enim ex illa tentatione divino iudicio inter tentatum et tentatorem debebat inimicitia exoriri; ideo tentatio hominis in serpente debuit fieri, quem post lapsum maxime exhorret, et qui maxime sua caliditate insidiatur hominem laedere.'

[90] *Comm. in Sent.*, Bk 2, D. 21, A. 1, Q. 2; vol. 2, p. 494: 'Item, tanto tentatio est efficacior, quanto tentans est in suggerendo affabilior; sed actus locutionis proprie debetur humanae effigiei: ergo videtur quod diabolus ad tentandum magis debuit assumere effigiem hominis quam bruti animalis, cum brutum animal sua locutione potius esset ad terrorem quam ad persuasionem.'

[91] *Comm. in Sent.*, Bk 2, D. 21, A. 1, Q. 2; vol. 2, p. 495: 'Ad illud de maiori affabilitate iam patet responsio. Verum est enim quod, si fuisset in effigie humana, affabilior fuisset; sed divina providentia non debuit hoc permittere, sed cautelam diaboli debuit temperare, et ideo concessum est sibi corpus serpentis, quod tamen habebat faciem virginis, sicut dicit Beda, et reliquum corpus erat serpentis, ut sic ex una parte posset latere, ex altera deprehendi.'

Whenever Bonaventure discussed animals, their lack of rationality in contrast with humans usually featured somewhere in his analysis. He expanded on the significance of this difference when he considered 'whether free judgment is only in creatures that have reason or also in brute animals'.[92] According to Bonaventure, there was no doubt that free judgment was to be found only in rational substances, and this could be demonstrated with regard to both freedom and judgment. Freedom, he argued, was opposed to servitude, hence a power was only said to be free if it had full dominion with respect to its object and its own proper act. A power that had dominion with respect to its object was not limited to any type of desirable thing but was born desiring all desirable things and rejecting all that was to be avoided. Three types of good were desirable and whose opposites were to be avoided: the good, which could also be called the honourable good, the expedient and the pleasurable. Since the expedient and the pleasurable good were sought by irrational and rational creatures, and the honourable good could only be sought by the rational, it was only in the rational that a power could be found that was not limited to any type of desirable thing and thus had freedom with respect to its object.[93] A power that had freedom with respect to its own proper act was also

---

[92] *Comm. in Sent.*, Bk 2, D. 25, P. 1, A. 1, Q. 1; vol. 2, pp. 592–5: 'Utrum liberum arbitrium sit in solis habentibus rationem, an etiam sit in animalibus brutis.' See Annabel S. Brett, *Liberty, Right and Nature: Individual Rights in Later Scholastic Thought* (Cambridge, 2003), p. 15; Theodor W. Köhler, *Homo animal nobilissimum: Konturen des spezifisch Menschlichen in der naturphilosophischen Aristoteleskommentierung des dreizehnten Jahrhunderts*, vols. 2.1 and 2.2 (Leiden, 2014), pp. 604–5.

[93] *Comm. in Sent.*, Bk 2, D. 25, P. 1, A. 1, Q. 1; vol. 2, p. 593: 'Dicendum quod absque dubio liberum arbitrium reperitur in solis substantiis rationalibus. Et ratio huius sumitur tum ex parte libertatis, tum ex parte arbitrationis. Ex parte libertatis: libertas enim opponitur servituti. Unde illa sola potentia dicitur esse libera quae dominium habet plenum tam respectu obiecti quam respectu actus proprii. Illa autem potentia dominium habet ex libertate respectu obiecti quae non est arctata ad aliquod genus appetibilis, sed nata est omnia appetibilia appetere et omne fugibile respuere. Tria autem sunt quae sunt in appetitibus et quorum opposita sunt in fugis, videlicet bonum, conferens et delectabile; et nomine boni ibi intelligitur honestum. Cum autem bonum conferens et delectabile nata sint appeti ab irrationalibus, bonum honestum a solis rationalibus potest appeti; et ideo in eis solum reperitur virtus quae non est ad aliquod genus appetibilis arctata, ac per hoc habens libertatem respectu obiecti.' See Boyd Taylor Coolman, *Knowing God by Experience: The Spiritual Senses in the Theology of William of Auxerre* (Washington, D.C., 2004), p. 62 for the roots of this division of the good.

to be found only in rational beings because the will in rational creatures not only restrained the exterior hand and foot, but also restrained
and curbed itself, frequently beginning to hate what it previously loved,
so that it had dominion over itself. In brute animals, however, although
there was dominion with respect to exterior acts which they could
sometimes restrain effectively, as was apparent with domestic animals,
there was no dominion with respect to their own proper interior acts,
namely their appetites. Thus, if they loved something, they could not
do otherwise, although they might be held back from the pursuit of
what they loved by fear of suffering being inflicted upon them. Brute
animals therefore lacked freedom with respect to their own proper
acts, just as they lacked it with respect to their objects, and so they
could not exercise freedom of judgment.[94]

Consideration of judgment led to the same conclusion. Judgment
moved and was obeyed by other powers, discerning between the just
and the unjust, between what was one's own and what belonged to
another. No power, however, could distinguish between the just and
the unjust except that which participated in reason and was created to
know the highest justice from which every law derived. This rational
power was only to be found in the substance which was made in the
image of God, for no substance could discern what was its own and
what belonged to another unless it knew itself and its own acts. No
power which was bound to matter, however, could know itself or
reflect on itself. If therefore all powers were bound to matter and
corporeal substance except only the rational, only the rational could
reflect on itself and had the full power of judgment to discern what was
just and what was unjust, what belonged to itself and what to another.
Consideration of judgment thus led to the same conclusion as

---

[94] *Comm. in Sent.*, Bk 2, D. 25, P. 1, A. 1, Q. 1; vol. 2, p. 593: 'In eis etiam solis
reperitur potentia habens libertatem respectu actus proprii; quod patet. Nam
voluntas in rationalibus non solum compescit manum exteriorem vel pedem, sed
etiam compescit se ipsam et refrenat, incipiens odire frequenter quod prius
diligebat; et hoc ex sui ipsius imperio et dominio. In brutis autem animalibus,
etsi aliquo modo sit reperire dominium respectu actus exterioris, quia bene
refrenant aliquando, sicut patet in animalibus domesticis, respectu tamen actus
proprii interioris, videlicet appetitus, dominium non est. Unde si aliquid amant,
non possunt illud non amare, licet a prosecutione alicuius rei amatae arceantur
timore alicuius passionis inflictivae. [...] ac per hoc, cum non possint actum
proprium reprimere, respectu actus proprii non habent libertatem nec etiam
respectu obiecti; et ideo, deficiente in eis libertate, liberum arbitrium non
possunt participare.'

consideration of freedom: freedom of judgment was only to be found in rational substances.[95]

Bonaventure's reply to one of the opening objections also addressed the issue of foresight. It had been argued that a power was free especially if it acted providentially not only for the present but also for the future, and this was the case in brute animals such as ants and others that were irrational.[96] Bonaventure replied that some foresight stemmed from an act of deliberation and foreknowledge, some from 'natural instinct'. The first involved freedom of judgment and was found only in the rational. The second was a matter of natural sagacity and industry, for nature was most prudent, and this was found in brute animals, and no freedom of judgment was involved.[97] Bonaventure was therefore adamant that, unlike humans, animals lacked reason and free judgment, were not made in the image of God and could neither distinguish between right and wrong nor engage in self-reflection and self-control, were bound to the material world, and exercised foresight only through natural instinct rather than deliberation.

[95] *Comm. in Sent.*, Bk 2, D. 25, P. 1, A. 1, Q. 1; vol. 2, p. 593: 'Sumitur etiam ratio ex parte arbitrationis. Arbitrium enim idem est quod iudicium, ad cuius nutum caeterae virtutes moventur et obediunt. Iudicare autem illius est secundum rationem completam, cuius est discernere inter iustum et iniustum et inter proprium et alienum. Nulla autem potentia novit quid iustum et quid iniustum nisi illa sola quae est particeps rationis et nata est cognoscere summam iustitiam, a qua est regula omnis iuris. Haec autem solum est in ea substantia quae est ad imaginem Dei, qualis est tantum potentia rationalis. Nulla enim substantia discernit quid proprium et quid alienum nisi cognoscat se ipsam et actum suum proprium. Sed nunquam aliqua potentia se ipsam cognoscit vel super se ipsam reflectitur quae sit alligata materiae. Si igitur omnes potentiae sunt alligatae materiae et substantiae corporali praeter solam rationalem, sola illa est quae potest se super se ipsam reflectere; et ideo ipsa sola est in qua est plenum iudicium et arbitrium in discernendo quid iustum et quid iniustum, quid proprium et quid alienum. Tam igitur ratione libertatis quam ratione arbitrationis liberum arbitrium in solis substantiis rationalibus reperitur.'
[96] *Comm. in Sent.*, Bk 2, D. 25, P. 1, A. 1, Q. 1; vol. 2, p. 592: 'Item, illa potentia libera est praecipue cuius est gerere providentiam, non solummodo circa praesentia, sed etiam circa futura; sed talis est in brutis animalibus, sicut patet in formicis et aliis animalibus irrationalibus: ergo etc.'
[97] *Comm. in Sent.*, Bk 2, D. 25, P. 1, A. 1, Q. 1; vol. 2, p. 594: 'Ad illud quod obicitur, quod liberi arbitrii est providere, dicendum quod providentia quaedam provenit ex actu deliberationis et praecognitionis, quaedam provenit ex instinctu naturali. Prima est libertatis arbitrariae et reperitur in solis rationalibus; secunda vero est naturalis sagacitatis et industriae: natura enim prudentissima est; et haec reperitur in brutis animalibus, et talis non ponit liberum arbitrium.'

The hard boundary that divided humans and animals was apparent once again when Bonaventure considered whether plants and brute animals would be renewed after the Last Judgment.[98] He was clear that they would not. They were corruptible by nature and originated in matter, so they were not fit to live eternally, in contrast to the supercelestial bodies and the elements.[99] It had been argued in the opening objections that plants and animals must be renewed because the ornament of the heavens was to be renewed in the form of the supercelestial bodies, so the same must apply to the ornament of the earth, namely plants and animals; if plants and animals were not renewed, the earth would be renewed without ornament and thus imperfectly.[100] Furthermore, because plants and animals existed to praise God, they must be renewed after the Last Judgment when praise of God should increase rather than diminish.[101] Moreover, things that contributed to the perfection of the universe should not cease to exist, and it was clear that plants and animals fell into this category because they had been created in the first six days when the world was set up before the fall, because they would otherwise now be superfluous, and because with them the universe would be more perfect after the Last Judgment.[102] Bonaventure dismissed these arguments, explaining that plants and animals existed for the service of humans, and only as the ornament of the earth, to praise God, and for the perfection of the universe through their current status which was corruptible and changeable,

[98] *Comm. in Sent.*, Bk 4, D. 48, A. 2, Q. 4; vol. 4, pp. 994–5: 'Utrum innovabuntur plantae et animalia bruta'.
[99] *Comm. in Sent.*, Bk 4, D. 48, A. 2, Q. 4; vol. 4, p. 994: 'Dicendum, quod plantae et animalia non innovabuntur, propter hoc quod ultima eorum perfectio est corruptibilis per naturam et ortum et radicem habet a materia; unde non sunt idonea ad vivendum sive durandum aeternaliter.'
[100] *Comm. in Sent.*, Bk 4, D. 48, A. 2, Q. 4; vol. 4, p. 994: 'Caeli ornatus innovabitur, ut patet in corporibus supercaelestibus: ergo pari ratione ornatus terrae; sed ornatus terrae sunt plantae et animalia: ergo etc. Alioquin, si non innovabuntur, ergo remunerabitur terra sine ornatu, et ita imperfecte: ergo etc.'
[101] *Comm. in Sent.*, Bk 4, D. 48, A. 2, Q. 4; vol. 4, p. 994: 'Item, plantae et animalia sunt ad laudem Dei [...]; ergo si laus Dei post iudicium non debet minui nec decescere, sed augeri; ergo non debent cessare plantae et animalia.'
[102] *Comm. in Sent.*, Bk 4, D. 48, A. 2, Q. 4; vol. 4, p. 994: 'Item, quae sunt de perfectione universi non debent cessare; sed plantae et animalia sunt huiusmodi: ergo etc. Prima patet, quia tunc universum erit perfectius. Secunda patet, quia nunc superfluerent, si non essent de perfectione; et praeterea sunt creata inter opera sex dierum, in quibus mundus est constitutus ante hominis lapsum.'

so they did not have to be renewed after the Last Judgment.[103] Animals were not to share an eternal future with humans.

However low the relative status and worth of animals, Bonaventure recognised that humans might have affection for animals, and he asked 'whether irrational creatures ought to be loved out of charity'.[104] Bonaventure distinguished between loving out of 'charity command- ing' and out of 'charity eliciting'. Explaining what it was to love out of 'charity commanding', he observed that all meritorious works could be said to derive from charity because charity commanded every good work. Thus, out of charity he could go to Saint James or pluck a weed from the earth. He conceded that irrational creatures ought to be loved out of charity in this sense. Just as charity commanded and moved one to do, say and know all things that pertained to human salvation and praise of the divine, it also commanded one to love these things. Thus, because many irrational creatures were given to humans to assist with the performance of meritorious deeds and they were ordered to the praise of God, it followed that charity commanded that such creatures be loved. As for loving out of 'charity eliciting', Bonaventure explained that an act was said to derive from charity in this sense when nothing other than the habit of charity was involved, when it was directed at God and those close to God, at that which contained the formal act of charity itself, which was only the highest good or something that could be united with the highest good through cognition and love. Because irrational creatures, not being made in God's image, were incapable of relating to God in this way, they could not desire the highest good through charity, they could not love out of charity according to its proper act and form, and therefore they could not themselves be loved out of charity in this second and more profound sense.[105]

---

[103] *Comm. in Sent.*, Bk 4, D. 48, A. 2, Q. 4; vol. 4, p. 994: 'plantae et animalia non sunt ad ornatum terrae, sed ad hominis obsequium, nec ad Dei laudem nec ad universi perfectionem nisi secundum statum eum, qui est corruptibilis et variabilis; et ideo non oportet innovari.'

[104] *Comm. in Sent.*, Bk 3, D. 28, A. 1, Q. 1; vol. 3, pp. 621–4: 'Utrum ex caritate diligendae sint creaturae irrationales'.

[105] *Comm. in Sent.*, Bk 3, D. 28, A. 1, Q. 1; vol. 3, p. 622: 'Ad praedictorum intelligentiam est notandum quod, cum aliquis actus dicitur esse ex aliqua virtute, hoc potest intelligi dupliciter: uno modo sicut a movente et imperante, alio modo sicut ab eliciente et informante. Primo modo potest dici quod omnia opera meritoria sunt ex caritate, quia caritas imperat omne opus bonum; sicut ex caritate possum ire ad sanctum Iacobum et ex caritate levare festucam de terra. Secundo modo ille actus dicitur esse ex caritate quem habitus caritatis

Bonaventure recognised, however, that people sometimes loved animals, but this, he explained, was through a sort of natural affection. It was by this sort of natural affection that humans loved dogs that they saw obeying them. Before the fall, humans had been born to love and cherish other beasts and irrational creatures with this sort of affection. Since the fall, the more that a human was reformed and returned to the state of innocence, the more creatures of this kind behaved gently towards that individual, and that individual was moved by greater affection towards them. Unsurprisingly, Bonaventure had Francis in mind. Accounts of his life related how he overflowed with a wonderful tenderness towards irrational creatures because he had in some way recovered innocence in this life. Irrational creatures had provided a sign in this regard.[106]

Bonaventure explained that there was another way of analysing the whole issue, which was entirely compatible with the one that he had

respicit formaliter et directe, sicut diligere Deum et proximum, quem non habet anima elicere mediante alio habitu quam habitu caritatis. Secundum hoc intelligendum quod aliquid diligi ex caritate potest dupliciter intelligi: uno modo ex caritate imperante; et sic concedi potest quod irrationales creaturae diligendae ex caritate. Sicut enim caritas imperat et movet ad faciendum et dicendum et cognoscendum omnia quae spectant ad salutem nostram et laudem divinam, sic etiam imperat ad amandum. Unde, quia multae irrationales creaturae datae sunt nobis in adiutorium ad exercendum opera meritoria, ordinatae sunt etiam ad laudandum Deum, hinc est quod caritas, quae est amatrix Dei et proximi, imperat tales creaturas diligi. Alio modo dicitur aliquid diligi ex caritate eliciente et informante; et sic diligitur ex caritate illud in quod est formalis et proprius actus ipsius caritatis; tale autem non est nisi illud quod est summum Bonum vel cui summum Bonum natum est aliquo modo uniri per cognitionem et amorem. Ideo, cum creaturae irrationales non sint hoc modo Dei capaces, quia non sunt ad Dei imaginem, per caritatem non potest eis exoptari summum Bonum; et ideo caritas non descendit ad illa diligenda secundum suum actum proprium et formalem: ac per hoc talia non diliguntur ex caritate elicitive.'

[106] *Comm. in Sent.*, Bk 3, D. 28, A. 1, Q. 1; vol. 3, p. 622: 'Et si tu quaeras: quae virtus elicit illum actum dilectionis quo quis diligit creaturas, in quantum sunt de Deo et ad Deum, dicendum quod hoc est cuiusdam pietatis et affectionis naturalis. Sicut enim homo diligit canem quadam pietate naturali, quia videt eum sibi obedientem, sic et ceteras alias bestias et irrationales creaturas naturaliter ex quadam pietate natus erat diligere et fovere, quantum erat ex prima conditione. Unde secundum quod homo plus reformatur et reducitur ad statum innocentiae, secundum hoc magis sibi mansuescunt huiusmodi creaturae et ipse circa eas maiori pietate movetur, sicut de beato Francisco legitur quod erga huiusmodi creaturas mira pietatis teneritudine affluebat, quia iam quodam modo innocentiam recuperaverat. In cuius rei signum creaturae irrationales eidem obtemperabant.'

already presented. According to this second analysis, something could
be loved out of charity in three ways. First, there could be affection
towards the beloved as an end; only God was to be loved out of charity
in this way. Second, there could be affection towards the beloved, but
not as an end; those who were closest were to be loved in this way,
wishing the highest good for them, not for their own sake, but for the
sake of God. Third, there could be an affection that was not towards
the beloved as an end or even towards the beloved itself, but solely by
reason of another for whose sake there was love; it was in this way that
irrational creatures, in which God shone forth, were to be loved
because God was loved in them. Bonaventure illustrated this third
way of loving out of charity by referring to the proverbial man who
loved his friend's dog not because of any special affection for the dog
but because of the way he felt about his friend. This showed how
charity did not bind humans to irrational creatures in the way that it
bound and connected them to fellow humans and to God. Thus, the
love that was part of friendship, which was directed to a friend,
extended to the friend's son, so that the son too was loved as a friend,
but did not extend to the friend's puppy. Charity, which was love of
God, extended to those who were born to be his children through
grace; because irrational creatures were not of this kind, they were not,
properly speaking, born to be loved out of charity, although through
charity God could be loved in them.[107]

[107] *Comm. in Sent.*, Bk 3, D. 28, A. 1, Q. 1; vol. 3, pp. 622–3: 'Est et alius hic
modus dicendi praedicto modo non contrarius, sed potius consonus, quod
aliquid diligi ex caritate potest esse tripliciter: vel ita quod caritas faciat circa
ipsum dilectum ponere affectionem et finem; et sic solus Deus diligitur ex
caritate. Alio modo ita quod caritas circa ipsum dilectum faciat ponere
affectionem, non tamen finem; et sic diligitur proximus ex caritate, quia circa
proximum affectu caritatis afficitur, optando ei summum Bonum, non propter
ipsum, sed propter Deum. Tertio modo dicitur aliquid ex caritate diligi ita quod
caritas circa illud non ponit finem nec etiam affectionem intuitu sui, sed solum
ratione illius propter quod diligit; et hoc modo creaturae irrationales, in quibus
Deus relucet, diliguntur ex caritate, quia Deus diligitur in illis; per quem
modum quis dicitur diligere canem amici sui, non quia afficiatur circa canem
speciali affectione, sed quia afficitur circa amicum. Et huius signum est, quia
affectus caritatis non alligat hominem creaturae irrationali secundum quod
alligat et connectit hominem ipsi proximo vel etiam ipsi Deo. Unde sicut
amor amicitiae, qui est in amicum, se extendit ad amici filium, ita quod filius
amici amicus est et dilectus, non autem sic se extendit ad amici catulum, ut canis
diligatur consimili affectu, sic intelligendum est quod caritas, quae est amor
Dei, se extendit ad illos qui sunt nati esse eius filii per gratiam adoptionis.'

For Bonaventure, human love of animals was always of a lower order compared with love for other humans and for the divine. Affection for animals invariably reflected something higher that had nothing to do with animals themselves: they assisted in the performance of good deeds, their existence constituted praise of God, affectionate behaviour on their part could signal the recovered innocence of the human at which it was directed, and they could be loved entirely for God's sake. Fundamentally, however, they could not relate to God in the way that humans could, so the standing of humans' relationships with them was correspondingly diminished.

In all the above, Bonaventure saw very little similarity between humans and animals. Metaphorically, those who thought that souls transmigrated between humans and animals were 'bestial humans'. There was a restricted sense in which animals should be loved out of charity. When the devil tempted the first humans, he had wanted to make them more like animals in their adherence to changeable good, and the serpent that he used had a maidenly face. Bonaventure did, however, recognise that there was something sensible and animal in humans, a point that received more substantial treatment when he discussed animal bodies, primarily with animals in mind but with the recognition that his analysis applied to human animals too.

Bonaventure discussed, for example, 'whether the bodies of animals are composed of the four elements or from one of them'.[108] He held that without doubt the bodies of animals contained 'the nature of the four elements', and this for four reasons: so that they were fit for sensing, fit for movement, fit to perform many operations, and had dignity of complexion.[109] Each reason was explained in the opening arguments. First, sensing was an operation of the soul in the body that involved

---

Et quia creaturae irrationales non sunt huiusmodi, ideo proprie loquendo, non sunt natae ex caritate diligi, ita quod caritas circa illas ponat affectum, bene tamen potest caritas in illis diligere Deum.'

[108] *Comm. in Sent.*, Bk 2, D. 15, A. 1, Q. 2; vol. 2, pp. 377–9: 'utrum corpora animalium sint composita ex quatuor elementis, an ex uno'. See Gilson, *Philosophie de Saint Bonaventure*, pp. 294–6.

[109] *Comm. in Sent.*, Bk 2, D. 15, A. 1, Q. 2; vol. 2, p. 378: 'Dicendum quod absque dubio corpora animalium habent in se naturam quatuor elementorum, sicut ostensum est per quatuor rationes, tum propter hoc ut sint idonea ad sensum; tum propter hoc ut sint idonea ad motum; tum propter hoc ut sint idonea ad multiplicitatem operationis; tum propter hoc ut in se habeant dignitatem completionis, quae omnia competunt illi corpori quod perficitur anima sensibili.'

conformity of the organ to what was sensed. Every animal had the sense of touch by means of which it perceived the four qualities rooted in the four elements. Every animal was therefore was made up of the four elements.[110] Second, every animal was mobile in some way, but no element on its own was mobile. It was therefore necessary that an animal be made up of several elements.[111] Third, the more spiritual the form, the more it was the principle of many operations. The sensible soul was a highly spiritual form, so it was the principle of many operations. The body was given to aid the soul, so it had to be fit to perform many operations, but it could only perform diverse operations through diverse powers which required diverse natures which required that they be composed from diverse elements.[112] Fourth, the more complex the form, the more noble it was because less complex forms were contained within the more complex. The form of something made up of the elements was therefore nobler than a form of a single element. Because the sensible soul was a noble form, it had to have a noble body, and this meant that the body of an animal was not simple but had to be composed of diverse elements.[113] That all this applied to humans as well as to brute animals was indicated in a reply to one of the objections where the human was described as 'the most perfect' of all animals.[114]

---

[110] *Comm. in Sent.*, Bk 2, D. 15, A. 1, Q. 2; vol. 2, p. 377: 'Sensus est operatio animae in corpore secundum conformitatem organi ad obiectum; sed quodlibet animal habet tactum, qui est perceptibilis quatuor qualitatum, quae radicantur in quatuor elementis: ergo quodlibet animal constat ex quatuor elementis.'

[111] *Comm. in Sent.*, Bk 2, D. 15, A. 1, Q. 2; vol. 2, p. 377: 'Item, omne animal aliquo motu est mobile, ut progressionis vel constrictionis vel dilatationis; sed nullum elementum de se est sic mobile: ergo necesse est animal constare ex pluribus elementis.'

[112] *Comm. in Sent.*, Bk 2, D. 15, A. 1, Q. 2; vol. 2, pp. 377–8: 'Item, quanto forma est spiritualior tanto est plurium operationum principium; sed anima sensibilis est forma valde spiritualis: ergo est principium multiplicis operationis. Sed corpus datum est ad subministrandum ei: ergo necesse est quod corpus sit aptum et idoneum ad diversas operationes; sed non est aptum ad diversas operationes nisi per diversas virtutes, nec ad diversas virtutes nisi per diversas naturas, nec habet diversas naturas nisi quia ex diversis compositum: ergo etc.'

[113] *Comm. in Sent.*, Bk 2, D. 15, A. 1, Q. 2; vol. 2, p. 378: 'Item, quanto forma posterior et ulterior tanto nobilior, pro eo quod anteriora sunt materialia respectu posteriorum: ergo nobilior est forma mixti quam forma elementi. Si ergo anima sensibilis, cum sit forma nobilis, debet habere corpus nobile, ergo corpus animalis non tantum non est corpus simplex, sed constans ex diversis elementis.'

[114] *Comm. in Sent.*, Bk 2, D. 15, A. 1, Q. 2; vol. 2, p. 378: 'homo, qui inter caetera animalia est perfectissimus'.

Bonaventure also considered whether the bodies of animals were composed more of passive elements than active elements, in other words whether they contained more earth and water than air and fire.[115] He argued that just as quantity had to be understood in two ways, with regard to mass and with regard to power, so the predominance of elements had to be understood in terms of mass and power. With regard to mass, the passive elements were predominant in animal bodies, and so they were said to be mostly made of these elements. With regard to power, however, the active elements were predominant because the body was constituted to be ruled by the soul through their mediation. Bonaventure explained that the active and passive elements were predominant in these different ways because of the end of the body, which was the soul insofar as the soul gave life, sense and movement to the body. He then considered how the body had to be composed if it were to receive each of these from the soul.[116]

The body would not be suitable for life if the passive elements were predominant with regard to both mass and power because this entailed coarseness and solidity, as in mineral bodies. Similarly, the

---

[115] *Comm. in Sent.*, Bk 2, D. 15, A. 1, Q. 3; vol. 2, pp. 379–81: 'Utrum corpora animalium magis constent ex elementis passivis quam activis'. See Gilson, *Philosophie de Saint Bonaventure*, pp. 296–7. The question is heavily dependent on Augustine, *De Genesi ad litteram libri duodecim*, book 3, chapters 4–5.

[116] *Comm. in Sent.*, Bk 2, D. 15, A. 1, Q. 3; vol. 2, p. 380: 'Respondeo: Dicendum quod secundum quod duplex est quantitas, videlicet molis et virtutis, secundum hoc dupliciter potest attendi elementorum praedominantia, videlicet quantum ad molem et quantum ad virtutem. Si enim loquamur de praedominantia quantum ad molem, sic in corporibus animalium praedominantur elementa passiva, et ideo ex eis maxime dicuntur esse facta. Si autem loquamur quantum ad quantitatem virtutis, cum corpus complexionatum sit natum regi ab anima mediantibus elementis activis, sic praedominantur in eis elementa activa. Ratio autem huius, quare elementa activa et passiva secundum hanc duplicem quantitatem virtutis et molis vicissim praedominantur, sumitur ex parte finis. Finis enim imponit necessitatem his quae sunt ad finem; finis autem corporis complexionati anima est, in quantum dat ei vitam et sensum et motum.' *Quantitas molis* and *quantitas virtutis* are usually considered insofar as they featured in Bonaventure's ideas about infinity; see, for example, J. Isaac Le Goff, 'Divine infinity in Bonaventure's disputed questions on the mystery of the Trinity', in Michael F. Cusato, Timothy J. Johnson and Steven J. McMichael (eds.), *Ordo et Sanctitas: The Franciscan Spiritual Journey in Theology and Hagiography: A Festschrift in Honour of J. A. Wayne Hellman O.F.M. Conv.* (Brill, 2017), pp. 165–85 at 171–2.

body would not be suitable for life if the active powers were predominant with regard to both mass and power because the passive elements would be consumed immediately and the body could not be aroused by the soul. For the body to be fit to receive life, therefore, there had to be balance and a sort of harmony between the active and passive elements.[117]

The body would not be suitable for sense unless the nature of a passive element was predominant with regard to mass because touch was the first among all the animal senses and earth was predominant in this sense. It followed that if earth were not predominant in the body, it would not be fit for touch and therefore not for any sense. With regard to power, however, for the body to be suitable for sense it was necessary that fire be predominant, for heat and the spirit were the instruments of the sensitive power. For the body to be suitable for sense, it was therefore necessary for the active and passive elements to be predominant in different but complementary ways.[118]

For the body to be suitable for movement, the active elements had to be predominant with regard to power because it was through their mediation that the motive force of the soul reached the limbs. It was also necessary, however, that the passive elements be predominant with regard to mass because they made the limbs solid enough to move. So, for the animal body to move, it was again necessary that active and passive elements be predominant in different but

---

[117] *Comm. in Sent.*, Bk 2, D. 15, A. 1, Q. 3; vol. 2, p. 380: 'Ad vitam autem corpus illud non esset habile, si praedominarentur ibi elementa passiva quantum ad quantitatem et virtutem, propter sui grossitiem et soliditatem, sicut sunt corpora mineralia. Similiter nec esset habile, si praedominarentur ei elementa activa quantum ad virtutem et quantitatem, quia statim consumerentur elementa passiva, nec esset quod posset vegetari ab anima. Et ita oportuit quod ex quadam mutua praedominantia consurgeret quaedam mutua concordia et proportio, ex qua corpus illud esset aptum ad vitam suscipiendam et animam, quae est quasi quaedam harmonia.'

[118] *Comm. in Sent.*, Bk 2, D. 15, A. 1, Q. 3; vol. 2, p. 380: 'Ad sensum similiter idoneum non esset nisi praedominaretur natura passivi elementi quantum ad molem, quia tactus est primus inter omnes sensus animalis, in quo sensu praedominatur terra; et ita, si non praedominaretur terra in corpore, non esset idoneum ad tactum: ergo nec ad aliquem sensum. Similiter oportet ad hoc quod sit idoneum ad sensum, quod praedominetur in eo ignis quantum ad virtutem sive calorem. Calor enim et spiritus sunt instrumenta virtutis sensitivae [...]. Et ita ex hoc patet quod ad hoc quod corpus sit idoneum ad sensum, necesse est elementorum activorum et passivorum esse mutuum praedominium.'

complementary ways, the limbs gaining vigour and agility from air and fire, but solidity from the predominance of water and earth.[119]

With regard to the body and its elemental composition, therefore, the bodies of humans and animals were the same. Beyond this, Bonaventure was not struck by much in the way of similarity, and of all the theologians considered here he was perhaps the most relentlessly insistent on difference. He took it for granted that humans were the most perfect animals, unlike all other animals in their possession of reason. Made in the image of God, humans related to God very differently from animals. The rational souls of humans were created and immortal, whereas brute animal souls were produced from seminal reasons and corruptible. Even though both humans and animals had sensible souls, the human sensible soul was a power of the rational soul, while the animal sensible soul was rooted in corporeal matter. Despite being the same with regard to elemental composition, even human bodies were superior to animal bodies in their multitude of parts, order and complexity. In addition to reason, humans had free will and judgment. Unlike animals, they could exercise self-reflection and self-control, they could discriminate between good and evil, and be punished for sin, and they could look to the future though deliberation rather than just natural instinct. Animals served humans, answering to their bodily and even emotional needs. Bearing symbolic meaning, they were God's tools. Many had become hostile to humans after the fall, but humans might hold some animals in affection, though only the lowest form of charity could be involved. While none of this would have appeared strange, let alone incorrect, to other Parisian scholars, Bonaventure did not see any of the similarities that underpinned more complex understandings in the work of others. For Bonaventure, the boundary between humans and animals was always clear-cut.

---

[119] *Comm. in Sent.*, Bk 2, D. 15, A. 1, Q. 3; vol. 2, pp. 380–1: 'Similiter ad hoc quod sit idoneum ad motum, necesse est quod elementa activa virtualiter praedominentur, mediantibus quibus animae vis motiva ad membra pertingat; necesse est etiam quod dominentur passiva secundum quantitatem molis, ex quibus constituantur membra solida ad movendum idonea. [...] Sic igitur propter motum necesse est esse mutuam activorum et passivorum elementorum in corpore animalis praedominantiam, ut membra sint mobilia, ita quod vigorem et agilitatem habeant ex aere et igne, soliditatem vero habeant ex praedominio aquae et terrae secundum quantitatem.'

3 | *Albert the Great and Thomas Aquinas*

This chapter focuses on the two most influential Dominican theologians of the thirteenth century, Albert the Great and Thomas Aquinas. Albert was probably born around 1200, although the precise date is uncertain. He came from a German family of knightly status and studied the arts in Padua. When and where he joined the Dominican order is unclear, but he studied theology as a Dominican in Cologne. He was sent to Paris in the early 1240s where he became a master of theology. In 1248 he went to Cologne to establish a Dominican *studium generale*. From 1254 to 1257 he was prior provincial of the German Dominicans, after which he resumed his teaching in Cologne. He became bishop of Regensberg in 1260, resigning in 1262. Thereafter he served the papacy and the order in many capacities until his death in 1280.[1]

Albert the Great is generally held to have completed his *De animalibus* between 1256 and 1260.[2] The first nineteen books were a commentary on Aristotle's *Historia animalium*, *De partibus animalium* and *De generatione animalium*, three texts that were translated into Latin in the thirteenth century and treated subsequently in the middle ages as a single work entitled *De animalibus*. When reading Albert's commentary, it is difficult to know when Albert was expounding Aristotle and when he was articulating his own views. Books 20 and 21 of Albert's *De animalibus*, however, are regarded as his 'original contribution'.[3] Moreover, in these books he made explicit and

---

[1] On Albert's life, see Irven M. Resnick, 'Albert the Great: biographical introduction', in Irven M. Resnick (ed.), *A Companion to Albert the Great: Theology, Philosophy, and the Sciences* (Leiden, 2013), pp. 1–11.

[2] Kenneth F. Kitchell Jr. and Irven Michael Resnick, 'Introduction: the life and works of Albert the Great', in Albertus Magnus, *On Animals: A Medieval Summa Zoologica*, trans. Kenneth F. Kitchell Jr. and Irven Michael Resnick (Baltimore, 2 vols., 1999), vol. 1, pp. 1–42 at 35.

[3] Kitchell and Resnick, 'Introduction', pp. 39–40 (quotation at 40). For summaries of the process by which Aristotle's zoological works became available in Latin,

systematic comparisons between humans and animals, so the focus here is on this part of his work.

Thomas Aquinas was born to a noble family in southern Italy in 1224 or 1225. As a child he was sent as an oblate to the abbey of Monte Cassino. From 1239 to 1244, he studied the arts at the university of Naples. He joined the Dominican order in 1244, but his family held him captive for over a year because they wished him to enter a traditional monastic order. Once set free, he was sent by the Dominican order to Paris where, from 1245 to 1248, he was taught in the convent of Saint-Jacques by Albert the Great. He moved to Cologne in 1248 where he continued his studies under Albert. In 1252 he returned to Paris where he studied theology until 1256. From 1256 to 1259 he was a master of theology in Paris. He spent the years between 1259 and 1269 in Italy, at Naples, at Orvieto and in Rome, where he set up a *studium* at the convent of Santa Sabina. From 1269 to 1272 he was once again a master of theology in Paris. He left in 1272 to establish a provincial *studium* at the priory of San Domenico in Naples where his lectures were also open to members of the university. Already in poor health, he died in March 1274 at the Cistercian abbey of Fossanova while on his way to attend the Council of Lyons.[4]

It was towards the end of his first spell as master of theology at Paris in the 1250s that Aquinas began his *Summa contra gentiles*, completing it in Orvieto in 1264 or perhaps 1265. According to a fourteenth-century chronicle, he wrote it at the request of Raymund of Pennaforte, a former master general of the Dominican order, to assist Dominicans who were preaching in Spain in opposition to Moslems, Jews and heretics, though this missionary purpose was probably attributed to

---

see Pieter Beullens, 'Like a book written by God's finger: animals showing the path toward God', in Brigitte Resl (ed.), *A Cultural History of Animals in the Medieval Age* (Oxford, 2007), pp. 127–51 at 136–8; Pieter de Leemans and Matthew Klemm, 'Animals and anthropology in medieval philosophy', in Resl (ed.), *Cultural History of Animals*, pp. 153–77 at 162.

[4] Amongst many accounts of Aquinas's life, see especially Brian Davies, *Thomas Aquinas's* Summa Theologiae: *A Guide and Commentary* (Oxford, 2014), pp. 3–7; Thomas F. O'Meara, *Thomas Aquinas: Theologian* (Notre Dame, Ind., 1997), pp. 1–40; Jean-Pierre Torrell, *Saint Thomas Aquinas*, trans. Robert Royal (Washington, D.C., 2 vols., 2005), vol. 1: *The Person and his Work*; James A. Weisheipl, *Friar Thomas d'Aquino: His Life, Thought and Works* (New York, 1974).

the work later by others.[5] Aquinas began the *Summa theologiae* in Rome in 1266. It was a summary of theology for beginners, although there has been some debate about the level at which he intended to pitch the work. The third and final part was unfinished at his death and his followers added a *Supplement* made up of extracts taken from his Commentary on the *Sentences*.[6]

Albert the Great, *De animalibus*, Books 20 and 21

In Books 20 and 21 of Albert the Great's *De animalibus*, the emphasis, at least initially, was very much on difference, with a very hard boundary separating humans and all other animals. At the end of Book 20, Albert noted that animals differed from each other by species, each species having a body and organs of a distinct shape. Because their bodies and organs varied in shape, their souls necessarily differed by species too.[7] According to Albert, however, humans seemed to differ from other animals by more than just species. This was because differentiation by species occurred even when there was no difference with regard to sense or motion, and yet humans differed from other animals with regard to the senses, as was proved by the shapes of their sense organs and the shape of the human body as a whole. More than this, however, they possessed the distinct characteristic of reason. A sign that humans differed from other animals by more than species was that the irrational powers of a human, such as desire and anger, could be

---

[5] On the nature and dating of the *Summa contra gentiles*, see Davies, *Thomas Aquinas's* Summa Theologiae, pp. 6, 16; René-Antoine Gauthier, *Saint Thomas d'Aquin: Somme Contre les Gentils: Introduction* (Paris, 1993), pp. 10–18, 101–8, 142–63, 165–76; Matthew Kostelecky, *Thomas Aquinas's* Summa Contra Gentiles: *A Mirror of Human Nature* (Leuven, 2013), pp. viii, 1–5; Torrell, *Saint Thomas Aquinas*, vol. 1, pp. 101–16.

[6] On the nature and dating of the *Summa theologiae*, see Leonard Boyle, *The Setting of the* Summa Theologiae *of Saint Thomas* (Toronto, 1982); Davies, *Thomas Aquinas's* Summa Theologiae, pp. 7–17; O'Meara, *Thomas Aquinas*, pp. 41–86; Jean-Pierre Torrell, *Aquinas's* Summa: *Background, Structure, and Reception*, trans. Benedict M. Guevin (Washington, D.C., 2005), pp. 17–62.

[7] Albertus Magnus, *De Animalibus Libri XXVI*, ed. Hermann Stadler, Beiträge zur Geschichte der Philosophie des Mittelalters 15–16 (Münster, 1916–1920), 20.2.6, p. 1319: 'animalia a se invicem specie sunt differentia. Unius enim forma et specie una est figura corporis et organorum. Cum igitur diversae sint figurae corporum animalium et organorum ipsorum, oportebit et animas ipsorum specie alteras ab invicem esse.' See also Albertus Magnus, *On Animals*, vol. 2, p. 1407.

overcome by reason, which was not the case with other animals. Humans therefore differed from brute animals by more than species, and seemingly in some way by genus, because they participated in animality itself according to a different power from other animals.[8] Albert thus argued that bodily difference alone was enough to establish that humans were different in species from other animals, and their possession of reason prompted him to suggest that the difference between humans and animals was so great that humans belonged in a different genus altogether. He was aware that a technical objection might be raised: it could be argued that a genus had to include several species and that a human genus must therefore be made up of several species. He dismissed this view, maintaining that a form that was in itself communicable to several things that differed by species or number was not necessarily communicated at all, but perhaps existed in just one thing, as was apparent with the sun, the moon and other things that had only one individual in their species because they were made up of all its matter. Thus, if there were just one ass and one tree, animal and animated body would nevertheless be different genera. A human therefore differed from brute animals by more than species. A lion and a horse differed by species, whereas a human differed from both by more than species.[9]

---

[8] *De Animalibus Libri XXVI*, 20.2.6, p. 1319: 'Homo autem ab aliis animalibus plus quam specie videtur differre: videmus enim ea quae nec sensu nec motu faciunt differentiam, tamen specie ab invicem differre. Cum igitur homo et in participatione sensuum differat specie ab aliis sicut probatur ex figuris organorum sensus et figura totius corporis, et insuper adiciat rationis differentiam, videtur plus quam specie homo ab aliis differre animalibus. Cuius signum est quia irrationales vires hominis persuasibiles sunt ratione sicut concupiscibile et irascibile: et hoc non est in aliis animalibus. Plus igitur quam specie differt a brutis, et videtur ad ipsa quamdam habere generis differentiam, cum ipsam animalitatem secundum differentem potestatem ab aliis animalibus participet.' See also *On Animals*, vol. 2, p. 1407.

[9] *De Animalibus Libri XXVI*, 20.2.6, p. 1320: 'Si quis autem opponat quod genus plures ambit species et sic homo plures deberet habere species, non valet quia forma de se communicabilis pluribus specie vel numero differentibus non necessario communicatur, se forte secundum esse non erit nisi in uno sicut apparet in sole et in luna et in aliis quae sub specie non nisi unum habent individuum eo quod sunt ex materia sua tota. Et si ponamus unum solum esse asinum et unam solam esse arborem, erunt tamen animal et corpus animatum genera diversa. Homo igitur plus quam specie differt ab hiis quae dicuntur bruta animalia. Specie enim differunt leo et equus: plus autem quam specie differt homo ab utroque ipsorum.' See also *On Animals*, vol. 2, pp. 1407–8.

At the beginning of Book 21, Albert continued to stress the difference between animals and humans by exploring the ways in which the
human was the most perfect animal. He explained that he would
analyse the perfection and imperfection of animals according to the
faculties and powers of the soul, and he would determine the cause of
imperfection and perfection. Since, however, every perfection and
imperfection reflected perfect or imperfect participation in the powers
of animals, and since the imperfect could only be known through the
perfect, it was necessary to begin by establishing the nature of the most
perfect animal. Every grade of imperfection in others could then be
located in relation to this.[10] He further explained that the nature of the
more perfect animal was to be sought by investigating the powers of
the soul. An animal that was perfect in the powers of its soul was
perfect in its organs because nature only made an organ for the sake of
the power of the soul which moved the organ.[11]

Albert then offered six reasons why the human was the most perfect
animal. He began with an analysis of the hierarchical relationship
between vegetative, sensible and intellectual souls. In beings where
the sensible soul was the highest act, that is to say in animals, the
vegetative soul was only 'a partial power' and existed according to
the being of the sensible soul.[12] In the same way, in beings where the
rational soul was the highest act, that is to say in humans, the vegetative and sensible powers existed according to the being of the rational
soul. Because the vegetative and sensible powers existed according to
the most perfect being that could exist in an organic body, they were

[10] *De Animalibus Libri XXVI*, 21.1.1, p. 1321: 'Determinandum autem nunc
videtur de perfectione et imperfectione animalium secundum animae facultates
et potestates et de causa imperfectionis et perfectionis. [...] Cum autem omnis
perfectio et imperfectio animalium sit secundum participationem virtutum
animalium perfectam vel imperfectam, nec imperfectum sciri possit, nisi per
rationem perfecti, oportet nos primum determinare quae sit ratio animalis
perfectissimi: quia secundum proportionem ad illud, omnem invenimus in aliis
gradum imperfectionis.' See also *On Animals*, vol. 2, p. 1409.

[11] *De Animalibus Libri XXVI*, 21.1.1, p. 1321: 'Ratio autem perfectioris animalis
secundum animae vires quaerenda est: quia [...] quod est perfectum in viribus
animae, perfectum est in organis, cum organum non faciat natura in animalibus,
nisi propter virtutem animae quae movet organum ipsum.' See also *On Animals*,
vol. 2, p. 1409.

[12] *De Animalibus Libri XXVI*, 21.1.1, p. 1321: 'in omnibus in quibus sensibilis
anima est actus ultimus sive enthelechya completiva, in hiis vegetativa non est
nisi sicut pars potestatis et est in eis secundum esse sensibilis.' For the translation,
see *On Animals*, vol. 2, p. 1409.

necessarily the most perfect they could be and participated somehow in reason. Evidence of this was that in humans both the vegetative and sensible powers were ordered according to reason. Temperance and chastity were present in the actions of the vegetative soul, while humility, mildness, fortitude and many other virtues were present in desires and angers of the sensible soul, and this was only possible because the vegetative and sensible souls existed in the human according to the being of the intellectual soul.[13] Humans were therefore the most perfect animals not only because they possessed reason, but because their rational souls caused their vegetative and sensible souls to take on their most perfect forms. Albert cited a maxim that he said many pronounced but perhaps did not understand, one which expressed an idea that William of Auvergne had also invoked: 'whatever an inferior power can do, a superior power can also do excellently and eminently'.[14] Even while stressing difference, Albert thus noted how difference was partly built on similarity: like animals, humans had vegetative and sensible souls, but these souls were more perfect in humans.

Albert explained more precisely how the sensible soul was more perfect in humans than in other animals when he responded to an objection that could be made to his argument thus far. Albert had just claimed that sensible souls in humans were superior to sensible souls in animals. But sight, smell, hearing and such like were powers of the sensible soul, and it was known that lynxes saw better than humans, vultures and dogs had a better sense of smell, and some other animals

[13] *De Animalibus Libri XXVI*, 21.1.1, pp. 1321–2: 'et cum eodem modo in quibuscumque rationalis anima est enthelechya completiva, in hiis vegetabilis et sensibilis potentiae naturales existentes, sunt secundum esse rationalis. [...] Cum autem vegetabilis et sensibilis potentiae insunt secundum esse perfectissimi quod potest esse in corpore organico, necessarium est ipsas perfectissimas esse, et ratione aliqualiter participare. Cuius signum est quod in homine tam in vegetativis quam in sensibilibus est ordo vitae secundum rationem. Nam temperantia et castitas insunt secundum opera vegetabilis: humilitas autem et mansuetudo, similiter autem fortitudo et plures aliae virtutes insunt secundum concupiscentias et iras sensibilis: quod esse non posset, nisi et vegetabilis et sensibilis inessent homini secundum esse animae intellectualis.' See also *On Animals*, vol. 2, pp. 1409–10.
[14] *De Animalibus Libri XXVI*, 21.1.1, p. 1323: 'Et hoc est quod quidem a multis dicitur, sed forte non a multis intelligitur, quod quidquid potest potentia inferior, potest et superior excellenter et eminenter.' See also *On Animals*, vol. 2, p. 1411. I have not identified the source of this maxim.

perhaps had better hearing. Albert did not consider this to undermine his previous argument, however, because seeing, smelling and hearing better could be understood in two ways. First, it could mean, for example, having sharper vision based on the complexion of the eye, and nothing prevented animals from having more acute senses than humans in this way. Second, it could refer to the application of a more noble sight, a larger power, to any object. In this way a sight that detected the distinguishing characteristics of the thing seen in a disciplined fashion ('disciplinabiliter') was larger than one that only did so in a sensory manner ('sensibiliter'). It was in this second way that humans had sight, hearing and the other senses which in them provided the basis of experience, memory and universal art and science. No animal used the senses in this way except the human.[15]

Albert was now in a position to explain more precisely what he meant when he said that humans differed from animals by more than species, and that in some way they differed by genus. The most perfect animal was one in which every power of the soul existed according to the being of a separate nature, and 'the human differed from other animals not only by specific difference but also according to the being of the proximate genus and according to the being of the remote genus'. The specific difference was reason, the characteristic which placed humans in a different species from other animals. The proximate genus was the sensible, which included all animals, rational and irrational. The remote genus was the living, which embraced animals and plants. Albert had shown that in humans the sensible and the living, the animal and the vegetative, participated somehow in reason,

---

[15] *De Animalibus Libri XXVI*, 21.1.1, p. 1323: 'Ex dictis tamen oritur quaestio quoniam visus et oderatus et auditus et cetera huiusmodi, sunt potentia quaedam sensibilis animae: et scimus lynces melius videre quam hominem, vultures autem melioris esse oderatus, similiter autem et canes, et quaedam animalia forte melius audiunt. Hoc autem quod inductum est, non obstat. Videre enim melius et oderare et audire, dupliciter dicitur. Melius enim videtur quod acutius visu accipitur: et talis potentia visus est ex complexione organi corporalis in quo est visus: et hoc modo nichil prohibit quaedam animalia acutiores quosdam sensus habere quam homo habeat. Dicitur ideo melius videre nobiliori uti visu sive largioris potentiae super quolibet obiectum: et hoc modo largior est visus disciplinabiliter differentias rei visae nuntians quam ille qui sensibiliter tantum nuntiat easdem: et sic homo habet visum et similiter auditum et alios sensus qui in ipso sunt principium experimenti et memoriae et universalis artis et scientiae: secundum quem modum animalia nulla praetor hominem sensibus utuntur.' See also *On Animals*, vol. 2, p. 1411.

despite their naturally irrational powers.[16] His point was that consequently humans did not entirely fit with other animals in the proximate
genus of the sensible, nor with plants in the remote genus of the living.
Human nature was indeed truly separate at every level.

A second argument for humans being more perfect than all other
animals focused on the sense of touch. Touch was the first of the senses
because of which an animal was an animal, which no animal whatsoever lacked. Examination of the nerves and sensible organs showed
that it was the foundation of all the other senses because it stretched
and freed all the nerves to sense its object. It followed that every sense
must exist in animals according to the strength and power of touch.
Humans, however, had the most subtle and certain sense of touch, and
the rest of the senses were therefore also more noble, certain and subtle
than in any other animals. Since an animal was said to derive its
perfection from the perfection of the senses, and indeed did so, humans
were the most perfect of all animals.[17]

A third argument concerned the hand, which Albert described as the
'organ of organs', the organ of the intellect. His point was that only
humans had hands, whereas other animals had organs which each
performed only one act; thus, all quadrupeds had their front feet just
for walking, and birds had their foremost members for flying. Humans,
however, used their upper members not for motion but universally for

[16] *De Animalibus Libri XXVI*, 21.1.1, p. 1323: 'Patet igitur quod diximus quod
videlicet perfectissimum animalium est, cuius omnis animae potentia est
secundum esse naturae separatae: et ideo diximus in antehabitis huius scientiae
quod homo non solum specifica differentia differt ab aliis animalibus, sed etiam
secundum esse generis proximi et secundum esse generis remoti. Genus enim
proximum est sensibile, et remotum est vivum: et nos ostendimus quod tam
sentiens quam vivum participant aliqualiter rationem, licet ipsae potentiae de
natura sua sint irrationales.' See also *On Animals*, vol. 2, p. 1411.
[17] *De Animalibus Libri XXVI*, 21.1.1, pp. 1323–4: 'primus enim sensuum propter
quem animal est animal et quo nullum omnino caret animal, est tactus: et hic si
ad nervos et organa sensibilia respiciamus, fundamentum est omnium sensuum
aliorum, et obiectum suum omnes nervos relaxat et solvit ad sentiendum. [...] Si
ergo tactus est in quo fundatur omnis sensus, oportebit necessario omnem
sensum inesse animalibus secundum virtutem et potentiam tactus. [...] Tactum
autem habet homo et subtilissimum et certissimum sicut a nobis in libro de
Anima probatum est. Igitur in homine sunt etiam ceteri sensus nobiliores
et aliqua certitudine certiores et subtiliores quam sint in aliquo aliorum
animalium. Cum igitur a perfectione sensuum dicatur et sit animal perfectum,
erit homo perfectissimum omnium animalium, eo quod perfectius et certius
sensus participat.' See also *On Animals*, vol. 2, p. 1412.

the practice of the arts and supporting the functions of the other members. Clearly, therefore, humans used certain organs in a superior way to all other animals, which made them more perfect in the organic composition of their bodies than other animal bodies and indeed the animals themselves.[18]

Fourth, the same conclusion could be reached by analysis of the shape of the body. Albert considered what he called three 'diameters': length from top to bottom, so height; width, by which he presumably meant from side to side; and depth, presumably meaning from front to back. In a variety of ways, the human body was more naturally proportioned than other animal bodies. Its height was greater than its width, and its depth was less than both its height and its width, for example. Moreover, the organs of the human body were more perfectly placed in relation to each other, the sense organs according to height and the organs of motion according to width.[19]

---

[18] *De Animalibus Libri XXVI*, 21.1.1, p. 1324: 'Amplius in organis sensuum et virium animae participat homo manum solus inter animalia, quae sola est organum organorum, et organum intellectus operativi [...]. Nullum autem omnino animalium praeter hominem in corpore suo habet organum organorum: sed potius habent omne organum ad unum actum tantum quia omnia quadrupedia habent anteriores pedes ad ambulandum tantum, et volatilia bipedia habent anteriora membra ad volatum. Homo autem huiusmodi membris superioribus non utitur ad motum, sed potius universaliter in usu artis et officii aliorum membrorum. Patet igitur quod ipse participat quaedam organa supra modum participandi omnium aliorum animalium, et sic etiam in compositione organica corporis perfectior est omnibus corporibus animalium et animalibus ipsis.' See also *On Animals*, vol. 2, p. 1412. For Albert on the human hand here and elsewhere in his work, see Theodor W. Köhler, *Homo animal nobilissimum: Konturen des spezifisch Menschlichen in der naturphilosophischen Aristoteleskommentierung des dreizehnten Jahrhunderts*, vols. 2.1 and 2.2 (Leiden, 2014), pp. 12–15.

[19] *De Animalibus Libri XXVI*, 21.1.1, pp. 1324–5: 'Amplius hoc ipsum ostendit figura corporis. Cum enim diametri tres constituant omne corpus, perfectius et naturalius erit corpus quod dyametrorum mensuram naturalium participat. Dyameter autem longitudinis mensurat a sursum in deorsum et in solo homine idem est sursum quod est sursum mundi, et idem deorsum quod est deorsum mundi. Similiter autem est de dyametro latitudinis. Solus enim homo inter omnia animalia latum habet corpus secundum mensuram suae quantitatis latitudine proportionata: quoniam etsi quidam vermes lati sunt, non habent latitudinem longitudini proportionatam. Longitudo enim in corpore naturali semper vincere debet latitudinem, si non sit vitium naturae. Quadrupedia autem spissiora habent corpora quam lata. Homo autem solus dyametrum profunditatis minorem habet ceteris dyametris. Cum igitur sensus organa ponantur secundum longitudinem descendendo, et motus organa secundum latitudinem,

Fifth, only the human was the image and likeness of the world with regard to both soul and body. Every other animal had too much or too little of something pertaining to perfection, which also showed that the human alone was the most perfect of all animals, for when any animal somehow lacked a symbolic relationship ('simbolum') with the things that caused the world, it was because it was not 'impressed', or stamped, by something. Thus, only the human was impressed by intelligence, and no animal was impressed by heaven in the same way as the human, for which reason the balance of the human complexion came closer to the nature and balance of heaven than that of any other animal.[20]

Finally, Albert presented an argument based on the role of the intellect as first mover. He began with a general principle: the second mover in all things which had a mover of the second order was imperfect unless it was joined to a first mover of the same order, because a first mover moved itself and was the cause of motion in all things. Albert had established elsewhere that the fantasy was related to the intellect as a second mover to a first mover. Only the human, however, was moved by intellect and therefore possessed perfectly ordered motion.[21]

---

perfectionem distinctionis maiorem habent organa corporis in homine quam in aliquo animalium aliorum.' See also *On Animals*, vol. 2, p. 1413.

[20] *De Animalibus Libri XXVI*, 21.1.1, p. 1325: 'Amplius solus homo [...] est ymago et similitudo mundi tam secundum animam quam secundum corpus: omne autem aliud animal deficit secundum plus vel minus, et defectus est ex carentia alicuius ad perfectionem pertinentis. Patet igitur etiam ex isto quod solus homo perfectissimum est omnium aliorum. In eo enim in quo quodcumque animalium non habet simbolum cum hiis quae universaliter causant mundum, in hoc non imprimatur ab illo: propter quod non imprimitur ab intelligentia nisi homo: nec est aliquod animalium quod ita a caelo imprimatur sicut homo: propterea quod aequalitas complexionis eius magis inter omnia animalia accedit ad naturam caeli et aequalitatem.' See also *On Animals*, vol. 2, p. 1413.

[21] *De Animalibus Libri XXVI*, 21.1.1, p. 1325: 'Amplius motor secundus in omnibus in quibus est motor secundi ordinis, imperfectus est nisi coniungatur motori primo eiusdem ordinis. Motor enim primus solus est qui a seipso movet, et est causa motus in omnibus [...]. Constat nobis ex hiis quae de Motibus animalium bene determinata sunt, quod fantasia movens se habet ad intellectum moventem sicut motor secundi ordinis se habet ad motorem primum. Nullum autem animalium perfecte et ordinatum habet motum, nisi in quo motus procedit secundum rationem motoris primi qui rectus est. Solus igitur homo cum per intellectum moveatur, perfectionem habet principiorum motivorum.' See also *On Animals*, vol. 2, p. 1413.

According to Albert, therefore, humans were profoundly different from all other animals because they were more perfect in a host of ways. When, however, Albert moved on to analyse perfection in other animals, similarities between humans and other animals came much more to the fore. While Albert clearly did not think that his previous arguments were undermined in the slightest, they were at the very least challenged, requiring him to do more intellectual work to sustain them.

Albert began the second chapter of Book 21 by discussing the different ways in which it was possible to speak about the perfection of animals, which involved making a series of distinctions. Some were more perfect than others according to the body, and some according to the powers of the soul. Perfection according to the body existed either with regard to the quantity of the body or to the quality of its complexion. Perfection with regard to quantity could mean either the magnitude of a continuous quantity or the number of organs. Glossing what he meant by the last category, Albert contradicted his earlier assertion that while the human hand performed many functions, no other animal had an organ that could carry out more than one task. He illustrated his explanation that the number of organs meant the number of a discrete quantity by citing the example of an elephant's trunk 'which it put to many uses instead of a hand'.[22] Albert did not apparently notice that he was undermining one of his arguments for human exceptionalism.

Turning to perfection according to the soul, Albert explained that it consisted of participation in either the interior powers of the soul or its exterior powers. Participation in the interior powers of the soul could be considered with regard to the number of powers or with regard to their mode and quality. This analysis led Albert to observe how closely some animals could resemble humans. Some animals, he noted, seemed to have few or no interior powers, while others were so

---

[22] *De Animalibus Libri XXVI*, 21.1.2, pp. 1325–6: 'Sunt enim quaedam illorum aliis perfectiora secundum corpus, sunt et quaedam aliis perfectiora secundum animae potentias. Et utraque istarum perfectionum est duplex: quoniam ea quae est secundum corpus, aut est secundum corporis quantitatem, aut secundum qualitatem aequalitatis sive complexionis. Et ea quidem quae est secundum corporis quantitatem, adhuc in duas distribuitur: quoniam perfectio quantitatis aut secundum magnitudinem continuae quantitatis, aut est secundum numerum organorum, qui numerus discretae est quantitatis sicut promuscidam habet elefas qua loco manus utitur in multis usibus.' See also *On Animals*, vol. 2, p. 1414.

vigorous in their interior powers that they seemed to have 'something resembling reason'.[23]

Albert then focused on the perfection of the soul and the number of its powers, identifying ever greater degrees of similarity between some animals and humans. The first power that he discussed was memory. Some animals had memory based on sense perception, others did not. Memory entailed the recall of what had previously been received by the senses in the absence of what had been sensed. Thus, vultures could be seen to leave a body when they had eaten enough and return later because they remembered the body and where it was located. Similarly, sheep returned to their folds and birds to their nests. Other animals, however, could only deal with what they currently sensed, lacking any memory of what they had sensed previously. Flies, for example, flew back after being driven away, not remembering the blow that they had previously received.[24]

Some animals had 'a sort of prudence' concerning things that they gathered for themselves, but they could not be taught. Bee and ants were good examples. Out of prudence, they provided stores for themselves, but that they did not come in response to the voices of humans, were not afraid of their threats, and did not seem to flee dreadful sounds, was a sign that they could not be taught by human instruction. Albert dismissed the view that they did not hear at all, emphasising that they did not hear sounds in such a way that they could be taught,

---

[23] *De Animalibus Libri XXVI*, 21.1.2, p. 1326: 'Adhuc et ea quae est secundum animam, dividitur et efficitur duplex. Aut est in participando vires plures animae interiores, aut in participando plures vires exteriores in numero sensuum. Et secundum participationem quidem potentiarum interius apprehendentium, adhuc sunt duo modi quorum unus est secundum numerum potentiarum et alter secundum modum et qualitatem. Quaedam enim animalium videntur de interioribus potentiis paucas aut nullas habere, et quaedam in tantum in hiis vigent quod etiam aliquid simile rationi habere videntur.' See also *On Animals*, vol. 2, p. 1414.

[24] *De Animalibus Libri XXVI*, 21.1.2, p. 1326: 'Ex sensu autem quibusdam fit memoria, quibusdam autem non. Et quod non fiat memoria quibusdam ex sensu, ex hoc scimus quod memoria est quae facit ex prius per sensum accepto redire in absens sensibile, sicut videmus vultures saturatos recedere a loco cadaveris, et postea iterum redire ex memoria loci et cadaveris: et hoc modo ad caulas revertuntur greges, et aves ad nidos et huiusmodi. Quaecumque autem animalium non persequuntur nisi praesens sensibile et ex prius accepto non revertuntur ad absens sensibile, scimus memoriam nullam prius acceptorum habere, sicut sunt muscae quae cum abiguntur, revolant immemores ictus prius accepti.' See also *On Animals*, vol. 2, pp. 1414–15.

which meant that they could not be called by name and instructed in the way that many other animals, like dogs and monkeys, could be instructed.[25]

The issue of being teachable led Albert to discuss hearing. While some animals possessed hearing only as a sense, others also possessed it as 'a sense capable of instruction'.[26] This teachable sense relied on sounds and voices as a sign of the intentions of the maker of the sound or voice, and these sounds and voices were sometimes a confused sign and sometimes a defined sign, confused in brute animals and defined in humans. Thus, some animals possessed hearing as a sense capable of instruction and a memory by which they retained the signs of instruction perceived confusedly or clearly, so that they were teachable and perceived confused or clear teaching. Consequently, many animals performed many actions in response to human commands; the elephant, for example, bent its knees before the king when instructed, and dogs did many such things.[27]

---

[25] *De Animalibus Libri XXVI*, 21.1.2, pp. 1326–7: 'Amplius videmus quaedam animalia quamdam habentia prudentiam circa res sibi conferentes, et tamen indisciplinabilia, sicut patet in apibus quae prudentiam habent magnam in rebus conferentibus, et tamen non disciplinantur, et similiter formicae. Ex prudentia enim contingit quod provident sibi thesauros. Sed quod non veniunt ad voces hominum, et non timent minas ipsorum, nec videntur fugere terribiles sonos, signum est quod sint indisciplinabilia per magisterium hominum: propter quod etiam quidam dicunt quod sonos non audiunt: hoc autem in antehabitis improbatum est, quia videntur sonos audire. Sed quidquid sit de auditu, hoc absque dubio verum est, quod sonos non audiunt ad disciplinam ut per nomina vocari possint et instrui sicut instruuntur multa animalia sicut canes et symye et alia quaedam.' See also *On Animals*, vol. 2, p. 1415.

[26] *On Animals*, vol. 2, p. 1415.

[27] *De Animalibus Libri XXVI*, 21.1.2, p. 1327: 'Duplicitur enim habetur auditus ab animalibus: a quibusdam enim habetur in quantum est sensus tantum, et a quibusdam habetur in quantum est sensus et in quantum est disciplinalis sensus. Et hoc secundo modo adhuc dupliciter participatur ab animalibus: quoniam hic sensus est disciplinalis, secundum quod per sonos et voces accipitur notitia intentionum sonantis et vocantis hoc enim modo soni et voces faciunt disciplinam. Hoc autem dupliciter fit. Faciunt enim quandoque soni et voces aliquando signum intentionis confusum et aliquando determinatum. Confusum autem signum faciunt in brutis, et determinatum faciunt in homine. Et ideo quaecumque animalia auditum habent prout est sensus disciplinalis, et cum hoc memoriam qua retinent signa disciplinae perceptae confuse vel determinate, sunt disciplinabilia et aut percipiunt disciplinam confusam aut determinatam. Et ideo multa animalia ad voces hominum multa faciunt, et elefas flectit genua coram rege ad vocem indicantis, et canes multa talia faciunt.' See also *On Animals*, vol. 2, p. 1415.

Some of these animals could do more, however. Some of them seemed to participate, 'although slightly', in experience (*experimentum*). By this, Albert meant the capacity to learn from remembered experience, especially many memories of the same thing. Many animals could be seen to have something of experiential knowledge in particular cases: when a weasel was wounded in a fight with a snake, for example, it used an endive leaf to counter the venom. Their participation was insufficient, however, to allow them to achieve universal art and reason.[28] Certain animals, however, were sufficiently elevated in these powers that they had 'a kind of imitation of art', although they did not attain art. Some seemed to be teachable by sight and hearing because they copied what they saw and retained what they heard, 'sicut symia': the monkey was like this. But some were so strong in their ability to learn through hearing that they even signified their intentions to each other, 'sicut pigmeus', like the pygmy, who talked, although an irrational animal. Albert's notion of the pygmy was rooted in ancient Greek accounts of a diminutive race that warred with cranes, and whose existence in upper Egypt was confirmed by Aristotle. In the hierarchy that Albert had been constructing, with regard to the animal powers, the pygmy seemed to be 'the most perfect animal after the human'. More than other animals, the pygmy seemed to bring its memories together and understand audible signs, so that it seemed 'to have something imitating reason', although it did not have reason.[29]

---

[28] *De Animalibus Libri XXVI*, 21.1.2, p. 1327: 'Quaedam autem animalium videntur aliquid licet parum experimenti participare. Experimentum namque ex multis nascitur memoriis quia eiusdem rei multae memoriae faciunt potentiam et facultatem experimenti: et nos videmus quod multa animalia praeter hominem aliquid experimentalis habent cognitionis in singularibus, sicut quod mustela pugnans cum serpente vulnerata contra venenum accipit folium endiviae [...]. Sufficienter autem non participant experimento quia non veniunt per experimentum ad universale et artem et rationem.' See also *On Animals*, vol. 2, p. 1416. For detailed consideration of how Albert envisaged the weasel's cognition, see Anselm Oelze, *Animal Rationality: Later Medieval Theories 1250–1350* (Leiden, 2018), pp. 75–7.

[29] *De Animalibus Libri XXVI*, 21.1.2, pp. 1327–8: 'Quaedam autem in tantum elevantur in hiis potentiis ut artis quamdam habeant imitationem, licet artem non attingant. Et hoc dupliciter videmus fieri in animalibus: quoniam quaedam et visu et auditu videntur esse disciplinalia quia faciunt quae vident, et reservant quae audiunt sicut symia. Quaedam autem in tantum vigent in disciplina auditus quod etiam sibi mutuo suas intentiones significant, sicut pigmeus qui loquitur, cum tamen sit irrationabile animal: et ideo quantum ad animales virtutes, post hominem videtur pigmeus esse perfectius animal; et videtur quod inter omnia

But why 'after the human', why did the pygmy only imitate reason, lacking the real thing? It depended on Albert's definition of reason:

Reason is a power of the soul for running through the experiences received from memories, drawing out the universal from the specific or syllogistic figure, and bearing from it principles of arts and sciences through similar figures. The pygmy does not do this. [...] And thus the pygmy, although it speaks, nevertheless does not argue or speak of the universals of things, but rather their voices are directed at the particular things of which they speak.[30]

Albert explained further that reason involved, first, reflection on sense and memory, that is to say experience, and, second, eliciting the principles of art and science from the universal; the pygmy could only do the first of these, and so, because 'the entire light of reason' lay in the second, the pygmy only possessed 'the shadow of reason'. The pygmy therefore grasped nothing of the quiddities of things or the figures of arguments.

animalia plus confert memorias suas et plus percipit de signis auditus, ita quod videtur aliquid habere imitans rationem, sed ratione caret.' For the translations, see *On Animals*, vol. 2, p. 1416. On Albert and animal speech, see Irven M. Resnick and Kenneth F. Kitchell, 'Albert the Great on the "language" of animals', *American Catholic Philosophical Quarterly* 70 (1996), pp. 41–61. On Albert's discussion of pygmies, see Udo Friedrich, *Menschentier und Tiermensch: Diskurse der Grenzziehung und Grenzüberschreitung im Mittelalter* (Göttingen, 2009), 138–41; Horst Woldemar Janson, *Apes and Ape Lore in the Middle Ages and the Renaissance* (London, 1952), pp. 84–94; Joseph Koch, 'Sind die Pygmäen Menschen? Ein Kapital aus der philosophischen Anthropologie der mittelalterlichen Scholastik', *Archiv für Geschichte der Philosophie* 40 (1931), pp. 194–213; Köhler, *Homo animal nobilissimum*, vols. 2.1 and 2.2, pp. 198–201, 236, 369, 388, 487–8, 663; Oelze, *Animal Rationality*, pp. 72–5, 114–15, 153–5; Bernd Roling, *Drachen und Sirenen: Die Rationalisierung und Abwicklung der Mythologie an den europäischen Universitäten* (Leiden, 2010), pp. 494–6; Peter G. Sobol, 'The shadow of reason: explanations of intelligent animal behaviour in the thirteenth century', in Joyce E. Salisbury (ed.), *The Medieval World of Nature: A Book of Essays* (New York, 1993), pp. 109–28 at 118–19; J. M. M. H. Thijssen, 'Reforging the great chain of being: the medieval discussion of the human status of "pygmies" and its influence on Edward Tyson', in Raymond Corbey and Bert Theunissen (eds.), *Ape, Man, Apeman: Changing Views since 1800* (Leiden, 1995), pp. 43–50 at 45–6.

30 *De Animalibus Libri XXVI*, 21.1.2, p. 1328: 'Ratio enim est vis animae discurrendo per experta ex memoriis accepta, per habitudinem localem aut sillogisticam, universale eliciens et ex illo priincipia artium et scientiarum per similes habitudines conferens: hoc autem non facit pigmeus. [...] Et ideo pigmeus licet loquatur, tamen non disputat nec loquitur de universalibus rerum, sed potius suae voces diriguntur ad res particulares de quibus loquitur.' For the translation, see *On Animals*, vol. 2, pp. 1416–17.

The pygmy's speech was like that of morons who were naturally stupid because they could not recognise reason, except that the pygmy lacked reason by nature whereas the moron lacked not reason but the use of reason for some accidental reason such as melancholy.[31]

According to Albert, the kind of perfection enjoyed by the pygmy was the closest below that of the human, and he proceeded to spell out some of the differences and similarities that this entailed. It meant that the pygmy did not maintain perfect civil society and laws, but rather followed natural urges in such matters, as did other brute animals. But then again, it walked upright. The pygmy did not use its hand as an instrument of the intellect, but rather as some animals used their front feet for many purposes; several types of mice, for example, took food in their front feet and put it in their mouths. The pygmy thus used its hand for several purposes, but not for works of art, so its hand did not have the full nature of a hand. But then again, because the pygmy always stood upright, it enjoyed greater clarity of spirit (literally, greater clarity of *spiritualia*) and therefore better apprehension than other brutes, although it did not feel shame at what was base, or glory in what was honourable. Its complete lack of rational judgment was indicated by the absence of rhetorical and poetic techniques when it talked, and these were the most imperfect of all rational devices. This was why it always lived in the woods without any civil society. But then again, the power of the soul, which had not been named by philosophers but which Albert had called the shadow of reason, went beyond the estimative power. The estimative power of brutes judged the intentions of things, by which he meant their basic characteristics, received from the senses, but this power did more because it moved

---

[31] *De Animalibus Libri XXVI*, 21.1.2, p. 1328: 'Ratio enim duo habet quorum unum est ex reflexione sua ad sensum et memoriam, et ibi est perceptio experimenti. Secundum autem est quod habet secundum quod exaltatur versus intellectum simplicem: et sic est elicitiva universalis quod est principium artis et scientiae. Pigmeus autem non habet nisi primum istorum: et ideo non habet nisi umbram rationis, quia totum lumen rationis est in secundo. Dico autem umbram idem quod resultationem obscuram a sensibilium materia et appendiciis materiae non separatam. Et ideo pigmeus nichil omnino percipit de rerum quidditatibus nec umquam percipit habitudines argumentorum: et sua locutio et sicut locutio morionum qui naturaliter stulti sunt eo quod non perceptibiles sunt rationum. Sed in hoc est differentia quod pigmeus habet privationem rationis ex natura, morio autem habet per accidens ex melancholia vel alio accidente non privationem rationis, sed potius privationem usus rationis.' See also *On Animals*, vol. 2, p. 1417.

things to the memory and drew out what was learned by experience to be used later.[32] Albert emphasised again that the pygmy lacked the contemplative ability to attain the universal and to use experience and memory to grasp the quiddity of things, but experience and memory could cause the pygmy to desire something or to run away from it.[33]

Having weighed up the similarities and the differences, Albert concluded that:

The pygmy is therefore [...] as if in the middle between the human which has divine intellect and other mute animals in which nothing of divine light is found to exist, insofar as it uses experiential cognition through the shadow of reason which no other animal receives. According to nature, however, it is closer to the brute than the human [...] because that which is known by experience has more to do with the universal and contemplation than with the particular and movement.[34]

---

[32] *De Animalibus Libri XXVI*, 21.1.2, pp. 1328–9: 'Huiusmodi autem perfectio proxima est sub homine: propter quod etiam pigmeus civilitatem perfectam et leges non custodit, sed potius in talibus sequitur naturae impetum sicut et alia bruta animalia, sed erectus incedit. Et manu utitur non prout manus est instrumentum intellectus [...], sed potius prout quaedam animalium utuntur pede anteriori ad multos usus sicut genera muris plurima anteriori pede cibum accipiunt et ad os porrigunt: ita etiam pigmeus utitur manu in pluribus usibus, sed non ad artis opera: et ideo etiam sua manus non plenam habet manus rationem. Quod autem erigitur semper, facit in eo spiritualium maiorem claritatem: et ideo melioris apprehensionis est inter cetera bruta sed verecundiam de turpi, et gloriam de honesto non attendit. Et hoc signum est quod nichil habet de iudicio rationis: propter quod etiam rethoricis persuasionibus in loquendo non utitur neque poeticis quae tamen imperfectiores sunt omnium rationum: et ideo semper silvestris manet nullam prorsus civilitatem custodiens. Virtus autem illa animae quam umbram rationis quamdam vocavimus superius, innominata quidem est a philosophis, sed circumloquendo cognoscimus quod haec vis aliquid potentiae addit super aestimativam. Cum enim aestimativa brutorum iudicet de intentionibus quae cum sensibilibus accipiuntur, ista plus facit quoniam res fert huiusmodi intentionis ad memoriam et elicit expertum et utitur illo postea ad quae confert.' See also *On Animals*, vol. 2, pp. 1417–18.

[33] *De Animalibus Libri XXVI*, 21.1.2, p. 1329: 'Est autem hic non praetermittendum quod aestimatum et expertum dupliciter referuntur ad universale, uno quidem modo contemplative prout ex expertis et memoratis in sensu acceptis, quiditas rerum quod est rerum veritas accipitur per se vel in signo communi: et hoc modo memoratum et expertum non est in pigmeo. Alio modo inest memoratum et expertum prout in ipso est conferens ad appetitum vel fugam: et hoc modo expertum et memoratum accipiuntur a pigmeo.' See also *On Animals*, vol. 2, p. 1418.

[34] *De Animalibus Libri XXVI*, 21.1.2, p. 1329: 'Pycmeus [*sic*] igitur [...] quasi medius est inter hominem divinum intellectum habentem et alia muta animalia

So, for Albert, there was a hierarchy of animals at the top of which some kinds of rational processes took place. Monkeys came close to humans, and pygmies came closest. But even they fell short because they could not argue syllogistically and so they could not go from the particular to the universal. Not all animals were the same, some were very like humans indeed, but a particular type of reason elevated humans above them all.

Having worked his way up the hierarchy by focusing on powers of the soul and increasing similarity with humans, Albert now worked his way down. Analysing monkeys in more detail, Albert offered a series of general reflections on what it was to be teachable, applying them to monkeys in each case. First, only the human was naturally teachable by means of both instruction and discovery (*inventio*), and teaching by instruction was a matter of intellect and what could be sensed. Monkeys seemed to have sagacity (*sagacitas*) beyond other animals in that they were teachable by means of what could be sensed.[35] Returning to the general, Albert explained that there were three stages in being taught: first, diligently noting and gathering what was seen and heard; second, drawing on what had been experienced and retained in the memory; and, third, taking from this the purified universal as a principle of science, art, prudence or another such intellectual virtue. The monkey only attained the first stage perfectly, and this only by means of imagination and memory. It did not draw further on experience, and thus ranked below the pygmy. For precisely this reason, however, the monkey found imitation easier because it did not refer what it saw or sensed to experiential cognition, focusing immediately on what it sensed and imitating what it saw straight away and without discrimination, which neither the pygmy nor the

---

in quibus nichil divinae lucis esse deprehenditur, in quantum experimentali cognitione utitur per umbram rationis, quam prae ceteris accepit animalibus: magis tamen secundum naturam vicinus est bruto quam homini [...]: quoniam expertum magis est ad universale et contemplationem, quam ad particulare et motum.' See also *On Animals*, vol. 2, p. 1418.

[35] *De Animalibus Libri XXVI*, 21.1.3, pp. 1329–30: 'Cum enim disciplina fiat in homine qui solus secundum naturam est animal disciplinae susceptibile, per doctrinam videlicet et per inventionem: ea autem quae per doctrinam est, duplex est, intellectiva videlicet et sensibilis: videntur symiae prae ceteris animalibus sagacitatem habere eam quod disciplinabiles sunt sensibilibus.' See also *On Animals*, vol. 2, p. 1419. For further analysis of Albert's views on what it was to be teachable, see Köhler, *Homo animal nobilissimum*, vols. 2.1 and 2.2, pp. 235–8.

human did.[36] Reverting once more to the general, Albert noted that the human had two teachable senses, sight and hearing. Sight served teaching by discovery. Because discovery could not take place unless reason brought memory and what had been sensed into play, no animal was teachable by sight alone. Some animals could be taught by hearing, however, because that process was based on comprehending signs. The monkey was therefore superior to other animals because through hearing it received teaching, and through sight it received representations of acts that it could imitate. Only humans, pygmies and monkeys could do this, so clearly these three animals constituted successive steps going down Albert's hierarchy.[37] Albert neatly summarised where humans, pygmies and monkeys thus stood in relation to each other and to other animals:

The human participates in teachable sense in every way, and in memory, experience, reason, science and art. The pygmy participates in teachable sense, memory, experience slightly, and not at all in reason, science and art. The monkey participates in the teachable sense of hearing, it perceives

[36] *De Animalibus Libri XXVI*, 21.1.3, p. 1330: 'Primum enim oportet eum qui disciplinae est perceptibilis ea quae videt et audit, diligenter attendere et conferre, et ex collatis memoria retentis experta sumere, et ex illis universale depuratum accipere, prout est principium scientiae vel artis vel prudentiae vel alicuius huiusmodi intellectualis virtutis. De hiis autem tribus gradibus perfecte non attingit symia nisi primum, et hunc non attingit nisi ymaginabiliter et memoriter: sed ulterius experientia non participat neque multam neque parum utens experientia: et in hoc deficit a pigmeo. Ymitatio autem tanto facilior est in ea, quanto rem visam vel sensam non refert ad experimentalem cognitionem: referens enim ad experimentalem cognitionem detinetur in collatione memoriarum sive per memoriam acceptorum: non conferens autem statim fertur in sensibile. Et ex hoc est quod symia primam facultatem disciplinae habens statim imitatur hoc quod videt: sed pygmeus et homo non statim imitantur. Habet enim symia sicut diximus, non nisi primam disciplinabilitatis facultatem. Cuius signum est quod non discernit in quo vel quem imitetur.' See also *On Animals*, vol. 2, p. 1419.

[37] *De Animalibus Libri XXVI*, 21.1.3, pp. 1330–1: 'Sed cum homo habeat sensus disciplinales duos, visum videlicet et auditum [...], visus deservit inventioni disciplinae: et cum huius inventio non fiat nisi ratione conferente memorias et sensata, non est aliquod animal disciplinabile visu quia non habet facultatem inventivae ex collatione sensibilium. Auditus autem sensus est disciplinalis ex signis rerum et ex alio et ideo animalia quaedam possunt disciplinari per auditum et nulla per solum visum. Et ex hoc cognoscitur symia maioris esse facultatis quam aliud animal quoniam disciplinam recipit per auditum et imitationem repraesentativam operum per visum: quod non facit aliud animal nisi homo et pigmeus et symia. Et ideo patet quod ista tria animalia continuis descendunt gradibus.' See also *On Animals*, vol. 2, p. 1420.

through sight something ordered to teaching, namely imitation, and it has memory of what has been sensed, but from that elicits absolutely nothing of experience. Other brutes, gaining nothing teachable through sight, only obtain some sort of teaching through hearing.[38]

Albert had more to say about what separated the monkey from animals lower in the hierarchy. Monkeys were better at using their estimative power to detect what was harmful and what was profitable, drawing on sense, imagination and memory. Other animals could estimate what was harmful and profitable to themselves, pursuing or running away from them accordingly, but monkeys could estimate what was of value to other animals as well. Thus, a monkey would show a youngster its mother's breasts, even showing a human child the breasts of a woman, if it were allowed to do so. In performing such actions, however, the monkey was only moved by sense-based phantasms so that it often made mistakes, as did other animals where phantasms were not joined to intellect; such animals were only capable of imperfect argument because they assessed only what they could perceive in the moment, reckoning that everything with the same accidental qualities in the here and now was to be fled or pursued.[39]

[38] *De Animalibus Libri XXVI*, 21.1.3, p. 1331: 'Homo quidem particeps sensus disciplinalis omni modo, et memoriae et experimenti et rationis et scientiae et artis, pigmeus autem particeps sensus disciplinalis et memoriae et parum experimenti et nichil rationis et scientiae et artis. Symia autem participans sensum disciplinae auditum et in visu aliquid percipiens ordinatum ad disciplinam, imitationem videlicet et memoriam habens sensibilium, sed ex ipsa omnino nichil experimenti eliciens. Alia autem bruta in visu quidem nichil disciplinale accipiendo, solum auditu aliquid disciplinae percipiunt.' See also *On Animals*, vol. 2, p. 1420.

[39] *De Animalibus Libri XXVI*, 21.1.3, pp. 1331–2: 'Videtur autem genus symiarum prae ceteris animalibus brutis aestimare de nocivo et conferente ex sensu et ymaginatione et memoria. Aliis enim aestimationem habentibus de sibi conferentibus et nocentibus, et illa persequentibus et fugientibus, symia estimat de conferentibus sibi et aliis animalibus: et ideo videns parvulum exhibet parvulo ubera, non propria, sed matris quae peperit eum si permittatur: puero enim exhibit ubera feminarum si permittatur: et hoc alia non faciunt animalia: et in hoc cognoscitur symia melioris esse aestimationis quam aliud animal. Sed in omnibus hiis non movetur nisi ex fantasmate: et ideo frequenter errat sicut et alia animalia quia [...] ubi fantasticum intellectui non coniungitur, frequens incidit error: et est in talibus animalibus non sillogismus operis, sed argumentatio imperfecta. [...] Fantastica autem aestimatio non est nisi ex eo quod videtur tantum: et ideo frequenter decipitur ex sophismate accidentis: quia non procedit nisi ex hiis quae hic et nunc videntur, reputans similiter fugienda vel persequenda quibus idem accidit accidens secundum hic et nunc.' See also *On Animals*, vol. 2,

According to Albert, monkeys and pygmies were called 'similitudines hominis', 'likenesses of the human'. Their similarity to humans was further indicated by similar physical characteristics, and he pointed to the similar shape and position of the head, ears, hands, arms, chest, neck, shoulders, female breasts and vulva, and the use of the same position for sexual intercourse. These external likenesses signified the internal likeness: as he had explained, the estimative power of pygmies and monkeys was more similar to reason than the estimative power of other animals.[40]

Having considered the two animals that were most similar to humans, Albert continued to work his way down the hierarchy, explaining how animals in each category were similar to and different from humans. With quadrupeds, he focused on hearing, estimation and memory with a view to understanding their different degrees of teachability. It was the capacity of birds to imitate human speech that caught his attention, as well as their teachability. He explored the shrewdness (*astutia*) and sagacity (*sagacitas*) of aquatic animals, the prudence (*prudentia*) and sagacity of serpents and crawling animals, and the great sagacity of insects, or 'ringed animals' as he called them, which were, however, unteachable.[41]

Albert therefore placed humans at the top of a hierarchy. He saw many similarities between animals and humans, the likeness diminishing with every step down the hierarchy. Even immediately below the human, the pygmy only possessed something that was like reason in some respects, 'the shadow of reason', as Albert put it. In spite of similarities, therefore, a hard boundary between humans and other animals remained. Strikingly, however, in Albert's overall analysis, the boundary between the pygmy and the human was only one of many boundaries. Another separated the pygmy and monkey, and yet another the monkey and quadrupeds, and so on. The boundary that defined the human was just one of many that divided animals into categories, and similarities were readily apparent.

---

pp. 1420–1. For further analysis of Albert's views on monkeys and imperfect argumentation, see Oelze, *Animal Rationality*, pp. 114–15, 150–3.

[40] *De Animalibus Libri XXVI*, 21.1.3, p. 1332. See also *On Animals*, vol. 2, p. 1422.

[41] *De Animalibus Libri XXVI*, 21.1.4–8, pp. 1332–47. See also *On Animals*, vol. 2, pp. 1422–37. See Köhler, *Homo animal nobilissimum*, vols. 2.1 and 2.2, p. 357.

Aquinas, *Summa theologiae*

The *Summa theologiae* will be considered before the earlier *Summa contra gentiles* because in the *Summa theologiae* Thomas Aquinas emphasised strong differences between humans and animals much more frequently. This was especially the case when he treated the closely related topics of free will and intellect. Discussing whether angels had free choice, for example, led him briefly to consider where animals stood in this regard.[42] He explained that some things did not act through any choice of their own, but as if acted upon and moved by others; as an example, he cited the arrow that was moved to its end by an archer. Others, however, acted according to 'a sort of choice', but that choice was not free, and irrational animals fell into this category. Thus, a sheep fled a wolf after making a kind of judgment by which it reckoned the wolf to be harmful to it, but this judgment was not free because it was 'implanted by nature'. Only that which had intellect could act according to free judgment insofar as it knew the universal reason of goodness by which it could judge this or that to be good. Thus, wherever there was intellect, there was free choice. Aquinas concluded that angels had free choice, and that it was more excellent than that of humans, just as their intellect was more excellent.[43] Along

---

[42] *Summa theologiae*, 1a.59.3; *Sancti Thomae Aquinatis Opera Omnia iussu Leonis XIII*, 4–12 (Rome, 1888–1906), vol. 5, p. 95: 'utrum in angelis sit liberum arbitrium.' Henceforth ST. On animals, choice, judgment and will in Aquinas, see Tobias Davids, *Anthropologische Differenz und animalische Konvenienz: Tierphilosophie bei Thomas von Aquin* (Leiden, 2017), pp. 180–201; Oelze, *Animal Rationality*, 106–11; Robert Pasnau, *Thomas Aquinas on Human Nature: A Philosophical Study of* Summa Theologiae *Ia 75–89* (Cambridge, 2002), pp. 209–14 (Pasnau translates 'liberum arbitrium' as 'free decision'). On the concept of 'liberum arbitrium' more generally, see Köhler, *Homo animal nobilissimum*, vols. 2.1 and 2.2, pp. 518–19.

[43] ST 1a.59.3; vol. 5, p. 95: 'Respondeo dicendum quod quaedam sunt quae non agunt ex aliquo arbitrio, sed quasi ab aliis acta et mota, sicut sagitta a sagittante movetur ad finem. Quaedam vero agunt quodam arbitrio, sed non libero, sicut animalia irrationalia: ovis enim fugit lupum ex quodam iudicio, quo existimat eum sibi noxium; sed hoc iudicium non est sibi liberum, sed a natura inditum. Sed solum id quod habet intellectum, potest agere iudicio libero, inquantum cognoscit universalem rationem boni, ex qua potest iudicare hoc vel illud esse bonum. Unde ubicumque est intellectus, est liberum arbitrium. Et sic patet liberum arbitrium esse in angelis etiam excellentius quam in hominibus, sicut et intellectum.'

the way, he had drawn a hard boundary between humans and animals: animals lacked both free will and the intellect that made free will possible. It was not that they had no will at all, but they made the judgments that they were bound by nature to make.

Aquinas also considered whether humans had free choice.[44] He began his response with a firm statement that they did, otherwise there would be no point to advice, precepts, prohibitions, rewards and punishments. To demonstrate this, he pointed out that some things acted without judgment, like a stone that fell downwards, and all things that lacked cognition were like this. Other things, however, acted with judgment, but not free judgment, and this was the case with brute animals. A sheep that saw a wolf judged that it should be fled, and it did so by 'natural judgment' and not by free judgment, because it reached its judgment not by making comparisons ('ex collatione') but by 'natural instinct'; all judgments made by brute animals were like this. Humans, however, acted through judgment in a different way altogether. It was through the capacity to know that they judged that something was to be fled or pursued. Because this judgment did not stem from natural instinct in relation to a particular action but from a sort of comparison in the reason, humans acted by free judgment that could have different outcomes, for reason with regard to contingent matters could go in different directions, as was apparent in the syllogisms of dialectic and the persuasions of rhetoric. Particular actions, however, were contingent, thus the judgment of reason about them could have different outcomes rather than being determined to just one. Thus, humans had free choice because they were rational.[45]

---

[44] ST 1a.83.1; vol. 5, pp. 307–8: 'utrum homo sit liberi arbitrii'. See Davies, *Thomas Aquinas's* Summa Theologiae, pp. 141–2; Pasnau, *Thomas Aquinas on Human Nature*, pp. 214–16 (he has 'free decision').

[45] ST 1a.83.1; vol. 5, p. 307: 'Respondeo dicendum quod homo est liberi arbitrii: alioquin frustra essent consilia, exhortationes, praecepta, prohibitiones, praemia et poenae. Ad cuius evidentiam, considerandum est quod quaedam agunt absque iudicio: sicut lapis movetur deorsum; et similiter omnia cognitione carentia. Quaedam autem agunt iudicio, sed non libero; sicut animalia bruta. Iudicat enim ovis videns lupum, eum esse fugiendum, naturali iudicio, et non libero: quia non ex collatione, sed ex naturali instinctu hoc iudicat. Et simile est de quolibet iudicio brutorum animalium. Sed homo agit iudicio, quia per vim cognoscitivam iudicat aliquid esse fugiendum vel prosequendum. Sed quia iudicium istud non est ex naturali instinctu in particulari operabili, sed ex collatione quadam rationis; ideo agit libero iudicio, potens in diversa ferri. Ratio enim circa contingentia habet viam ad opposita; ut patet in dialecticis

Aquinas again drew a hard boundary between humans and animals: humans had free will while animals did not because judgments made by animals in any particular circumstance were always going to be the same, and this was fundamentally because they lacked reason.

Aquinas explained his stance in greater detail when he considered 'whether choice is properly found in brute animals'.[46] Since choice meant taking one thing rather than another, choice had to be made with regard to several things that could be chosen. It followed that choice had no place in that which was completely determined to one thing. Aquinas went on to explain the difference between the sensitive appetite and the will. The sensitive appetite was determined to one particular thing, according to the order of nature; but the will, according to the order of nature, was determined to one general thing, namely the good, but was indeterminate with regard to particular goods. To choose was therefore proper to the will, but not to the sensitive appetite, which was all that was to be found in brute animals. Aquinas concluded that choice was not properly found in animals.[47] Previously Aquinas had allowed animals a sort of will, but now he made it clear that they had only sensitive appetite and no will at all, if the term were used properly.

But what if animals seemed to make choices, indeed rational choices? One of the opening objections argued that prudence was found in various animals, such as bees, spiders and dogs. It cited the

---

syllogismis, et rhetoricis persuasionibus. Particularia autem operabilia sunt quaedam contingentia: et ideo circa ea iudicium rationis ad diversa se habet, et non est determinatum ad unum. Et pro tanto necesse est quod homo sit liberi arbitrii, ex hoc ipso quod rationalis est.'

[46] ST 1a2ae.13.2; vol. 6, p. 99–100: 'Utrum electio conveniat brutis animalibus'. For analysis of Aquinas's argument, see Davids, *Anthropologische Differenz und animalische Konvenienz*, pp. 189–92; Köhler, *Homo animal nobilissimum*, vols. 2.1 and 2.2, pp. 600–1; Oelze, *Animal Rationality*, pp. 134–7.

[47] ST 1a2ae.13.2; vol. 6, p. 99: 'Respondeo dicendum quod, cum electio sit praeacceptio unius respectu alterius, necesse est quod electio sit respectu plurium quae eligi possunt. Et ideo in his quae sunt penitus determinata ad unum, electio locum non habet. Est autem differentia inter appetitum sensitivum et voluntatem, quia, ut ex praedictis patet, appetitus sensitivus est determinatus ad unum aliquid particulare secundum ordinem naturae; voluntas autem est quidem, secundum naturae ordinem, determinata ad unum commune, quod est bonum, sed indeterminate se habet respectu particularium bonorum. Et ideo proprie voluntatis est eligere: non autem appetitus sensitivi, qui solus est in brutis animalibus. Et propter hoc brutis animalibus electio non convenit.'

instance of a dog in pursuit of a stag, facing three possible paths, not picking up the scent on the first two paths, then choosing the third path without sniffing around, reckoning that the stag must have taken this path because it had not taken the other two, 'quasi utens syllogismo divisivo', 'as if using a disjunctive syllogism'.[48] It should not be supposed that Aquinas had joined hunting parties to observe the behaviour of dogs; this example had been given by Sextus Empiricus, writing in the second or third century, who credited it to Chrysippus, who lived in the third century BC.[49] For Aquinas, the dog was not reasoning at all, indeed Aquinas no longer treated animals as distinct from things that simply lacked will and were moved by others. He returned to the example of the arrow and the archer: the arrow moved towards its target as if it had reason to direct it, but in fact it was moved by the archer and the archer's reason. The same was apparent in the movements of clocks and all devices made by human art. Just as such artifices stood in relation to human art, so all natural things stood in relation to the divine art. Thus, an order was apparent in things moved by nature, and brute animals sometimes seemed wise insofar as they had 'a natural inclination to highly ordered processes', set up that way by the divine art. This was why some animals were called wise and prudent, but not because they possessed reason or made choices. This was clear from the fact that all animals of the same kind acted in the same way.[50] Once again, Aquinas stressed the fundamental difference

[48] ST 1a2ae.13.2.obj3; vol. 6, p. 99: 'Praeterea, ut dicitur in VI Ethic., ad prudentiam pertinet quod aliquis bene eligat ea quae sunt ad finem. Sed prudentia convenit brutis animalibus, unde dicitur in principio Metaphys., quod prudentia sunt sine disciplina quaecumque sonos audire non potentia sunt, ut apes. Et hoc etiam sensui manifestum videtur: apparent enim mirabiles sagacitates in operibus animalium, ut apum et aranearum et canum. Canis enim insequens cervum, si ad trivium venerit, odoratu quidem explorat an cervus per primam vel secundam viam transiverit: quod si invenerit non transisse, iam securus per tertiam viam incedit non explorando, quasi utens syllogismo divisivo, quo concludi posset cervum per illam viam incedere, ex quo non incedit per alias duas, cum non sint plures. Ergo videtur quod electio brutis animalibus conveniat.'
[49] See Luciano Floridi, 'Scepticism and animal rationality: the fortune of Chrysippus' dog in the history of western thought', *Archiv für Geschichte der Philosophie* 79 (1997), pp. 27–57.
[50] ST 1a2ae.13.2.ad3; vol. 6, pp. 99–100: 'in omnibus quae moventur a ratione, apparet ordo rationis moventis, licet ipsa rationem non habeant: sic enim sagitta directe tendit ad signum ex motione sagittantis, ac si ipsa rationem haberet dirigentem. Et idem apparet in motibus horologiorum, et omnium ingeniorum humanorum, quae arte fiunt. Sicut autem comparantur artificialia ad artem

between humans and animals. Any seeming capacity on the part of animals to make choices or act rationally simply reflected the pattern of behaviour that God had established for them, however complex.

Aquinas applied the same argument, expressed slightly differently, when he considered whether there was hope in brute animals.[51] He began by noting that the interior passions of animals could be detected from their exterior movements, and from these it appeared that there was hope in brute animals. If a dog saw a hare, or a hawk saw a bird, that was too distant, it did not move towards it, as if it had no hope of catching it. If, however, the hare or bird were close, it moved, as if it had hope of catching it. This gave Aquinas the opportunity to compare inanimate objects, animals and humans, and to explain why hope in animals was not like hope in humans. The sensitive appetite of brute animals and the natural appetite of non-sentient things followed the apprehension of some intellect, as did the appetite of an intellectual nature, the latter appetite being called the will. There was, however, a difference between the will and the other two. The will was moved by the apprehension of an intellect that was joined to it, whereas the natural appetite was moved by the apprehension of a separate intellect that had established its nature, as was the sensitive appetite of brute animals which acted 'by some sort of natural instinct'. In other words, humans operated with their own intellects whereas animals and inanimate objects depended on an intellect that was not their own, the intellect of the creator. In the case of animals this meant their behaviour was set by a natural instinct that had been implanted in them. Aquinas repeated the point that he had made when comparing the relationship between animals

---

humanam, ita comparantur omnia naturalia ad artem divinam. Et ideo ordo apparet in his quae moventur secundum naturam, sicut et in his quae moventur per rationem, ut dicitur in II Physic. Et ex hoc contingit quod in operibus brutorum animalium apparent quaedam sagacitates, inquantum habent inclinationem naturalem ad quosdam ordinatissimos processus, utpote a summa arte ordinatos. Et propter hoc etiam quaedam animalia dicuntur prudentia vel sagacia: non quod in eis sit aliqua ratio vel electio. Quod ex hoc apparet, quod omnia quae sunt unius naturae, similiter operantur.'

[51] ST 1a2ae.40.3; vol. 6, p. 267: 'utrum spes sit in brutis animalibus'. See Davids, *Anthropologische Differenz und animalische Konvenienz*, pp. 210–11; Köhler, *Homo animal nobilissimum*, vols. 2.1 and 2.2, p. 214; Oelze, *Animal Rationality*, pp. 185–8, where Oelze sums up Aquinas's view by referring to 'quasi-hope'.

and God to the relationship between humans and their machines, such as the clock. In the actions of brute animals and other natural things, there was a similar process to that found in works of art, and it was in this way that there was hope and despair in brute animals.[52] Animals thus experienced hope only insofar as it was part of the pattern of behaviour established for them by their creator. Unlike humans, they had no will and no intellect of their own. The hard boundary was very much in place.

In Aquinas's understanding of animals, it was of decisive importance that animals of the same species always behaved in the same way in any particular situation. He commented again on how this was the case when discussing prudence and whether it was present in humans by nature.[53] Replying to an opening objection, he explained that in brute animals the ways of reaching any particular end were 'determined', by which he meant 'fixed', which is why it could be seen that all animals of the same species behaved similarly. This could not be the case with humans because of their reason, which knew universals and therefore extended to an infinite number of singulars.[54] In other words, humans behaved differently from each other because they had reason and could think with universals, which meant that they did not all come to the same conclusions and thus acted differently, whereas animals lacked

---

[52] ST 1a2ae.40.3; vol. 6, p. 267: 'Respondeo dicendum quod interiores passiones animalium ex exterioribus motibus deprehendi possunt. Ex quibus apparet quod in animalibus brutis est spes. Si enim canis videat leporem, aut accipiter avem, nimis distantem, non movetur ad ipsam, quasi non sperans se eam posse adipisci: si autem sit in propinquo, movetur, quasi sub spe adipiscendi. Ut enim supra dictum est, appetitus sensitivus brutorum animalium, et etiam appetitus naturalis rerum insensibilium, sequuntur apprehensionem alicuius intellectus, sicut et appetitus naturae intellectivae, qui dicitur voluntas. Sed in hoc est differentia, quod voluntas movetur ex apprehensione intellectus coniuncti: sed motus appetitus naturalis sequitur apprehensionem intellectus separati, qui naturam instituit; et similiter appetitus sensitivus brutorum animalium, quae etiam quodam instinctu naturali agunt. Unde in operibus brutorum animalium, et aliarum rerum naturalium, apparet similis processus sicut et in operibus artis. Et per hunc modum in animalibus brutis est spes et desperatio.'

[53] ST 2a2ae.47.15; vol. 8, pp. 362–3: 'utrum prudentia insit nobis a natura'.

[54] ST 2a2ae.47.15.ad3; vol. 8, p. 363: 'Ad tertium dicendum quod in brutis animalibus sunt determinatae viae perveniendi ad finem: unde videmus quod omnia animalia eiusdem speciei similiter operantur. Sed hoc non potest esse in homine, propter rationem eius, quae, cum sit cognoscitiva universalium, ad infinita singularia se extendit.'

reason, so that animals of the same species always pursued a given end in the same way.

Consideration of reason, intellect and will thus led Aquinas to identify fundamental differences between humans and animals. He came to similar conclusions when he explored the interior senses. He discussed, for example, whether the interior senses were appropriately distinguished.[55] This prompted him to explain why it was necessary to posit the existence of the common sense, imagination (or fantasy), estimation and memory, and also to set out the differences between humans and animals in this regard. His first point was that the life of a perfect animal required it to apprehend not only things that were present to be sensed, but also things that were not there, in other words, to be able to consider what it had sensed previously. If this were not the case, given that movement and action followed apprehension, the animal would not be moved to take account of anything that was absent. In fact, it was apparent that perfect animals were moved by the apprehension of absent things. Such an animal therefore had not only to receive the species of things that could be sensed when they were actually affecting it, but also to retain those species. In bodies, however, receiving and retaining were very different processes because moist things received well but retained badly, and the opposite was the case with dry things. Since sensing was the act of a corporeal organ, there had to be one power to receive species and another to retain them.[56]

---

[55] ST 1a.78.4; vol. 5, pp. 255–7: 'Utrum interiores sensus convenienter distinguantur'. See Davids, *Anthropologische Differenz und animalische Konvenienz*, pp. 166–9; Oelze, *Animal Rationality*, pp. 57–69; Dominik Perler, 'Intentionality and action. Medieval discussions on the cognitive capacities of animals', in Maria Cândida Pacheco and José F. Meirinhos (eds.), *Intellect et imagination dans la philosophie médiévale* (Turnhout, 3 vols., 2006), vol. 1, pp. 73–98 at 80–8; Dominik Perler, 'Why is the sheep afraid of the wolf? Medieval debates on animal passions', in Martin Pickavé and Lisa Shapiro (eds.), *Emotion and Cognitive Life in Medieval and Early Modern Philosophy* (Oxford, 2012), pp. 32–52 at 39–44.

[56] ST 1a.78.4; vol. 5, pp. 255–6: 'Est autem considerandum quod ad vitam animalis perfecti requiritur quod non solum apprehendat rem apud praesentiam sensibilis, sed etiam apud eius absentiam. Alioquin, cum animalis motus et actio sequantur apprehensionem, non moveretur animal ad inquirendum aliquid absens; cuius contrarium apparet maxime in animalibus perfectis, quae moventur motu processivo; moventur enim ad aliquid absens apprehensum. Oportet ergo quod animal per animam sensitivam non solum recipiat species sensibilium, cum praesentialiter immutatur ab eis; sed etiam eas retineat et conservet. Recipere

Aquinas's second point was that if an animal were moved only by what was pleasurable or saddening according to the senses, it would not be necessary to posit anything but the apprehension of forms which were perceived by the senses and which the animal would like or dislike. It was necessary, however, that animals pursue or flee things, not only because they were or were not agreeable to the senses, but because they were either useful or harmful. Thus, a sheep fled when it saw a wolf coming, not because the wolf's colour or shape were unbecoming, but 'as if it were an enemy by nature'. Similarly, a bird collected straw, not because it pleased the senses, but because it was useful for nest-building. It was therefore necessary for the animal to perceive 'intentions' or characteristics of this kind, but they were not perceived by any exterior sense, which meant that there had to be some other basis for their perception.[57]

Aquinas was now in a position to explain the need for and the function of the interior senses. The common sense received the sensible forms, distinguishing between and combining the forms that came from different exterior senses, thus also perceiving that sense perception was taking place. The sensible forms were retained in the imagination, which could also be termed the fantasy. The estimation apprehended the intentions that could not be perceived by the senses, and these intentions were retained by the memory.[58]

---

autem et retinere reducuntur in corporalibus ad diversa principia: nam humida bene recipiunt, et male retinent; e contrario autem est de siccis. Unde, cum potentia sensitiva sit actus organi corporalis, oportet esse aliam potentiam quae recipiat species sensibilium, et quae conservet.'

[57] ST 1a.78.4; vol. 5, p. 256: 'Rursus considerandum est quod, si animal moveretur solum propter delectabile et contristabile secundum sensum, non esset necessarium ponere in animali nisi apprehensionem formarum quas percipit sensus, in quibus delectatur aut horret. Sed necessarium est animali ut quaerat aliqua vel fugiat, non solum quia sunt convenientia vel non convenientia ad sentiendum, sed etiam propter aliquas alias commoditates et utilitates, sive nocumenta: sicut ovis videns lupum venientem fugit, non propter indecentiam coloris vel figurae, sed quasi inimicum naturae; et similiter avis colligit paleam, non quia delectet sensum, sed quia est utilis ad nidificandum. Necessarium est ergo animali quod percipiat huiusmodi intentiones, quas non percipit sensus exterior. Et huius perceptionis oportet esse aliquod aliud principium: cum perceptio formarum sensibilium sit ex immutatione sensibilis, non autem perceptio intentionum praedictarum.' For the translation of 'quasi inimicum naturae', see Oelze, *Animal Rationality*, p. 62.

[58] ST 1a.78.4; vol. 5, p. 256: 'Sic ergo ad receptionem formarum sensibilium ordinatur sensus proprius et communis: de quorum distinctione post dicetur.

Thus far it might have seemed that humans and animals perceived in the same ways, but Aquinas now explained how this was not the case. There was no difference with regard to sensible forms: they came from the exterior senses in both humans and animals. With regard to intentions, however, there was a significant difference. Animals perceived intentions solely 'by a certain natural instinct', whereas humans did so 'through a sort of collation', by which Aquinas meant 'a process of making comparisons'. Thus, what was called 'natural estimation' in animals was called 'cogitation' in humans. The difference between humans and animals extended to the memory. Like animals, humans had memory which involved sudden recall of past intentions, but they also had reminiscence which was a quasi-syllogistic process of inquiry amongst individual intentions.[59] As Aquinas saw it, humans did far more with intentions than animals, using cogitation rather than estimation, and possessing the power of reminiscence as well as that of memory.

When it came to actual relations between humans and animals, Aquinas was entirely conventional in his views about human dominion and

> Ad harum autem formarum retentionem aut conservationem ordinatur phantasia, sive imaginatio, quae idem sunt: est enim phantasia sive imaginatio quasi thesaurus quidam formarum per sensum acceptarum. Ad apprehendendum autem intentiones quae per sensum non accipiuntur, ordinatur vis aestimativa. Ad conservandum autem eas, vis memorativa, quae est thesaurus quidam huiusmodi intentionum.' And 1a.78.4.ad2; vol. 5, p. 256: 'sensus proprius iudicat de sensibili proprio, discernendo ipsum ab aliis quae cadunt sub eodem sensu, sicut discernendo album a nigro vel a viridi. Sed discernere album a dulci non potest neque visus neque gustus: quia oportet quod qui inter aliqua discernit, utrumque cognoscat. Unde oportet ad sensum communem pertinere discretionis iudicium, ad quem referantur, sicut ad communem terminum, omnes apprehensiones sensuum; a quo etiam percipiantur intentiones sensuum, sicut cum aliquis videt se videre.'

[59] ST 1a.78.4; vol. 5, p. 256: 'Considerandum est autem quod, quantum ad formas sensibiles, non est differentia inter hominem et alia animalia: similiter enim immutantur a sensibilibus exterioribus. Sed quantum ad intentiones praedictas, differentia est: nam alia animalia percipiunt huiusmodi intentiones solum naturali quodam instinctu, homo autem etiam per quandam collationem. Et ideo quae in aliis animalibus dicitur aestimativa naturalis, in homine dicitur cogitativa, quae per collationem quandam huiusmodi intentiones adinvenit. [...] Ex parte autem memorativae, non solum habet memoriam, sicut cetera animalia, in subita recordatione praeteritorum; sed etiam reminiscentiam, quasi syllogistice inquirendo praeteritorum memoriam, secundum individuales intentiones.' For 'per quandam collationem' translated as 'by a process of comparison', see Thomas Aquinas, *Summa Theologiae: Latin Text and English Translation*, ed. T. Gilby et al., 61 vols. (London, 1964–80), vol. 11, p. 141. See also Köhler, *Homo animal nobilissimum*, vols. 2.1 and 2.2, pp. 160, 194.

use of animals. Was it illicit to kill anything that lived?[60] Aquinas
explained that no one sinned by using something for the purpose for
which it existed. In the order of things, moreover, the more imperfect
existed for the sake of the more perfect, just as in the process of generation nature proceeded from the imperfect to the perfect. Thus, just as in
the generation of a human there was first something living, then an
animal, and finally a human, so things that only lived, such as plants,
existed collectively for the sake of animals, and all animals existed for the
sake of humans. It was not therefore illicit for a human to use plants for
the benefit of animals, and animals for the benefit of humans. Amongst
various uses, however, it seemed most necessary that animals use plants
and humans use animals for food, which could not be done without
killing them. It was therefore licit to kill plants for the use of animals, and
animals for the use of humans. This was confirmed by divine ordinance,
and Aquinas cited Genesis 1:29–30 and 9:3.[61] Aquinas thus invoked a
conception of hierarchy in which humans were higher than animals, and
their entitlement to use animals extended to killing and eating them.

Two of his replies to the opening arguments further revealed his
thinking about animals. One argument was that homicide was a sin
because a human was deprived of life, but life was shared by all
animals and plants, so killing them had to be a sin too.[62] Aquinas

[60] ST 2a2ae.64.1; vol. 9, pp. 67–8: 'utrum occidere quaecumque viventia sit
illicitum'. See Francisco Benzoni, 'Thomas Aquinas and environmental ethics:
a reconsideration of providence and salvation', *The Journal of Religion* 85
(2005), pp. 446–76 at 456–7.
[61] ST 2a2ae.64.1; vol. 9, p. 67: 'Respondeo dicendum quod nullus peccat ex hoc
quod utitur re aliqua ad hoc ad quod est. In rerum autem ordine imperfectiora
sunt propter perfectiora: sicut etiam in generationis via natura ab imperfectis ad
perfecta procedit. Et inde est quod sicut in generatione hominis prius est vivum,
deinde animal, ultimo autem homo; ita etiam ea quae tantum vivunt, ut plantae,
sunt communiter propter omnia animalia, et animalia sunt propter hominem. Et
ideo si homo utatur plantis ad utilitatem animalium, et animalibus ad utilitatem
hominum, non est illicitum [. . .]. Inter alios autem usus maxime necessarius esse
videtur ut animalia plantis utantur in cibum, et homines animalibus: quod sine
mortificatione eorum fieri non potest. Et ideo licitum est et plantas mortificare in
usum animalium, et animalia in usum hominum, ex ipsa ordinatione divina:
dicitur enim Gen. I: *Ecce, dedi vobis omnem herbam et universa ligna, ut sint
vobis in escam et cunctis animantibus.* Et Gen. IX dicitur: *Omne quod movetur
et vivit, erit vobis in cibum.*'
[62] ST 2a2ae.64.1.obj2; vol. 9, p. 67: 'homicidium est peccatum ex eo quod homo
privatur vita. Sed vita communis est omnibus animalibus et plantis. Ergo eadem
ratione videtur esse peccatum occidere bruta animalia et plantas.'

dismissed this view because animals and plants did not have rational life. They did not therefore shape their own lives but were always led by 'a kind of natural impulse', as if by another. This was a sign that they were naturally servile and accommodated to the uses of others.[63] Lack of reason thus underpinned the status of animals in relation to humans. Another opening argument was that divine law had set a penalty for killing someone else's ox or sheep, which would not have been the case unless the act was sinful.[64] Aquinas explained, however, that sin lay not in killing the animal but in damaging someone else's property.[65] He thus reinforced the view that animals belonged to humans as property.

Aquinas addressed a very specific way of using animals when he considered whether divination through auguries, omens and other such observations of exterior things was illicit.[66] He explained that the movements and calling of birds, or anything else of this sort, were manifestly not the causes of future events, so future things could not be known from them as from their causes. If therefore any future things were known from them, this was insofar as they were the effects of causes which were also the causes of future events or had foreknow-ledge of them. The cause of the actions of brute animals was 'a sort of instinct' by which they were naturally moved, for they did not have control of their actions. This instinct could stem from either a corpor-eal cause or a spiritual cause. Aquinas considered corporeal causes

---

[63] ST 2a2ae.64.1.ad2; vol. 9, pp. 67–8: 'Ad secundum dicendum quod animalia bruta et plantae non habent vitam rationalem, per quam a seipsis agantur, sed semper aguntur quasi ab alio, naturali quodam impulsu. Et hoc est signum quod sunt naturaliter serva, et aliorum usibus accommodata.'

[64] ST 2a2ae.64.1.obj3; vol. 9, p. 67: 'in lege divina non determinatur specialis poena nisi peccato. Sed occidenti ovem vel bovem alterius statuitur poena determinata in lege divina, ut patet Exod. XXII. Ergo occisio brutorum animalium est peccatum.'

[65] ST 2a2ae.64.1.ad3; vol. 9, p. 68: 'Ad tertium dicendum quod ille qui occidit bovem alterius peccat quidem, non quia occidit bovem, sed quia damnificat hominem in re sua. Unde non continetur sub peccato homicidii, sed sub peccato furti vel rapinae.'

[66] ST 2a2ae.95.7; vol. 9, pp. 324–5: 'Utrum divinatio quae est per auguria et omina et alias huiusmodi observationes exteriorum rerum, sit illicita'. See Köhler, *Homo animal nobilissimum*, vols. 2.1 and 2.2, pp. 209–10. On Aquinas's approach to the future, see Ian P. Wei, 'Predicting the future to judge the present: Paris theologians and attitudes to the future', in John A. Burrow and Ian P. Wei (eds.), *Medieval Futures: Attitudes to the Future in the Middle Ages* (Woodbridge, 2000), pp. 19–36 at 28–33.

first. Since brute animals only had a sensitive soul and all of its powers were acts of bodily organs, their souls were subject to the disposition of adjacent and especially celestial bodies. Nothing therefore prevented some of their actions from being signs of future events insofar as they were shaped by the disposition of celestial bodies and the air around them, from which some future events arose. Two considerations had to be borne in mind, however. First, actions of this kind only extended to foreknowledge of future events that were caused by the movement of celestial bodies. Second, they only extended to things that somehow pertained to animals of this kind, for they derived from the celestial bodies a sort of natural and instinctual cognition of things that were necessary to their lives, such as changes made by rain, wind and such like. Aquinas then turned to the spiritual causes of animal instinct. That meant God, as was the case with many animals that featured in the bible, for example the dove that descended above Christ, the raven that fed Elias, and the whale that swallowed and ejected Jonah. It also meant demons who used the actions of brute animals to entangle souls with empty opinions. Aquinas held this analysis as a whole to apply to all forms of divination except omens because human words, which were received as omens, were not subject to the disposition of the stars. Rather, they were ordered according to divine providence and some-times the work of demons. Indeed, all divination that went beyond that to which it could pertain according to the order of nature or divine providence was superstitious and illicit.[67] Animals could therefore be

---

[67] ST 2a2ae.95.7; vol. 9, p. 325: 'Respondeo dicendum quod motus vel garritus avium, vel quaecumque dispositiones huiusmodi in rebus consideratae, manifestum est quod non sunt causa futurorum eventuum: unde ex eis futura cognosci non possunt sicut ex causis. Relinquitur ergo quod si ex eis aliqua futura cognoscantur, hoc erit inquantum sunt effectus aliquarum causarum quae etiam sunt causantes vel praecognoscentes futuros eventus. Causa autem operationum brutorum animalium est instinctus quidam quo moventur in modum naturae: non enim habent dominium sui actus. Hic autem instinctus ex duplici causa potest procedere. Uno quidem modo, ex causa corporali. Cum enim bruta animalia non habeant nisi animam sensitivam, cuius omnes potentiae sunt actus corporalium organorum, subiacet eorum anima dispositioni continentium corporum, et primordialiter caelestium. Et ideo nihil prohibet aliquas eorum operationes esse futurorum signa, inquantum conformantur dispositionibus corporum caelestium et aeris continentis, ex qua proveniunt aliqui futuri eventus. In hoc tamen duo considerari oportet. Primum quidem, ut huiusmodi operationes non extendantur nisi ad praecognoscenda futura quae causantur per motus caelestium corporum, ut supra dictum est. Secundo, ut non extendantur nisi ad ea quae aliqualiter possunt ad huiusmodi

'read' by humans in various ways because they lacked will and their instinct was shaped by the corporeal, by God and by demons. The hard boundary was in place here, and a particular use of animals by humans was accepted.

Like Bonaventure, Aquinas also considered whether irrational creatures ought to be loved out of charity.[68] Charity was a type of friendship, and Aquinas distinguished between love of a friend and love of the good things that one desired for a friend. With regard to love of a friend, he declared that no irrational creature could be loved out of charity, and this for three reasons, of which two pertained to friendship in general. First, friendship was a relationship with someone to whom one wished good. Properly speaking, however, it was not possible to wish good to an irrational creature because it could not, properly speaking, have good; this was only possible for a rational creature which, through free will, could control the use of any good that it possessed. Second, all friendship was based on some kind of shared life, but irrational creatures could not share in human life, which was rational; consequently, no friendship was possible with irrational creatures, except perhaps metaphorically speaking. The third reason was particular to charity. Charity was based on sharing eternal beatitude, of which irrational creatures were incapable, so the friendship of charity could not be directed towards an irrational creature. As good things that one desired for others, however, irrational creatures could be loved out of charity, insofar as, out of charity, one wished them to be conserved for the honour of God and the use of humans. In this way

animalia pertinere. Consequuntur enim per caelestia corpora cognitionem quandam naturalem et instinctum ad ea quae eorum vitae sunt necessaria: sicut sunt immutationes quae fiunt per pluvias et ventos, et alia huiusmodi. Alio modo instinctus huiusmodi causantur ex causa spirituali. Scilicet vel ex Deo, ut patet in columba super Christum descendente, et in corvo qui pavit Eliam, et in cete qui absorbuit et eiecit Ionam. Vel etiam ex daemonibus, qui utuntur huiusmodi operationibus brutorum animalium ad implicandas animas vanis opinionibus. Et eadem ratio videtur esse de omnibus aliis huiusmodi, praeterquam de ominibus. Quia verba humana, quae accipiuntur pro omine, non subduntur dispositione stellarum. Disponuntur tamen secundum divinam providentiam; et quandoque secundum daemonum operationem. Sic igitur dicendum quod omnis huiusmodi divinatio, si extendatur ultra id ad quod potest pertingere secundum ordinem naturae vel divinae providentiae, est superstitiosa et illicita.'

68 ST 2a2ae.25.3; vol. 8, pp. 199–200: 'utrum etiam creaturae irrationales sint ex caritate diligendae'.

God too loved them out of charity.[69] Aquinas thus limited the feelings that humans might properly have for animals: friendship was not possible, and they existed for use by humans. Moreover, his argument supposed that animals were irrational, lacked free will, and could not enjoy eternal happiness, thus showing how the major differences between humans and animals dictated the relations that were possible between them.[70]

While difference and a hard boundary between humans and animals dominated Aquinas's treatment of animals in the *Summa theologiae*, there were some occasions when similarities were recognised at least implicitly, and the boundary was no longer entirely immutable. This was the case, for example, when he offered further explanation of the response of sheep to wolves while considering the nature of hatred and specifically the relationship between hate and universals.[71] He wanted to understand how it was that sheep fled all wolves rather than making a 'natural judgment' about each individual wolf, and did so without the capacity to grasp universals. Aquinas explained that a universal could be spoken of in two ways: in one way, with regard to its being

---

[69] ST 2a2ae.25.3; vol. 8, pp. 199–200: 'Respondeo dicendum quod caritas [...] est amicitia quaedam. Per amicitiam autem amatur uno quidem modo, amicus ad quem amicitia habetur; et alio modo, bona quae amico optantur. Primo ergo modo nulla creatura irrationalis potest ex caritate amari. Et hoc triplici ratione. Quarum duae pertinent communiter ad amicitiam, quae ad creaturas irrationales haberi non potest. Primo quidem, quia amicitia ad eum habetur cui volumus bonum. Non autem proprie possum bonum velle creaturae irrationali: quia non est eius proprie habere bonum, sed solum creaturae rationalis, quae est domina utendi bono quod habet per liberum arbitrium. [...] Secundo, quia omnis amicitia fundatur super aliqua communicatione vitae, nihil enim est ita proprium amicitiae sicut convivere [...]. Creaturae autem irrationales non possunt communicationem habere in vita humana, quae est secundum rationem. Unde nulla amicitia potest haberi ad creaturas irrationales, nisi forte secundum metaphoram. Tertia ratio est propria caritati: quia caritas fundatur super communicatione beatitudinis aeternae, cuius creatura irrationalis capax non est. Unde amicitia caritatis non potest haberi ad creaturam irrationalem. Possunt tamen ex caritate diligi creaturae irrationales sicut bona quae aliis volumus: inquantum scilicet ex caritate volumus eas conservari ad honorem Dei et utilitatem hominum. Et sic etiam ex caritate Deus eas diligit.'

[70] For insightful comments on this question, see Karl Steel, *How to make a Human: Animals and Violence in the Middle Ages* (Columbus, Ohio, 2011), p. 130.

[71] ST 1a2ae.29.6; vol. 6, pp. 207–8: 'utrum aliquid possit haberi odio in universali'. For a general account of the question, see Robert Miner, *Thomas Aquinas on the Passions: A Study of* Summa Theologiae *1a2ae 22–48* (Cambridge, 2009), pp. 148–9.

universal ('secundum quod subest intentioni universalitatis'), in another way, with regard to the nature of that to which being universal was attributed ('de natura cui talis intentio attribuitur'). Thus, for example, applying this distinction to the universal 'human', there was consideration of the universal 'human' itself, and there was consideration of humans as humans. Aquinas then explained that while the intellect could grasp universals in both ways, the sensitive powers could grasp them only in the second. No sensitive power could grasp universals in the first sense because the universal was abstracted from individual matter in which every sensitive power was rooted. Sensitive powers could, however, grasp things universally in the second sense. For example, when we say that colour as genus is the object of vision, this is not because vision recognises the universal 'colour', but because it recognises colour in general rather than just a particular colour. Turning to the question of hatred, it was in this way that hatred in the sensitive powers could be directed at a universal: an animal could hate something that was hostile not just as a particular thing but because of the nature that this thing shared with others of its kind, from their 'common nature'. It was in this way that the wolf was hated by the sheep. The sheep hated the wolf 'generally'.[72] Thus, according to Aquinas, sheep could perceive that all wolves had something in common, namely their hostility to sheep, but could not go further and conceive of 'wolf' as a universal. He preserved a hard boundary between humans and animals: animals lacked intellect and a grasp of universals as such. This did not mean that they were necessarily incapable of recognising types of other animals or at least perceiving

---

[72] ST 1a2ae.29.6; vol. 6, pp. 207–8: 'Respondeo dicendum quod de universali dupliciter contingit loqui: uno modo, secundum quod subest intentioni universalitatis; alio autem modo, de natura cui talis intentio attribuitur: alia est enim consideratio hominis universalis, et alia hominis in eo quod homo. Si igitur universale accipiatur primo modo, sic nulla potentia sensitivae partis, neque apprehensiva neque appetitiva, potest in universale: quia universale fit per abstractionem a materia individuali, in qua radicatur omnis virtus sensitiva. Potest tamen aliqua potentia sensitiva, et apprehensiva et appetitiva, ferri in aliquid universaliter. Sicut dicimus quod obiectum visus est color secundum genus, non quia visus cognoscat colorem universalem; sed quia quod color sit cognoscibilis a visu, non convenit colori inquantum est hic color, sed inquantum est color simpliciter. Sic ergo odium etiam sensitivae partis, potest respicere aliquid in universali: quia ex natura communi aliquid adversatur animali, et non solum ex eo quod est particularis, sicut lupus ovi. Unde ovis odit lupum generaliter.'

their general characteristics, but this could be explained without challenge to the boundary. At least in some species, the sensitive powers included the capacity to generalise about what they perceived. A limited ability to deal with universals was in effect allocated to the sensitive powers whose scope was thus expanded.[73]

Aquinas was also very much aware of the way in which similarities between humans and animals could shape the language that was used metaphorically of humans. This was the case when he considered whether cruelty differed from savagery or wildness.[74] He explained that the terms 'savagery' and 'wildness' were based on human likeness to wild animals which were also called 'savage'. Animals of this kind harmed humans so that they could feed on their bodies, not for some just cause which could only be considered through reason. Properly speaking, therefore, the terms wildness and savagery were applicable to humans when someone imposed a penalty without considering any fault on the part of the person thus punished, but only delighting in the torture of humans. It followed that wildness and savagery were types of bestiality because such delight was not human but bestial, stemming from evil practice or corrupt nature, just like other bestial affections. Cruelty, on the other hand, took account of the fault of the person being punished but was excessive in the punishment, so that cruelty differed from savagery and wildness in the way that human evil differed from bestiality.[75] The irrationality of animals thus rendered

---

[73] For differing interpretations of Aquinas's views on this issue as discussed throughout his works, see Oelze, *Animal Rationality*, pp. 57–69. On the strategy of expanding the scope of the sensitive powers, see Oelze, *Animal Rationality*, p. 231: 'None of the authors covered in this book would deny that every process relies on a faculty. What some of them seem to suggest is simply that not all of those processes that were usually taken to depend on rational faculties, actually require those faculties. Again, this does not mean that they do not require any faculties at all. Rather, they do not require the faculties of intellect and reason but can take place in the sensory soul (or some part of the sensory soul). Therefore, one could say that the sensory soul is "upgraded" in the sense that the scope of its cognitive operations is widened.'

[74] ST 2a2ae.159.2; vol. 10, pp. 286–7: 'Utrum crudelitas a saevitia sive feritate differat.'

[75] ST 2a2ae.159.2; vol. 10, pp. 286–7: 'Respondeo dicendum quod nomen saevitiae et feritatis a similitudine ferarum accipitur, quae etiam saevae dicuntur. Huiusmodi enim animalia nocent hominibus ut ex eorum corporibus pascantur: non ex aliqua iustitiae causa, cuius consideratio pertinet ad solam rationem. Et ideo, proprie loquendo, feritas vel saevitia dicitur secundum quam aliquis in poenis inferendis non considerat aliquam culpam eius qui punitur, sed

them incapable of acting for a just cause or sinning through cruelty. Human behaviour could, however, be like that of animals, and perception of this similarity could shape the language used of humans.

In the *Summa theologiae* Aquinas consistently stressed differences between humans and animals. Humans were more perfect, exercising reason, intellect and free will, and grasping universals whereas animals relied on natural judgment, instinct and their sensitive appetites. While individual humans would respond to the same circumstances very differently, animals of the same species would always behave in the same way, following a pattern of behaviour established for them by the creator. Humans and animals also differed in their interior senses: animals deployed estimation and memory, but humans had cogitation and reminiscence which enabled them to think by making comparisons and to begin syllogistic argument. Humans were entitled to use animals as property, and animals had no prospect of an eternal future. On the other hand, there were significant similarities and continuities between humans and animals. Even if they could not grasp universals, some animals could nevertheless think generally about types of other animal, a capacity included in the sensitive powers that were expanded in conception accordingly. Similarities between the human and animal behaviour also inspired the use of metaphorical language about humans. The perception of similarities could therefore generate more complex approaches to an apparently straightforward boundary, and this was much more evident in Aquinas's earlier work, the *Summa contra gentiles*.

Aquinas, *Summa contra gentiles*

Although the *Summa contra gentiles* made much more of similarities between humans and animals than the *Summa theologiae*, there were occasions when difference was to the fore. For example, the huge significance that Aquinas attributed to the boundary between the rational human and the irrational animal was very clear when he

solum hoc quod delectatur in hominum cruciatu. Et sic patet quod continetur sub bestialitate: nam talis delectatio non est humana, sed bestialis, proveniens vel ex mala consuetudine vel ex corruptione naturae, sicut et aliae huiusmodi bestiales affectiones. Sed crudelitas attendit culpam in eo qui punitur, sed excedit modum in puniendo. Et ideo crudelitas differt a saevitia sive feritate sicut malitia humana a bestialitate.'

argued that while divine providence extended to all things, it applied in a special way to intellectual and rational natures, beyond its application to other creatures. This was because rational creatures excelled other creatures in the perfection of their nature and in the dignity of their end. They excelled in the perfection of their nature because only a rational creature had dominion over its acts, freely acting on itself so that it did things, whereas other creatures were more acted upon than acting when doing things. Rational creatures excelled in the dignity of their end because only an intellectual creature attained the ultimate end of the universe by its own actions, namely knowing and loving God, whereas other creatures could not attain the ultimate end except through a kind of participation in its likeness.[76]

The first distinctive way in which providence applied to rational creatures was that the very constitution of an intellectual nature, according to which it was master of its actions, required providential care that would enable it to look after itself for its own sake. The constitution of other things, which did not have dominion over their acts, meant that they did not receive care for their own sake but as they were ordered to others. Aquinas likened irrational creatures to instruments and rational creatures to principal agents. His point was that instruments were sought not for their own sake but for use by principal agents. It followed that all attention paid to the instrument was for the sake of the principal agent, whereas that paid to the principal agent as such was for the sake of that principal agent. Intellectual creatures were therefore set up by God to be looked after for their own sakes, but other creatures to be subordinated to rational creatures.[77]

---

[76] *Summa contra gentiles*, 3.111.1; *Sancti Thomae Aquinatis Opera Omnia iussu Leonis XIII*, 13–15 (Rome, 1918–30), vol. 14, p. 355: 'manifestum est quod divina providentia ad omnia se extendit. Oportet tamen aliquam rationem providentiae specialem observari circa intellectuales et rationales naturas, prae aliis creaturis. Praecellunt enim alias creaturas et in perfectione naturae, et in dignitate finis. In perfectione quidem naturae, quia sola creatura rationalis habet dominium sui actus, libere se agens ad operandum; ceterae vero creaturae ad opera propria magis aguntur quam agant [...]. In dignitate autem finis, quia sola creatura intellectualis ad ipsum finem ultimum universi sua operatione pertingit, scilicet cognoscendo et amando Deum: aliae vero creaturae ad finem ultimum pertingere non possunt nisi per aliqualem similitudinis ipsius participationem.' Henceforth SCG.

[77] SCG 3.112.1; vol. 14, p. 356: 'Primum igitur, ipsa conditio intellectualis naturae, secundum quam est domina sui actus, providentiae curam requirit qua sibi propter se provideatur: aliorum vero conditio, quae non habent

Intellectual creatures also received providential care for their own sake, while other creatures received it for the sake of intellectual creatures, because having dominion over their own acts meant that intellectual creatures were free whereas others, which were necessarily acted upon when doing something, were subject to servitude, and in any regime different provision had to be made for the free and the unfree.[78] Those who supposed that it was a sin for humans to kill brute animals were therefore in error, for by divine providence animals were established in the natural order for human use, and could be used by humans, either by killing them or in any other way, without injustice.[79]

A further consequence was that the individual human mattered in a way that the individual animal did not. As rational creatures, individual humans could direct their own acts, and not just follow the natural inclination common to all members of a species.[80] This was because, having reason and understanding, they could perceive the diverse ways

dominium sui actus, hoc indicat, quod eis non propter ipsa cura impendatur, sed velut ad alia ordinatis. Quod enim ab altero tantum agitur, rationem instrumenti habet: quod vero per se agit, habet rationem principalis agentis. Instrumentum autem non quaeritur propter seipsum, sed ut eo principale agens utatur. Unde oportet quod omnis operationis diligentia quae circa instrumenta adhibetur, ad principale agens referatur sicut ad finem: quod autem circa principale agens vel ab ipso vel ab alio adhibetur, inquantum est principale agens, propter ipsum est. Disponuntur igitur a Deo intellectuales creaturae quasi propter se procuratae, creaturae vero aliae quasi ad rationales creaturas ordinatae.' See Vojtěch Novotný, *Cur Homo? A History of the Thesis concerning Man as a Replacement for Fallen Angels*, trans. Pavlína Morgan and Tim Morgan (Prague, 2014), pp. 144–6. For discussion of SCG 3.112, see Benzoni, 'Thomas Aquinas and environmental ethics', pp. 453–5, 467–8.

[78] SCG 3.112.2; vol. 14, p. 356: 'Quod dominium sui actus habet, liberum est in agendo, liber enim est qui sui causa est: quod autem quadam necessitate ab alio agitur ad operandum, servituti subiectum est. Omnis igitur alia creatura naturaliter servituti subiecta est: sola intellectualis natura libera est. In quolibet autem regimine, liberis providetur propter seipsos: servis autem ut sint in usum liberorum. Sic igitur per divinam providentiam intellectualibus creaturis providetur propter se, ceteris autem creaturis propter ipsas.'

[79] SCG 3.112.12; vol. 14, p. 357: 'Per haec autem excluditur error ponentium homini esse peccatum si animalia bruta occidat. Ex divina enim providentia naturali ordine in usum hominis ordinantur. Unde absque iniuria eis utitur homo, vel occidendo, vel quolibet alio modo.'

[80] SCG 3.113.2; vol. 14, p. 360: 'Si igitur homo haberet directionem in suis actibus solum secundum congruentiam speciei, non esset in ipso agere vel non agere, sed oporteret quod sequeretur inclinationem naturalem toti speciei communem, ut contingit in omnibus irrationalibus creaturis. Manifestum est igitur quod rationalis creaturae actus directionem habet non solum secundum speciem, sed etiam secundum individuum.'

in which something might be good or bad, according to variations in individuals, times and locations.[81] They could also in some way know the workings of divine providence and therefore properly govern others as well as themselves.[82] God therefore exercised care of human acts not only as they pertained to the species but also as personal acts.[83] Moreover, whereas irrational creatures were directed by natural inclination, humans needed divine law to govern their personal acts.[84] A host of fundamental differences between humans and animals thus stemmed from the contrast between human rationality and animal irrationality. Animals had a lower degree of perfection and dignity, did not possess free will, could not truly know and love God, were subject to human control and use, and did not receive providential care for their own sakes, either as species or individuals.

Aquinas acknowledged similarities between humans and animals, however, when discussing how an intellectual substance could be the form of a body, and these similarities took on meaning in the context of hierarchy.[85] Aquinas drew attention to the 'wonderful connection of things' ('mirabilis rerum connexio'). The lowest in the higher genus, he

---

[81] SCG 3.113.4; vol. 14, p. 360: 'Sola autem creatura rationalis est capax directionis qua dirigitur ad suos actus non solum secundum speciem, sed etiam secundum individuum: habet enim intellectum et rationem, unde percipere possit quomodo diversimode sit aliquid bonum vel malum secundum quod congruit diversis individuis, temporibus et locis.'

[82] SCG 3.113.5; vol. 14, p. 360: 'Creatura rationalis sic providentiae divinae subiacet quod non solum ea gubernatur, sed etiam rationem providentiae utcumque cognoscere potest: unde sibi competit etiam aliis providentiam et gubernationem exhibere. Quod non contingit in ceteris creaturis, quae solum providentiam participant inquantum providentiae subduntur. Per hoc autem quod aliquis facultatem providendi habet, potest etiam suos actus dirigere et gubernare.'

[83] SCG 3.113.7; vol. 14, p. 360: 'de humanis actibus Deus curam habet non solum prout ad speciem pertinent, sed etiam secundum quod sunt actus personales.'

[84] SCG 3.114.1; vol. 14, p. 363: 'Ex hoc autem apparet quod necessarium fuit homini divinitus legem dari. Sicut enim actus irrationalium creaturarum diriguntur a Deo ea ratione qua ad speciem pertinent, ita actus hominum diriguntur a Deo secundum quod ad individuum pertinent, ut ostensum est. Sed actus creaturarum irrationalium, prout ad speciem pertinent, diriguntur a Deo quadam naturali inclinatione, quae naturam speciei consequitur. Ergo, supra hoc, dandum est aliquid hominibus quo in suis personalibus actibus dirigantur. Et hoc dicimus legem.'

[85] SCG 2.68; vol. 13, pp. 440–1. See Davids, *Anthropologische Differenz und animalische Konvenienz*, pp. 72–4; Antonia Fitzpatrick, *Thomas Aquinas on Bodily Identity* (Oxford, 2017), p. 128.

explained, was always found to touch the highest of the lower genus. Thus, some of the lowest in the genus of animals barely rose above the life of plants. Oysters, for example, were immobile, only had the sense of touch, and were bound to the earth like plants. This was why Dionysius, in Book 7 of *The Divine Names*, had said that divine wisdom had joined the ends of superior things to the beginnings of inferior ones. This was immensely significant for humans, as Aquinas immediately pointed out. The human body, highest in the genus of bodies, was in contact with the human soul, which held the lowest position in the higher genus of intellectual substances. Thus, the human soul was said to be like a horizon or boundary of the corporeal and the incorporeal, insofar as it was an incorporeal substance but the form of a body. Aquinas stressed, however, that the presence of this profoundly important boundary within the human did not undermine the unity of human being. As he put it, something made up of intellectual substance and corporeal matter was no less one thing than something made up of the form of fire and its matter. Indeed, its unity was perhaps greater because the more form conquered matter, the greater the unity between them.[86]

Aquinas proceeded to set out a hierarchy of forms, beginning at the bottom: the forms of the elements, the forms of mixed bodies, the souls

---

[86] SCG 2.68.6; vol. 13, pp. 440–1: 'Hoc autem modo mirabilis rerum connexio considerari potest. Semper enim invenitur infimum supremi generis contingere supremum inferioris generis: sicut quaedam infima in genere animalium parum excedunt vitam plantarum, sicut ostrea, quae sunt immobilia, et solum tactum habent, et terrae in modum plantarum adstringuntur; unde et beatus Dionysius dicit, in VII cap. de Div. Nom., quod divina sapientia coniungit fines superiorum principiis inferiorum. Est igitur accipere aliquid supremum in genere corporum, scilicet corpus humanum aequaliter complexionatum, quod attingit ad infimum superioris generis, scilicet ad animam humanam, quae tenet ultimum gradum in genere intellectualium substantiarum, ut ex modo intelligendi percipi potest. Et inde est quod anima intellectualis dicitur esse quasi quidam horizon et confinium corporeorum et incorporeorum, inquantum est substantia incorporea, corporis tamen forma. Non autem minus est aliquid unum ex substantia intellectuali et materia corporali quam ex forma ignis et eius materia, sed forte magis: quia quanto forma magis vincit materiam, ex ea et materia efficitur magis unum.' For Latin translations of the relevant part of Pseudo-Dionysius, *De divinis nominibus*, 7, see *Dionysiaca: recueil donnant l'ensemble des traductions latines des ouvrages attribués au Denys de l'aréopage*, ed. Philippe Chevallier (Bruges, 2 vols., 1937), vol. 1, p. 407. For a modern translation from the Greek, see *De divinis nominibus*, ed. Salvatore Lilla and Claudio Moreschini (Alessandria, 2018), p. 157.

of plants, the souls of brute animals, and the intellective soul, by which he meant the human soul.[87] The forms of the elements could only perform operations consistent with qualities that were dispositions of matter, such as hot and cold.[88] Higher up the hierarchy, the forms were less and less dependent upon these qualities. When it came to the souls of brute animals, they were similar to superior substances not only in moving but even 'in knowing in some way' ('aliqualiter in cognoscendo'). They were thus able to carry out operations that were independent of material qualities even though they were only performed through a corporeal organ, for feeling and imagining were not achieved by getting hotter or colder, although these were necessary conditions for the proper disposition of the bodily organ.[89] The intellective soul was superior again in that it was similar to even higher substances with regard to the genus of knowledge because it could understand ('intelligere'), an operation that was entirely independent of any corporeal organ. It still needed the powers of imagination and sense, however, which worked through certain corporeal organs, for which reason it was naturally united to the body.[90]

---

[87] SCG 2.68.7–12; vol. 13, p. 441.

[88] SCG 2.68.8; vol. 13, p. 441: 'Invenimus enim aliquas infimas formas, quae in nullam operationem possunt nisi ad quam se extendunt qualitates quae sunt dispositiones materiae, ut calidum, frigidum, humidum et siccum, rarum, densum, grave et leve, et his similia: sicut formae elementorum. Unde istae sunt formae omnino materiales, et totaliter immersae materiae.'

[89] SCG 2.68.11; vol. 13, p. 441: 'Supra has formas inveniuntur aliae formae similes superioribus substantiis non solum in movendo, sed etiam aliqualiter in cognoscendo; et sic sunt potentes in operationes ad quas nec organice qualitates praedictae deserviunt, tamen operationes huiusmodi non complentur nisi mediante organo corporali; sicut sunt animae brutorum animalium. Sentire enim et imaginari non completur calefaciendo et infrigidando: licet haec sint necessaria ad debitam organi dispositionem.'

[90] SCG 2.68.12; vol. 13, p. 441: 'Super omnes autem has formas invenitur forma similis superioribus substantiis etiam quantum ad genus cognitionis, quod est intelligere: et sic est potens in operationem quae completur absque organo corporali omnino. Et haec est anima intellectiva: nam intelligere non fit per aliquod organum corporale. Unde oportet quod illud principium quo homo intelligit, quod est anima intellectiva, et excedit conditionem materiae corporalis, non sit totaliter comprehensa a materia aut ei immersa, sicut aliae formae materiales. Quod eius operatio intellectualis ostendit, in qua non communicat materia corporalis. Quia tamen ipsum intelligere animae humanae indiget potentiis quae per quaedam organa corporalia operantur, scilicet imaginatione et sensu, ex hoc ipso declaratur quod naturaliter unitur corpori ad complendam speciem humanam.'

Aquinas thus identified an important similarity between animals and humans: animals were similar to humans in that they could know in some way. This was entirely consistent with the fashion in which he envisaged the boundaries between grades in the hierarchy, such that the lowest animals were barely distinguishable from plants. Indeed, the hierarchy required that similarities as well as differences should inform the boundaries between grades. The boundaries were not undermined by the similarities because fundamental differences were established by other similarities with the grades even higher up and lower down. In the case of humans, their difference from animals was established by the capacity to understand without use of the body, which they had in common with higher grades, although for humans the body still supplied some relevant powers. The nature of the hierarchy thus ensured that similarities did not threaten boundaries, indeed the consistent presence of similarities across *all* boundaries was what generated difference.

Aquinas again addressed the relationship between similarity and hierarchy when considering how divine providence provided rational order, which led him to explain the value of diversity and how that diversity was structured in a hierarchy that included similarities at every level. Through providence, God ordered everything to divine goodness, as to an end, so that likeness ('similitudo') of his goodness was impressed on things as far as possible. Every created substance, however, necessarily lacked the perfection of divine goodness. For likeness of divine goodness to be communicated to things more perfectly, diversity amongst things was required so that what could not be perfectly represented by one thing could be represented more perfectly by diverse things in diverse ways, and for things to be diverse they had to have diverse forms.[91]

---

[91] SCG 3.97.2; vol. 14, p. 299: 'Ostensum enim est quod Deus per suam providentiam omnia ordinat in divinam bonitatem sicut in finem [...] ut similitudo suae bonitatis, quantum possibile est, imprimatur in rebus. Quia vero omnem creatam substantiam a perfectione divinae bonitatis deficere necesse est, ut perfectius divinae bonitatis similitudo rebus communicaretur, oportuit esse diversitatem in rebus, ut quod perfecte ab uno aliquo repraesentari non potest, per diversa diversimode perfectiori modo repraesentaretur. [...] Res autem per hoc diversae sunt, quod formas habent diversas.' On this approach elsewhere in Aquinas's works, see Benzoni, 'Thomas Aquinas and environmental ethics', pp. 460–3; John H. Wright, *The Order of the Universe in the Theology of St Thomas Aquinas* (Rome, 1957), pp. 46–7.

Having presented the need for diversity, Aquinas explained why hierarchical structure was also necessary. Likeness to one simple thing, by which he meant God, could not be diversified unless likeness were more or less close or remote. The closer something was to divine likeness, the more perfect it was, so difference among forms required that one exist more perfectly than another. Diversity of forms therefore required diverse grades of perfection.[92] Aquinas considered the presence of such grades to be readily apparent. A diligent observer would discover plants above inanimate bodies, irrational animals above plants, and intellectual substances above irrational animals. Moreover, in each of these categories diversity would be found, with some things being more perfect than others, to the extent that the highest of a lower genus seemed to be 'close' ('propinqua') to the higher genus, and vice versa.[93] Thus, for example, immobile animals were similar to plants, and Dionysius said in book 7 of *The Divine Names* that divine wisdom had 'joined' those at the bottom of a first class to those at the top of a second class.[94] Aquinas thus asserted hierarchical difference that was based on degrees of likeness to divine goodness, and that supposed similarity and closeness between members of different grades at the boundaries.

Similarities as well as differences between animals and humans were also an important part of Aquinas's discussion of happiness (*felicitas*), but here he took an entirely different approach. He referred to animals in order to establish that pleasure could not be the ultimate end, and

---

[92] SCG 3.97.3; vol. 14, p. 299: 'Similitudo autem ad unum simplex considerata diversificari non potest nisi secundum quod magis vel minus similitudo est propinqua vel remota. Quanto autem aliquid propinquius ad divinam similitudinem accedit, perfectius est. Unde in formis differentia esse non potest nisi secundum quod una perfectior existit quam alia [...] ut ex hoc detur intelligi quod formarum diversitas diversum gradum perfectionis requirit.'

[93] The things that Aquinas had in mind were species rather than individual things; see Benzoni, 'Thomas Aquinas and environmental ethics', pp. 462–4.

[94] SCG 3.97.3; vol. 14, p. 299: 'Et hoc evidenter apparet naturas rerum speculanti. Inveniet enim, si quis diligenter consideret, gradatim rerum diversitatem compleri: nam supra inanimata corpora inveniet plantas; et super has irrationalia animalia; et super has intellectuales substantias; et in singulis horum inveniet diversitatem secundum quod quaedam sunt aliis perfectiora, in tantum quod ea quae sunt suprema inferioris generis, videntur propinqua superiori generi, et e converso, sicut animalia immobilia sunt similia plantis; unde et Dionysius dicit, VII cap. de Div. Nom., quod divina sapientia coniungit fines primorum principiis secundorum.' See Wright, *Order of the Universe*, pp. 59–60.

that pleasure was therefore quite different from happiness. He explained that the right order of things was consistent with the order of nature, because natural things were ordered to their end without error. In natural things, however, pleasure existed for the sake of operation, and not the other way round. Nature thus attached pleasure to the operations of animals that were manifestly ordered to necessary ends, like the use of food, which was ordered to the preservation of the individual, and the use of sexual apparatus, which was ordered to the preservation of the species. Unless pleasure were attached in this way, animals would abstain from these necessary uses. It was therefore impossible that pleasure should be the ultimate end.[95] These pleasures, moreover, were common to humans and brute animals whereas happiness was possible for humans but not animals: 'Happiness is a certain good proper to humans, for brutes cannot be said to be happy, except through misapplication of the term.'[96] Happiness could not therefore consist in goods of the body precisely because they were common to humans and other animals.[97] Furthermore, many animals were physically more powerful than humans because they were, for example, faster or stronger. If the highest human good had to do with the body, the human would not be the best of animals, which was patently false.[98] Similarly, human happiness did not lie in the senses because goods relating to sensation were also common to humans and other

---

[95] SCG 3.26.14; vol. 14, p. 72: 'Rectus ordo rerum convenit cum ordine naturae: nam res naturales ordinantur in suum finem absque errore. In naturalibus autem est delectatio propter operationem, et non e converso. Videmus enim quod natura illis operationibus animalium delectationem apposuit quae sunt manifeste ad fines necessarios ordinatae, sicut in usu ciborum, qui ordinatur ad conservationem individui, et in usu venereorum, qui ordinatur ad conservationem speciei: nisi enim adesset delectatio, animalia a praedictis usibus necessariis abstinerent. Impossibile ergo est quod delectatio sit ultimus finis.'

[96] SCG 3.27.4; vol. 14, p. 82: 'Felicitas est quoddam bonum hominis proprium: non enim bruta possunt dici felicia, nisi abusive. Delectationes autem praemissae sunt communes hominibus et brutis.'

[97] SCG 3.32.3; vol. 14, p. 88: 'Haec bona sunt homini et aliis animalibus communia. Felicitas autem est proprium hominis bonum. Non est igitur in praemissis bonis hominis felicitas.'

[98] SCG 3.32.4; vol. 14, p. 88: 'Multa animalia, quantum ad bona corporis, sunt homine potiora: quaedam enim sunt velociora homine, quaedam robustiora, et sic de aliis. Si igitur in his esset summum hominis bonum, non esset homo optimum animalium: quod patet esse falsum. Non est igitur felicitas humana in bonis corporis consistens.'

animals.[99] The same argument even applied to morally virtuous acts. As he had already indicated, happiness was the good proper to humans. The ultimate happiness of humans was therefore to be sought in that which, amongst all human goods, was most proper to humans in comparison with other animals. A morally virtuous act did not fall into this category because some animals participated somehow in either liberality or fortitude.[100] Again, one of the reasons why ultimate human happiness did not lie in the act of prudence was that some irrational animals participated somehow in prudence.[101] Having ruled out all other possibilities, Aquinas was left to conclude that ultimate human happiness consisted in the contemplation of truth, for this was the only human operation proper to humans in which nothing was shared in any way with other animals.[102] That humans could only attain this ultimate happiness in an afterlife denied to animals reinforced its status as the defining characteristic of the human.[103]

These were by no means Aquinas's only arguments regarding happiness, but he clearly found the comparison with animals valuable, and the defining characteristic of the human had to be something that humans and animals did not share in any way at all. This was a very different strategy from his deployment of the Dionysian hierarchy. All similarities had now to be set aside in order to establish the boundary, and it was striking that these similarities included not only corporeal pleasure, bodily goods and the senses, but also morally virtuous acts and prudence in which some animals participated in some way so that differences in these fields were not decisive in separating humans from animals.

---

[99] SCG 3.33.1; vol. 14, p. 89: 'Per eadem etiam apparet quod neque summum hominis bonum est in bonis sensitivae partis. Nam haec etiam bona sunt homini et aliis animalibus communia.'

[100] SCG 3.34.6; vol. 14, p. 90: 'Felicitas est proprium hominis bonum. Illud igitur quod est maxime proprium hominis inter omnia bona humana respectu aliorum animalium, est in quo quaerenda est eius ultima felicitas. Huiusmodi autem non est virtutum moralium actus: nam aliqua animalia aliquid participant vel liberalitatis vel fortitudinis [...]. Non est igitur ultima hominis felicitas in actibus moralibus.'

[101] SCG 3.35.5; vol. 14, p. 91: 'Animalia irrationabilia non participant aliquid felicitatis: sicut probat Aristoteles in I Ethicorum. Participant autem quaedam eorum aliquid prudentiae: ut patet per eundem in I Metaphysicae. Igitur felicitas non consistit in operatione prudentiae.'

[102] SCG 3.37.1–2; vol. 14, pp. 92–3: 'relinquitur quod ultima hominis felicitas sit in contemplatione veritatis. Haec enim sola operatio hominis est sibi propria; et in ea nullo modo aliquod aliorum animalium communicat.'

[103] SCG 3.48.10; vol. 14, p. 131.

Aquinas recognised another similarity between animals and humans, and gave yet another account of difference, when he discussed whether the human soul was formed from the father's semen.[104] Animals and humans both possessed sensitive souls, which seemed to raise the possibility that they were the same in significant ways. It could be argued, for example, that because humans were animals insofar as they had a sensitive soul, and the term animal could be applied univocally to humans and other animals, the human sensitive soul was of the same genus as souls of other animals. Things belonging to the same genus, however, had the same mode of coming into being. This meant that the human sensitive soul, just like the souls of other animals, must come into being through a power existing in semen. Since, however, the intellective and sensitive soul were the same in substance, it seemed that the intellective soul must also be produced through the power of semen.[105] In response, Aquinas explained that the development of a human embryo involved a succession of different forms. Initially the embryo had a vegetative soul, by which it lived the life of a plant. This was corrupted to be succeeded by a more perfect soul which was both nutritive and sensitive, and then the embryo lived the life of an animal. When this soul was corrupted in its turn, it was succeeded by a rational soul. Whereas the previous souls, the vegetative and the sensitive, had come into being by the power of semen, this rational soul was introduced from outside.[106] It was therefore very different in its origins

---

[104] SCG 2.88–89; vol. 13, pp. 539–43. Only a small part of an extended discussion is considered here. For accounts of Aquinas's views on embryos and the human soul, see Fabrizio Amerini, *Aquinas on the Beginning and End of Human Life* (Cambridge, Mass., 2013), esp. pp. 58–78 for analysis of this part of the *Summa contra gentiles* and his treatment of the same issues in other works; Pasnau, *Thomas Aquinas on Human Nature*, pp. 100–25, esp. 122–3.

[105] SCG 2.88.2; vol. 13, p. 539: 'Cum enim homo sit animal inquantum habet animam sensitivam; ratio autem animalis univoce homini et aliis animalibus conveniat; videtur quod anima sensitiva hominis sit eiusdem generis cum animabus aliorum animalium. Quae autem sunt unius generis, eundem modum habent prodeundi in esse. Anima igitur sensitiva hominis, sicut et aliorum animalium, per virtutem quae est in semine in esse procedit. Est autem idem secundum substantiam anima intellectiva et sensitiva in homine, ut supra ostensum est. Videtur igitur quod etiam anima intellectiva per virtutem seminis producatur.'

[106] SCG 2.89.11; vol. 13, p. 542: 'Quanto igitur aliqua forma est nobilior et magis distans a forma elementi, tanto oportet esse plures formas intermedias, quibus gradatim ad formam ultimam veniatur, et per consequens plures generationes medias. Et ideo in generatione animalis et hominis, in quibus est forma

from the vegetative and sensitive souls, although it was vegetative and
sensitive too.

Aquinas then explained that while 'animal' was predicated univocally of both humans and brute animals, it did not follow that the
sensitive souls must have the same mode of origin in both. For,
although the sensitive souls of humans and brute animals belonged to
the same genus, they differed according to species, just like the things
of which they were forms. Just as the human animal differed in species
from other animals in that it was rational, so the sensitive human soul
differed in species from the sensitive animal soul in that it was also
intellective. The soul in a brute animal had nothing beyond the sensitive, and consequently neither its being nor its operation rose above the
body, so that it had to be generated when the body was generated and
to be corrupted at the same time as the body. The sensitive soul in a
human, however, had intellective power beyond its sensitive nature,
and consequently the substance of the soul was necessarily elevated
above the body in being and operation, so that it was neither generated
through the generation of the body nor corrupted by its corruption.
The diverse mode of origin of human and brute animal souls did not
derive from the sensitive, according to which they belonged to the same
genus, but from the intellective, according to which they belonged to
different species.[107]

---

perfectissima, sunt plurimae formae et generationes intermediae, et per
consequens corruptiones, quia generatio unius, est corruptio alterius. Anima
igitur vegetabilis, quae primo inest, cum embryo vivit vita plantae, corrumpitur,
et succedit anima perfectior, quae est nutritiva et sensitiva simul, et tunc embryo
vivit vita animalis; hac autem corrupta, succedit anima rationalis ab extrinseco
immissa, licet praecedentes fuerint virtute seminis.'

[107] SCG 2.89.12; vol. 13, p. 542: 'Quod enim primo obiicitur, oportere animam
sensitivam eundem modum originis in homine et in brutis habere, ex eo quod
animal de eis univoce praedicatur:– dicimus hoc necessarium non esse. Etsi
enim anima sensitiva in homine et bruto conveniant secundum generis
rationem, differunt tamen specie, sicut et ea quorum sunt formae: sicut enim
animal quod est homo, ab aliis animalibus specie differt per hoc quod est
rationale, ita anima sensitiva hominis ab anima sensitiva bruti specie differt
per hoc quod est etiam intellectiva. Anima igitur in bruto habet id quod est
sensitivum tantum; et per consequens nec esse nec eius operatio supra corpus
elevatur; unde oportet quod simul cum generatione corporis generetur, et cum
corruptione corrumpatur. Anima autem sensitiva in homine, cum habeat supra
sensitivam naturam vim intellectivam, ex qua oportet ut ipsa substantia animae
sit secundum esse et operationem supra corpus elevata; neque per generationem
corporis generatur, neque per eius corruptionem corrumpitur. Diversus ergo

In sum, according to Aquinas, there was a stage in the development of a human embryo when its sensitive soul was no different from that of an animal, both coming into being through the power of semen. That soul perished, however, and an intellective soul was introduced from outside, a soul that was also vegetative and sensitive. Humans and animals were therefore similar in their possession of sensitive souls, but the significance of that similarity was limited by their different origins.

Similarities as well as differences again came into play when Aquinas discussed sex and marriage, and he used those similarities in yet another way. Stressing that marriage was natural, he attributed an exemplary function to animal behaviour. Emission of semen was contrary to human good, he argued, if it happened in such a way that generation could follow but an appropriate upbringing was impeded. He pointed out that with animals in which the female alone sufficed to bring up the offspring, the male and female did not remain together for any time after coitus, as was the case with dogs. With animals, however, in which the female did not suffice to raise the offspring, the male and female remained together after coitus for as long as was necessary for the upbringing and instruction of the offspring. This was the case with some birds whose chicks could not look for their own food immediately after birth. Since a bird did not feed its chicks with milk, but had to search for their food, and also had to keep them warm by sitting on them, the female alone did not suffice to do this. By divine providence, therefore, it was naturally impressed on the male of such animals that he should remain with the female to raise the offspring. It was manifest that in the human species the female certainly did not suffice to bring up offspring alone because human life necessarily required many things that could not be furnished by only one person. It was therefore appropriate, according to human nature, that a man should stay together with a woman after coitus and not depart at once, going indiscriminately to some other woman, as fornicators did.[108]

---

modus originis in animabus praedictis non est ex parte sensitivi, ex quo sumitur ratio generis: sed ex parte intellectivi, ex quo sumitur differentia speciei. Unde non potest concludi diversitas generis, sed sola diversitas speciei.'

[108] SCG 3.122.6; vol. 14, p. 379: 'oportet contra bonum hominis esse si semen taliter emittatur quod generatio sequi possit, sed conveniens educatio impediatur. Est enim considerandum quod in animalibus in quibus sola femina sufficit ad prolis educationem, mas et femina post coitum nullo tempore commanent, sicut patet in

A rationale that applied to brute animals was thus applicable to humans as well. Humans were subject to the same considerations as animals, and they should behave accordingly.

Even the differences between humans and animals could be deployed within this model. Human offspring required not only corporeal nutrition, but also instruction for the soul. While other animals naturally had their own kinds of prudence by which they could provide for themselves, humans lived by reason, which had to be brought to prudence by experience over a long period of time, so that it was necessary for children to be instructed by their parents who were already trained. Moreover, they only became capable of being instructed a long time after their birth, especially when they attained the age of discretion, after which a long time was then required for this instruction. As well as instruction, children also needed discipline because the passions undermined the judgment of prudence. For this a woman alone did not suffice and the man had to contribute because his reason was more perfect for instruction and his strength greater for administering punishment. Humans therefore had to devote a large part of life to developing offspring, not a short time, as in birds. Since in all animals it was necessary for the male to stay with the female for as long as the father's work was necessary for the offspring, it was natural for humans that the man should have a long-lasting rather than a short union with a specific woman. This union was termed marriage, and marriage was therefore natural to humans while fornication, which occurred outside marriage, was contrary to the good of humans and therefore had to be a sin.[109]

---

canibus. Quaecumque vero animalia sunt in quibus femina non sufficit ad educationem prolis, mas et femina simul post coitum commanent quousque necessarium est ad prolis educationem et instructionem: sicut patet in quibusdam avibus, quarum pulli non statim postquam nati sunt possunt sibi cibum quaerere. Cum enim avis non nutriat lacte pullos, quod in promptu est, velut a natura praeparatum, sicut in quadrupedibus accidit, sed oportet quod cibum aliunde pullis quaerat, et praeter hoc, incubando eos foveat: non sufficeret ad hoc sola femella. Unde ex divina providentia est naturaliter inditum mari in talibus animalibus, ut commaneat femellae ad educationem fetus. Manifestum est autem quod in specie humana femina minime sufficeret sola ad prolis educationem: cum necessitas humanae vitae multa requirat quae per unum solum parari non possunt. Est igitur conveniens secundum naturam humanam ut homo post coitum mulieri commaneat, et non statim abscedat, indifferenter ad quamcumque accedens, sicut apud fornicantes accidit.'

[109] SCG 3.122.8; vol. 14, p. 379: 'Rursus considerandum est quod in specie humana proles non indiget solum nutritione quantum ad corpus, ut in aliis animalibus; sed etiam instructione quantum ad animam. Nam alia animalia

Aquinas continued to grant animals an exemplary function, and to
build on both similarities and differences, when explaining why marriage should not just be long lasting, but indivisible and lifelong. If
paternal concern for offspring caused male and female to remain
together even in the case of birds, the natural order required that in
the human species father and mother should stay together for life.[110]
Humans were therefore like animals but had a natural obligation to
meet more exacting standards. That humans possessed reason made a
difference, however, because it introduced issues of fairness. Women
needed men not just for procreation, as was the case with other
animals, but also for governance because men were more perfect in
reason as well as stronger. A woman who united with a man for
procreation and then lost her fecundity and good looks would not be
taken by another man. If, therefore, a man who took a woman when
she was young, beautiful and fecund, could dismiss her when she was
old, he would inflict an injury on the woman contrary to natural
fairness.[111] Humans were just the same as animals, however, in

naturaliter habent suas prudentias, quibus sibi providere possunt: homo autem
ratione vivit, quam per longi temporis experimentum ad prudentiam pervenire
oportet; unde necesse est ut filii a parentibus, quasi iam expertis, instruantur.
Nec huius instructionis sunt capaces mox geniti, sed post longum tempus, et
praecipue cum ad annos discretionis perveniunt. Ad hanc etiam instructionem
longum tempus requiritur. Et tunc etiam, propter impetus passionum, quibus
corrumpitur aestimatio prudentiae, indigent non solum instructione, sed etiam
repressione. Ad haec autem mulier sola non sufficit, sed magis in hoc requiritur
opus maris, in quo est et ratio perfectior ad instruendum, et virtus potentior ad
castigandum. Oportet igitur in specie humana non per parvum tempus insistere
promotioni prolis, sicut in avibus, sed per magnum spatium vitae. Unde, cum
necessarium sit marem feminae commanere in omnibus animalibus quousque
opus patris necessarium est proli, naturale est homini quod non ad modicum
tempus, sed diuturnam societatem habeat vir ad determinatam mulierem. Hanc
autem societatem matrimonium vocamus. Est igitur matrimonium homini
naturale: et fornicarius coitus, qui est praeter matrimonium, est contra
hominis bonum. Et propter hoc oportet ipsum esse peccatum.'
[110] SCG 3.123.2; vol. 14, p. 382: 'Si igitur sollicitudo patris de filio causat etiam in
avibus commanentiam maris et feminae, ordo naturalis requirit quod usque ad
finem vitae in humana specie pater et mater simul commaneant.'
[111] SCG 3.123.3; vol. 14, p. 382: 'Videtur etiam aequitati repugnare si praedicta
societas dissolvatur. Femina enim indiget mare non solum propter
generationem, sicut in aliis animalibus, sed etiam propter gubernationem:
quia mas est et ratione perfectior, et virtute fortior. Mulier vero ad viri
societatem assumitur propter necessitatem generationis. Cessante igitur
fecunditate mulieris et decore, impeditur ne ab alio assumatur. Si quis igitur,
mulierem assumens tempore iuventutis, quo et decor et fecunditas ei adsunt,

possessing natural instinct, though it was directed towards different behaviour. Men had a natural concern to be certain of their offspring which was necessary because the child needed paternal guidance for a long time. Whatever undermined certainty about offspring was therefore contrary to the natural instinct of the human species. If a man could dismiss a woman, or a woman could dismiss a man, and have sex with another, certainty about offspring would be lost because the woman would have had sex first with one man and then with another. Thus, it was contrary to the natural instinct of the human species for a woman to be separated from a man, and the joining of male and female in the human species had to be not only long lasting but indivisible.[112]

There were also similarities in the effects that sexual intercourse had on the relationship between female and male, though human relationships were more complex. Sexual intercourse resulted in 'a certain tender fellowship' even between brute animals. Husband and wife, however, were united not only by sex but in the whole of domestic life, so there seemed to be 'the greatest friendship' between them. The greater the friendship, the firmer and longer lasting it was, and it was therefore appropriate that marriage should be entirely indissoluble.[113] The uniquely human obligation for sexual intercourse to be part of a lifelong union also reflected human responsibility for more than producing offspring. For humans, generation was the only natural act ordered to the common good and it was therefore subject to divine

eam dimittere possit postquam aetate provecta fuerit, damnum inferet mulieri, contra naturalem aequitatem.'

[112] SCG 3.123.5; vol. 14, p. 382: 'Hominibus naturalis quaedam sollicitudo inest de certitudine prolis: quod propter hoc necessarium est, quia filius diuturna patris gubernatione indiget. Quaecumque igitur certitudinem prolis impediunt, sunt contra naturalem instinctum humanae speciei. Si autem vir posset mulierem dimittere, vel mulier virum, et alteri copulari, impediretur certitudo prolis, dum mulier a primo cognita, postmodum a secundo cognosceretur. Est igitur contra naturalem instinctum speciei humanae quod mulier a viro separetur. Sic igitur non solum diuturnam, sed etiam individuam oportet esse in humana specie maris et feminae coniunctionem.'

[113] SCG 3.123.6; vol. 14, p. 382: 'Amicitia, quanto maior, tanto est firmior et diuturnior. Inter virum autem et uxorem maxima amicitia esse videtur: adunantur enim non solum in actu carnalis copulae, quae etiam inter bestias quandam suavem societatem facit, sed etiam ad totius domesticae conversationis consortium [...]. Conveniens igitur est quod matrimonium sit omnino indissolubile.'

and human laws.[114] Marriage was also a matter of good behaviour
which affected the family and civil society more widely.[115] Humans
were thus similar to animals in displaying natural concern for offspring, in having natural instincts and in that sexual relations resulted
in affection. Human relationships were further shaped, however, by
their rational nature and more complex social relationships, domestic,
familial and social.

When Aquinas explained why marriage had to be between one man
and one woman, he again turned to animals. In the minds of all animals
that had sexual intercourse it was innate not to share one's partner with
a rival, so that animals fought over sex. Indeed, there was 'one common
reason' in all animals because every animal desired to enjoy the pleasure
of sex with freedom, a freedom that was impeded if many males
approached one female, or vice versa, hence the fighting. In men, however, there was 'a special reason' because they naturally wished to be
certain of their offspring, and such certainty would be totally removed if
several men had sex with one woman. It therefore followed from natural
instinct that one woman should be with one man.[116] Furthermore, in
every species of animal in which the father cared for his offspring in
some way, each male had only one female. This was apparent in all birds
which fed their chicks together, for one male would not suffice to help

---

[114] SCG 3.123.7; vol. 14, p. 382: 'Ulterius autem considerandum est quod inter
naturales actus sola generatio ad bonum commune ordinatur: nam comestio,
et aliarum superfluitatum emissio, ad individuum pertinent; generatio vero ad
conservationem speciei. Unde, cum lex instituatur ad bonum commune, ea quae
pertinent ad generationem, prae aliis oportet legibus ordinari et divinis et
humanis.'

[115] SCG 3.123.8; vol. 14, p. 383: 'Quia vero necesse est ad id quod est optimum in
homine, alia omnia ordinari, coniunctio maris et feminae non solum sic
ordinata est legibus secundum quod ad prolem generandam pertinet, ut est in
aliis animalibus, sed etiam secundum quod convenit ad bonos mores, quos ratio
recta disponit vel quantum ad hominem secundum se, vel secundum quod
homo est pars domesticae familiae, aut civilis societatis. Ad quos quidem
bonos mores pertinet individua coniunctio maris et feminae.'

[116] SCG 3.124.1; vol. 14, p. 385: 'Considerandum etiam videtur quod innatum est
mentibus omnium animalium quae coitu utuntur, quod consortium in compari
non compatiuntur: unde propter coitum pugnae in animalibus existunt. Et
quidem quantum ad omnia animalia est una communis ratio, quia quodlibet
animal desiderat libere frui voluptate coitus [...]: quae quidem libertas
impeditur per hoc quod ad unam plures accedunt, aut e converso [...]. In
hominibus autem est ratio specialis: quia, ut dictum est, homo naturaliter
desiderat certus esse de prole; quae quidem certitudo omnino tolleretur si
plures essent unius. Ex naturali igitur instinctu procedit quod sit una unius.'

with raising the broods of several females. With species in which the males did not care for their offspring, however, the male had sex indiscriminately with several females, and the females with several males, as was the case with dogs, chickens and such like. Because, amongst all animals, male care for offspring was greater in the human species, it was clearly natural for humans that one male should have one female, and vice versa.[117] Aquinas thus deployed his view that humans and animals were the same in their desire for sexual pleasure and in possessing natural instinct. Human instinct was distinctive, however, because men had a special wish to be sure that their children were really theirs and they did more to look after their offspring than did the males of other species.

Aquinas thus approached similarities and differences between humans and animals in a range of different ways. Certainly, human possession and animal lack of reason underpinned many other fundamental differences, producing a straightforward boundary. For Aquinas, however, the relationship between similarity and difference was highly complex, and it was their combination that informed the boundary. Within the hierarchy of being, for example, difference might be generated by similarities. It was precisely because the members of any one grade were similar to the members of both the grade above and the grade below that they were different from both, and members at the top and bottom of a grade were very close to the members of the bottom and top of adjacent grades respectively. Then again, the hierarchy might be viewed entirely in terms of degrees of likeness to the divine, a pattern that generated hierarchy even within grades so that those at the top of any one grade were extremely close to those at the bottom of the grade above. Aquinas took an entirely different approach, however, when he set aside every aspect of the human which was in any way similar to the animal, and concluded that contemplation of the truth was the sole feature that defined the human

---

[117] SCG 3.124.3; vol. 14, p. 385: 'In omni animalis specie in qua patri inest aliqua sollicitudo de prole, unus mas non habet nisi unam feminam, sicut patet in omnibus avibus quae simul nutriunt pullos: non enim sufficeret unus mas auxilium praestare in educatione prolis pluribus feminis. In animalibus autem in quibus maribus nulla est sollicitudo de prole, indifferenter mas habet plures feminas, et femina plures mares: sicut in canibus, gallinis, et huiusmodi. Cum autem masculo inter omnia animalia maior sit cura de prole in specie humana, manifestum est quod naturale est homini quod unus mas unam feminam habeat, et e converso.'

absolutely, thus seeming to reject much that informed the hard boundary that he identified when simply accepting that humans were rational and animals were not. He handled the relationship between similarity and difference in still other ways when he pointed to the different origins of apparently similar features, and when he granted an exemplary function to animal behaviour, first drawing attention to what was similar, then shifting to what was particular to the human. Far from being limited by conventional parameters, Aquinas was varied and highly imaginative in the diverse ways he thought about the human and the animal.

Conclusion

When Parisian theologians of the thirteenth century wrote about animals and the similarities and differences between animals and humans, there was great variety and richness in their work. While 'the paradigm of the boundary' persisted, 'the plurality and density of medieval thought about animals' that Susan Crane so brilliantly identified in vernacular literature was equally characteristic of theological texts written in Latin.[1] With reference to bestiaries, Crane observed that 'With *ratio* as their distinguishing feature, humans are crucially differentiated from other animals; with *ratio* even slightly shared out among them, animal difference is shot through with similitude', and it is clear that for the masters 'animal difference' was indeed 'shot through with similitude'.[2] Moreover, while historians of philosophy like Anselm Oelze have, with immense precision and eloquence, explained the different ways in which some medieval scholars attributed various 'rational processes' to animals, it is also apparent that preoccupation with and desire to explore similarity between animals and humans extended into many different areas of the theologians' endeavours, including, as we have seen, discussions of creation, the fall, divine providence, the heavens, angels and demons, virtues and passions, to list just some of the topics that prompted theologians to assess continuity between the animal and the human.

Differences between humans and animals were always asserted, however, and indeed some texts relentlessly insisted on a hard boundary. Some differences, moreover, were articulated by all theologians. Every text studied here presented humans as more perfect, more noble or superior in dignity to animals, and insisted that humans possessed reason and intellect while animals did not. With the exception of Books

---

[1] Susan Crane, *Animal Encounters: Contacts and Concepts in Medieval Britain* (Philadelphia, 2013), p. 8.
[2] Crane, *Animal Encounters*, p. 100.

20 and 21 of Albert the Great's *De animalibus*, which was not a straightforwardly theological text, they all understood animals to be subject to human dominion, to be used by humans according to human needs. Most of them denied that animals had free will or the capacity to sin, and there are no grounds for thinking that this view was disputed. Many of them discussed differences pertaining to the soul, the body, and relations with God, and many explained how animals had no prospect of an eternal future. Even with regard to difference, there was diversity, however. In the sample analysed here, for example, only Bonaventure discussed the creation of animals, only the Summa Halensis and Albert dwelt on issues of genus and species, only Aquinas identified concern to be sure of paternity as unique to the human male, and a wider sense of social responsibility to family and society as distinctively human.

Because it is possible and legitimate at one level to assert simply that medieval theologians regarded humans as rational and animals as irrational, and to relate all other differences to this, there is a tendency to suppose that they found similarities between humans and animals threatening, and that their primary concern was in some sense to defend 'ideal boundaries', a task they performed by desperately trying to explain similarities away. There is, however, no evidence whatsoever to suggest that discussion of similarities was a matter of anxiety. Medieval academic texts very rarely offer clues as to the emotional state of the author, and there are none in the passages analysed here. An entirely different perspective is therefore more plausible. As long as reason, the capacity to grasp universals and the ability to argue syllogistically were acknowledged as belonging to humans and not animals, Parisian theologians were largely free to explore the boundary between humans and animals however they wished. Far from being restrictive, the acceptance of these defining characteristics opened up an intellectual space in which diverse ideas could be explored with imagination and without fear of condemnation.[3]

---

[3] For similar reflections with regard to thirteenth-century work on natural philosophy, see Theodor W. Köhler, *Homo animal nobilissimum. Konturen des spezifisch Menschlichen in der naturphilosophischen Aristoteleskommentierung des dreizehnten Jahrhunderts*, vols. 2.1 and 2.2 (Leiden, 2014), p. 919: 'Unter der Prämisse, dass allein der Mensch ein mit Vernunftvermögen ausgestattetes Sinnenwesen ist und damit unter der Annahme des Bestehens eines kategorialen Unterschieds zwischen Menschlichem und Tierischem, werden auf der

It is certainly clear that Parisian theologians explored a great range of similarities between humans and animals. To recapitulate only some of the main ones, they compared human and animal bodies, finding similarities with regard to needs, figure, composition and functions. A range of similarities in ways of knowing were considered: William of Auvergne pointed to the light of prophecy and to *solertia*; learning by experience was identified by William of Auvergne and by Albert, who also discussed memory and the capacity to be taught; Aquinas discussed the ability to know the general characteristics shared by members of other distinct species, and also instinct. William of Auvergne dwelt on the power of the will, and several masters considered prudence and other virtues.

Above all, however, what emerges from close reading of the texts produced by Parisian theologians is tremendous diversity and creativity in the strategies that they adopted for making sense of similarities in relation to difference, for holding similarity and difference in productive tension. First, there could be great variety between the different works of any one theologian or even within a single work. Thus, for example, differences were repeatedly identified in William of Auvergne's *De legibus* while similarities hardly featured, but similarities were of fundamental importance in his *De universo*. Likewise, Aquinas had little to say about similarity in his *Summa theologiae*, insisting relentlessly on difference, whereas similarities were treated in many different ways in his *Summa contra gentiles*. The Summa Halensis, on the other hand, was far from consistent in the significance that it granted to corporeal similarity. The purposes of each text evidently dictated how the boundary between humans and animals was treated, and absolute consistency was not required. Another approach was to emphasise the division between the soul and the body, between the material and the spiritual, and to confine similarities to the material realm of the body. This was very much how the Summa Halensis and

Analyseebene der konkreten leib-seelischen Existenzweisen von Mensch und Tieren in konstitutioneller und verhaltensmäßiger Hinsicht die *convenientiae et differentiae* ausgegrenzt und analysiert. Jene Prämisse gibt den Denkern gewissermaßen die Freiheit, unter "Einklammerung des Normativen" unbefangen sämtliche in Betracht kommenden Seiten menschlicher und tierischer Existenzweisen auf strukturelle Gemeinsamkeiten, Unterschiede und gegebenenfalls Übergänge im Einzelnen zu erkunden und den jeweiligen kategorialen Grenzverlauf darin "realitätsnah" zu bestimmen.'

Bonaventure proceeded. Similarities could also be characterised as either natural or in some way transgressive. This was the case in the Summa Halensis, for example, when similarity was sometimes unproblematic but at other times 'the mother of falsity'. Similarity could also be rendered consistent with difference when they were set within the overall pattern of creation, time and the Last Judgment. As Aquinas explained, both animals and humans had sensitive souls, but these souls had different origins, the animal soul stemming from semen and the mature human sensitive soul being an aspect of the rational soul that was created by God. As several masters pointed out, whatever their similarities with humans, animals would not exist after the Last Judgment, unlike humans who faced an eternal future.

Other strategies had more to do with how the theologian expressed himself. William of Auvergne moved playfully back and forth between assertions of similarity and difference, ridiculing others when they replied to his questions, and perhaps even mocking himself when his analysis fizzled out with the hope that 'if God grants that you see something better on these points, I would rejoice and wish that it would happen to me'. Were the lights that descended from the creator and by which animals learned the behaviours characteristic of their species the same as prophetic knowledge in humans or just very like it? William's ludic mode of writing firmly implanted ideas in the reader's mind without offering a definite conclusion. Another strategy at the level of discourse was the splitting of terms. A term applied to humans was applied to animals but with the qualification that it was 'a sort of' whatever the characteristic or quality might be. The effect was usually achieved by placing 'quidam' in the appropriate case before the relevant noun, less often 'aliqualiter' or 'aliquid simile' were deployed.[4] What was apparently the same thus became merely similar. A term was held in place while its applicability was queried so as to generate a new, though related, meaning. While greater clarity was sometimes achieved by means of a full distinction, Bonaventure distinguishing between 'charity commanding' and 'charity eliciting' for example, the less precise distinction was often preferred. The discourse of medieval masters was much more slippery than is generally appreciated.

---

[4] On linguistic strategies of this kind, see Köhler, *Homo animal nobilissimum*, vols. 2.1 and 2.2, pp. 138–40.

Some of the most remarkable strategies were developed when animals and humans were placed within an all-embracing hierarchy. Both William of Auvergne and Albert articulated and applied the principle that a power that could be exercised by something low in the hierarchy must also be exercised by things higher up, though more intensely and perhaps with additional powers. As Albert put it, 'whatever an inferior power can do, a superior power can also do excellently and eminently'. There were therefore similarities running through the hierarchy, though the strength of any given quality differed at different levels. Thus, in William's case, if animals could move bodies by the power of their will, so too could humans and spiritual substances higher up the hierarchy, whereas for Albert, animals and humans had vegetative and sensible souls, but these souls were more perfect in humans. Albert offered another technique for setting similarity and difference within hierarchy when he placed multiple boundaries close to each other. There was a boundary between the pygmy and the human, but another one between the pygmy and the monkey, and still another between the monkey and quadrupeds. The boundary separating the human from animals was just one of many boundaries. Similarities abounded, and that which demarcated the human no longer seemed so special. Aquinas presented a hierarchy in which everything had its place according to the degree of its likeness to the divine. Difference thus stemmed from different degrees of likeness, and that hierarchy was effective even within grades, so that at the boundaries the beings at the top of the lower grade were very close to those at the bottom of the higher grade. Aquinas offered yet another version of hierarchy in which any given grade was different from the grade above because of what it had in common with the grade below, and it was different from the grade below because of what it had in common with the grade above. Boundaries were thus generated by similarities across all boundaries.

The work of Aquinas was especially rich in the variety of ways used to handle similarities and differences between humans and animals. In addition to various treatments of hierarchy, Aquinas simply redefined what was on the animal side of the boundary by expanding the capacities of the sensitive powers in animals so that they could think generally about other types of animal, sheep thus perceiving a general characteristic of wolves, even though they could not grasp universals, something which humans could do. The boundary remained the same, but not what was on one side of it, so that there was greater similarity across the boundary. Aquinas took an entirely different approach, however, when he sought to identify a characteristic of the human that was in no way shared with animals. Only humans could enjoy happiness, and happiness could only consist of contemplation of the truth because everything else that humans did was in some way done by animals too. To define the boundary between humans and animals, Aquinas now set all similarities aside. Similarities were just as important as differences, however, when he gave animals an exemplary function for humans. With regard to sex and marriage, humans and animals were subject to the same natural imperatives, and humans could be directed to learn from animal behaviour, although because humans were different, further moral requirements applied naturally to humans.

There is no straightforward explanation for why accounts of similarities and differences between humans and animals were so varied. It is surely significant, however, that animals were not usually the main subject of discussion. Analysis of animals and their relationship with humans was almost invariably part of the treatment of another issue. While the theologians frequently stressed that animals had been created for use by humans, and sometimes treated them as tools employed by God to shape human behaviour, most powerfully in William of Auvergne's explanation of Old Testament laws, they were also analytical tools for the theologians themselves. Animals were brought into discussion when this helped solve problems that were often nothing to do with animals, and they were positioned in relation to humans in whatever way was helpful, hence the variety in the treatment of similarity and difference. This flexibility in the use of animals points to a significant continuity with preceding centuries. Writing about clerical discourse on animals from the fifth to twelfth centuries, Jacques Voisenet has identified a symbolic system that served to instruct and edify, and within which clerical authors were free to ascribe very different meanings to the same animals according to the moral issues that they wished to address.[5]

Were the discussions that included animals essentially part of a wider project to define the human? It is easy to appreciate why this might be so. For the masters, a profoundly important boundary ran through the human, although they did not doubt that unity prevailed.

---

[5] Jacques Voisenet, *Bêtes et hommes dans le monde médiéval: le bestiaire des clercs du ve au xiie siècle* (Turnhout, 2000), esp. 354, 361, 412–13.

The human was composed of body and soul, material and immaterial. As William of Auvergne put it, the human soul was 'on the horizon of eternity' or 'on the horizon of two worlds'.[6] For Aquinas, the human body was the highest in the genus of bodies and it touched the human soul, the lowest in the genus of intellectual substances, the human soul being 'like a horizon or boundary' between the corporeal and the incorporeal. The nature of the human was therefore far from obvious and it is hard to see how the human could be defined without reference to animals which were next to the human on the corporeal side of the human composite. Reviewing the occasions when theologians found it valuable to discuss animals, however, and especially the similarities and differences between humans and animals, it would seem that they had an even bigger project in mind. Animals were a crucial resource for understanding not just humans but the whole of creation and indeed the creator. It is striking that when discussing animals, the theologians made repeated use of the terms *convenientia* and *congruentia*, identifying what was *conveniens* and *inconveniens*, *congruens* and *incongruens*. Despite the seemingly casual frequency with which they were deployed, these terms bore complex meaning. They could refer just to what was 'fitting' in the sense of being consistent with something else. They could mean what was morally appropriate. They could also refer to a truth claim that fell between the necessary and the contingent.[7]

---

[6] See Ernest A. Moody, 'William of Auvergne and his treatise De Anima', in his *Studies in Medieval Philosophy, Science, and Logic: Collected Papers 1933–1969* (Berkeley, 1975), pp. 1–109 at 12.

[7] See Frederick Christian Bauerschmidt, *Thomas Aquinas: Faith, Reason, and Following Christ* (Oxford, 2013), pp. 160–5; Oliva Blanchette, *The Perfection of the Universe according to Aquinas: A Teleological Cosmology* (University Park, Pa., 1992), pp. 305–8, 312; Zachary Hayes, 'The meaning of *convenientia* in the metaphysics of St. Bonaventure', *Franciscan Studies* 34 (1974), pp. 74–100; C. H. Kneepkens, 'Roger Bacon's theory of the double *intellectus*: a note on the development of the theory of *congruitas* and *perfectio* in the first half of the thirteenth century,' in P. Osmund Lewry (ed.), *The Rise of British Logic: Acts of the Sixth European Symposium on Medieval Logic and Semantics, Balliol College, Oxford, 19–24 June 1983*, Pontifical Institute of Mediaeval Studies, Papers in Mediaeval Studies 7 (Toronto, 1985), pp. 115–43; Krystyna Krauze-Blachowicz, 'A survey of medieval concepts of congruity and completeness *ad sensum* and *ad intellectum*', trans. W. Wciórka, *Studia Semiotyczne – English Supplement* 25 (2004), pp. 130–44; Denys Turner, *Julian of Norwich, Theologian* (New Haven, Conn., 2011), pp. 34–51; Michael M. Waddell, 'Wisdom, fittingness and the relational transcendentals', in Jan A. Aertsen and Andreas Speer (eds.), *Was ist Philosophie im Mittelalter?* (Berlin, 1998), pp. 538–42.

Authorities did not explain everything, and the theologians tried to fill in the consequent gaps in their understanding by working out what fitted. That necessarily meant understanding similarity as well as difference. By understanding how animals were placed in relation to humans, they could work out what fitted all the way up the hierarchy of being to God. Animals provided not just food for the human body, but food for the human mind enabling it to generate 'convenient' truth.

Bibliography

Primary Sources

Albertus Magnus, *De Animalibus Libri XXVI*, ed. Hermann Stadler, Beiträge zur Geschichte der Philosophie des Mittelalters 15–16 (Münster, 1916–1920)

Albertus Magnus, *On Animals: A Medieval Summa Zoologica*, trans. Kenneth F. Kitchell Jr. and Irven Michael Resnick (Baltimore, 2 vols., 1999)

Alexander of Hales, *Doctoris Irrefragabilis Alexandri de Hales Ordinis Minorum Summa Theologica* (Quaracchi, 5 vols., 1924–48)

Ambrose, *Hexameron, Paradise, and Cain and Abel*, trans. John J. Savage (New York, 1961)

Aristotle, *Minor Works*, trans. W. S. Hett (Cambridge, Mass., 1936, reprinted 1963)

Aristotle, *Posterior Analytics*, trans. Hugh Tredennick (Cambridge, Mass., 1960, reprinted 1966)

Augustine, *The City of God against the Pagans*, trans. George E. McCracken (Cambridge, Mass., 7 vols., 1957, reprinted 1966)

Augustine, *Eighty-Three Different Questions*, trans. David L. Mosher, The Fathers of the Church: A New Translation 70 (Washington, D.C., 1982)

Augustine, *The Literal Meaning of Genesis*, trans. John Hammond Taylor (New York, 2 vols., 1982)

Augustine, *Soliloquies and Immortality of the Soul*, with introduction, translation and commentary by Gerard Watson (Warminster, 1990)

Bernard of Clairvaux, *On the Song of Songs II*, trans. Kilian Walsh (Kalamazoo, Mich., 1976)

Biblia latina cum glossa ordinaria (Strasbourg, 1480–81); *Biblia latina cum glossa ordinaria: Facsimile Reprint of the Editio Princeps, Adolph Rusch of Strassburg, 1480/81*, ed. with introduction by Karlfried Froehlich and Margaret T. Gibson (Turnhout, 4 vols., 1992)

Bonaventure, *Doctoris Seraphici S. Bonaventurae Opera Omnia* (Quaracchi, 10 vols., 1882–1902)

Bonaventure, *The Soul's Journey into God; The Tree of Life; The Life of St Francis*, trans. E. Cousins (New York, 1978)

Cicero, *Paradoxa Stoicorum* in Michele V. Ronnick, *Cicero's 'Paradoxa Stoicorum': A Commentary, an Interpretation and a Study of its Influence*, Studien zur klassischen Philologie 62 (Frankfurt am Main, 1991)

Gregory of Nyssa, *Dogmatic Treatises*, ed. and trans. Philip Schaff (Grand Rapids, Mich., 1892)

Gregory of Nyssa, 'Le "De imagine" de Grégoire de Nysse traduit par Jean Scot Érigène', ed. M. Cappuyns, *Recherches de théologie ancienne et médiévale* 32 (1965), pp. 205–62

Ovid, *Metamorphoses*, trans. Frank Justus Miller (Cambridge, Mass., 2 vols., third edition 1977, reprinted 1984)

Peter Comestor, *Scolastica Historica*, ed. Agneta Sylwan, Corpus Christianorum Continuatio Mediaeualis CXCI (Turnhout, 2005)

Peter Lombard, *In Epistolam I ad Corinthios*, Patrologia cursus completus, series Latina, ed. J.-P. Migne, 221 vols. (1844–61), vol. 191, cols. 1533–1696

Peter Lombard, *Sententiae in IV libris distinctae*, Spicilegium Bonaventurianum 4 and 5 (Grottaferrata, 1971 and 1981)

Pseudo-Dionysius, *Dionysiaca: recueil donnant l'ensemble des traductions latines des ouvrages attribués au Denys de l'aréopage*, ed. Philippe Chevallier (Bruges, 2 vols., 1937)

Pseudo-Dionysius, *De divinis nominibus*, ed. Salvatore Lilla and Claudio Moreschini (Alessandria, 2018)

Thomas Aquinas, *Summa contra gentiles*; Sancti Thomae Aquinatis Opera Omnia iussu Leonis XIII, 13–15 (Rome, 1918–30)

Thomas Aquinas, *Summa theologiae*, Sancti Thomae Aquinatis Opera Omnia iussu Leonis XIII, 4–12 (Rome, 1888–1906)

Thomas Aquinas, *Summa theologiae: Latin Text and English Translation*, ed. T. Gilby et al., 61 vols. (London, 1964–80)

William of Auvergne, *Opera Omnia*, ed. F. Hotot (Orléans and Paris, 2 vols., 1674)

William of Auvergne, *The Providence of God regarding the Universe: Part Three of the First Principal Part of the Universe of Creatures*, trans. Roland J. Teske (Milwaukee, Wis., 2007)

William of Auvergne, *The Universe of Creatures: Selections Translated from the Latin with an Introduction and Notes*, trans. Roland J. Teske (Milwaukee, Wis., 1998)

William of Saint Thierry, *De natura corporis et animae*, ed. and trans. Michel Lemoine (Paris, 1988)

William of Saint Thierry, *The Nature of the Body and the Soul*, in *Three Treatises on Man: A Cistercian Anthropology*, ed. Bernard McGinn (Kalamazoo, Mich., 1977)

Secondary Works

Amerini, Fabrizio *Aquinas on the Beginning and End of Human Life* (Cambridge, Mass., 2013)

Barad, Judith A. *Aquinas on the Nature and Treatment of Animals* (San Francisco, 1995)

Bauerschmidt, Frederick Christian *Thomas Aquinas: Faith, Reason, and Following Christ* (Oxford, 2013)

Benzoni, Francisco 'Thomas Aquinas and environmental ethics: a reconsideration of providence and salvation', *The Journal of Religion* 85 (2005), pp. 446–76

Berkman, John 'Towards a Thomistic theology of animality', in Celia Deane-Drummond and David Clough (eds.), *Creaturely Theology: On God, Humans and Other Animals* (London, 2009), pp. 21–40

Berlioz, Jacques 'Pouvoirs et contrôle de la croyance: la question de la procréation démonique chez Guillaume d'Auvergne (vers 1180–1249)', *Razo, Cahiers du Centre d'études médiévales de Nice* 9 (1989), pp. 5–27

Bernstein, Alan E. 'William of Auvergne and the Cathars', in Franco Morenzonni and Jean-Yves Tilliette (eds.), *Autour de Guillaume d'Auvergne* (Turnhout, 2005), pp. 271–89

Beullens, Pieter 'Like a book written by God's finger: animals showing the path toward God', in Brigitte Resl (ed.), *A Cultural History of Animals in the Medieval Age* (Oxford, 2007), pp. 127–51

Biller, Peter *The Measure of Multitude: Population in Medieval Thought* (Oxford, 2000)

Black, Winston 'William of Auvergne on the dangers of paradise: biblical exegesis between natural philosophy and anti-Islamic polemic,' *Traditio* 68 (2013), pp. 233–58

Blanchette, Oliva *The Perfection of the Universe according to Aquinas: A Teleological Cosmology* (University Park, Pa., 1992)

Boureau, Alain *Satan the Heretic: The Birth of Demonology in the Medieval West*, trans. Teresa Lavender Fagan (Chicago, 2006)

Boyle, Leonard *The Setting of the* Summa Theologiae *of Saint Thomas* (Toronto, 1982)

Brett, Annabel S. *Liberty, Right and Nature: Individual Rights in Later Scholastic Thought* (Cambridge, 2003)

Cohen, Jeffrey J. *Medieval Identity Machines* (Minneapolis, Minn., 2003)

Coolman, Boyd Taylor *Knowing God by Experience: The Spiritual Senses in the Theology of William of Auxerre* (Washington, D.C., 2004)

Corti, Guglielmo 'Le sette parti del Magisterium divinale et sapientiale di Guglielmo di Auvergne', in *Studi e Ricerche di Scienze Religiose in onore dei Santi Apostoli Pietro e Paulo nel xix centenario del loro martirio* (Rome, 1968), pp. 289–307

Cousins, Ewart H. *Bonaventure and the Coincidence of Opposites* (Chicago, 1978)

Crane, Susan *Animal Encounters: Contacts and Concepts in Medieval Britain* (Philadelphia, 2013)

Cullen, Christopher M. *Bonaventure* (Oxford, 2006)

Dales, Richard C. *The Problem of the Rational Soul in the Thirteenth Century* (Leiden, 1995)

Davids, Tobias *Anthropologische Differenz und animalische Konvenienz: Tierphilosophie bei Thomas von Aquin* (Leiden, 2017)

Davies, Brian *Thomas Aquinas's* Summa Theologiae: *A Guide and Commentary* (Oxford, 2014)

Fait, Paolo 'Fragments of Aristotle's modal syllogistic in the late medieval theory of consequences: the case of *consequentia ut nunc*', in Sten Ebbesen and Russell L. Friedman (eds.), *Medieval Analyses in Language and Cognition: Acts of the Symposium 'The Copenhagen School of Medieval Philosophy' January 10–13, 1996* (Copenhagen, 1999), pp. 139–61

Finger, Stanley and Marco Piccolino, *The Shocking History of Electric Fishes: From Ancient Epochs to the Birth of Modern Neurophysiology* (Oxford, 2011)

Fitzpatrick, Antonia *Thomas Aquinas on Bodily Identity* (Oxford, 2017)

Flores, Nona C. '"Effigies amicitiae ... veritas inimicitiae": antifeminism in the iconography of the woman-headed serpent in medieval art and literature', in Nona C. Flores (ed.), *Animals in the Middle Ages: A Book of Essays* (New York, 1996), pp. 167–95

Floridi, Luciano 'Scepticism and animal rationality: the fortune of Chrysippus' dog in the history of western thought', *Archiv für Geschichte der Philosophie* 79 (1997), pp. 27–57

Friedrich, Udo *Menschentier und Tiermensch: Diskurse der Grenzziehung und Grenzüberschreitung im Mittelalter* (Göttingen, 2009)

Gauthier, René-Antoine *Saint Thomas d'Aquin: Somme Contre les Gentils: Introduction* (Paris, 1993)

Gilson, Etienne *La Philosophie de Saint Bonaventure* (Paris, 1924)

Grant, Lindy *Blanche of Castille: Queen of France* (New Haven, 2016)

Hayes, Zachary 'The meaning of *convenientia* in the metaphysics of St. Bonaventure', *Franciscan Studies* 34 (1974), pp. 74–100

Hayes, Zachary *Bonaventure: Mystical Writings* (New York, 1999)

Janson, Horst Woldemar *Apes and Ape Lore in the Middle Ages and the Renaissance* (London, 1952)

Kay, Sarah *Animal Skins and the Reading Self in Medieval Latin and French Bestiaries* (Chicago, 2017)

Kelly, Henry Ansgar 'The metamorphoses of the Eden serpent during the middle ages and renaissance', *Viator* 2 (1971), pp. 301–29

Khanmohamadi, Shirin A. *In Light of Another's Word: European Ethnography in the Middle Ages* (Philadephia, 2014)

Kitchell Jr., Kenneth F. and Irven Michael Resnick, 'Introduction: the life and works of Albert the Great', in Albertus Magnus, *On Animals: A Medieval Summa Zoologica*, trans. Kenneth F. Kitchell Jr. and Irven Michael Resnick (Baltimore, 2 vols., 1999), vol. 1, pp. 1–42

Kneepkens, C. H. 'Roger Bacon's theory of the double *intellectus*: a note on the development of the theory of *congruitas* and *perfectio* in the first half of the thirteenth century', in P. Osmund Lewry (ed.), *The Rise of British Logic: Acts of the Sixth European Symposium on Medieval Logic and Semantics, Balliol College, Oxford, 19–24 June 1983*, Pontifical Institute of Mediaeval Studies, Papers in Mediaeval Studies 7 (Toronto, 1985), pp. 115–43

Koch, Joseph 'Sind die Pygmäen Menschen? Ein Kapital aus der philosophischen Anthropologie der mittelalterlichen Scholastik', *Archiv für Geschichte der Philosophie* 40 (1931), pp. 194–213

Köhler, Theodor W. *Homo animal nobilissimum: Konturen des spezifisch Menschlichen in der naturphilosophischen Aristoteleskommentierung des dreizehnten Jahrhunderts*, vol. 1 (Leiden, 2008)

Köhler, Theodor W. *Homo animal nobilissimum: Konturen des spezifisch Menschlichen in der naturphilosophischen Aristoteleskommentierung des dreizehnten Jahrhunderts*, vols. 2.1 and 2.2 (Leiden, 2014)

Kostelecky, Matthew *Thomas Aquinas's* Summa Contra Gentiles*: A Mirror of Human Nature* (Leuven, 2013)

Kramp, Josef 'Des Wilhelm von Auvergne "Magisterium divinale"', *Gregorianum* 1 (1920), pp. 538–616 and 2 (1921), pp. 42–103, 174–95

Krauze-Blachowicz, Krystyna 'A survey of medieval concepts of congruity and completeness *ad sensum* and *ad intellectum*', trans. W. Wciórka, *Studia Semiotyczne – English Supplement* 25 (2004), pp. 130–44

Leemans, Pieter de and Matthew Klemm, 'Animals and anthropology in medieval philosophy', in Brigitte Resl (ed.), *A Cultural History of Animals in the Medieval Age* (Oxford, 2007), pp. 153–77

Le Goff, J. Isaac 'Divine infinity in Bonaventure's disputed questions on the mystery of the Trinity', in Michael F. Cusato, Timothy J. Johnson and Steven J. McMichael (eds.), *Ordo et Sanctitas: The Franciscan Spiritual Journey in Theology and Hagiography: A Festschrift in Honour of J. A. Wayne Hellman O.F.M. Conv.* (Brill, 2017), pp. 165–85

Lugt, Maaike van der *Le ver, le démon et la Vierge: Les théories médiévales de la génération extraordinaire: Une étude sur les rapports entre théologie, philosophie naturelle et médecine* (Paris, 2004)

Lugt, Maaike van der '"Abominable mixtures": the "Liber Vaccae" in the medieval west, or the dangers and attractions of natural magic', *Traditio* 64 (2009), pp. 229–77

Marrone, Steven P. *William of Auvergne and Robert Grosseteste: New Ideas of Truth in the Early Thirteenth Century* (Princeton, N.J., 1983)

Mayo, Thomas B. de *The Demonology of William of Auvergne: By Fire and Sword* (Lewiston, N.Y., 2007)

McCracken, Peggy *In the Skin of a Beast: Sovereignty and Animality in Medieval France* (Chicago, 2017)

Miller, Michael 'William of Auvergne and the Aristotelians: the nature of a servant', in John Inglis (ed.), *Medieval Philosophy and the Classical Tradition in Islam, Judaism and Christianity* (Richmond, 2002), pp. 263–76

Miner, Robert *Thomas Aquinas on the Passions: A Study of* Summa Theologiae *1a2ae 22–48* (Cambridge, 2009)

Moody, Ernest A. 'William of Auvergne and his treatise De Anima', in his *Studies in Medieval Philosophy, Science, and Logic: Collected Papers 1933–1969* (Berkeley, 1975), pp. 1–109

Morenzoni, Franco 'Le monde animal dans le *De universo creaturarum* de Guillaume d'Auvergne', *Micrologus* 8 (2000), pp. 197–216

Murphy, Sean Eisen 'On the enduring impurity of menstrual blood and semen: Leviticus 15 in William of Auvergne's *De legibus*', in José Martínez Gázquez and John Victor Tolan (eds.), *Ritus Infidelium: Miradas Interconfesionales sobre las Prácticas Religiosas en la Edad Media*, Collection de la Casa de Velázquez 138 (Madrid, 2013), pp. 191–208

Murphy, Sean 'Pagans past and present: righteousness and idolatry in academic discussions of ancient religion *c.*1130–*c.*1230,' in Susanne Knaeble and Silvan Wagner (eds.), *Gott und die Heiden: Mittelalterliche Funktionen und Semantiken der Heiden* (Berlin, 2015), pp. 147–67

Murphy, Sean 'The corruption of the elements: the science of ritual impurity in the early thirteenth century', in Jack P. Cunningham and Mark Hocknull (eds.), *Robert Grosseteste and the Pursuit of Religious and Scientific Learning in the Middle Ages* (Cham, 2016), pp. 103–16

Novotný, Vojtěch *Cur Homo? A History of the Thesis concerning Man as a Replacement for Fallen Angels*, trans. Pavlína Morgan and Tim Morgan (Prague, 2014)

Oelze, Anselm *Animal Rationality: Later Medieval Theories 1250–1350* (Leiden, 2018)

Oesterle, John A. 'The significance of the universal *ut nunc*', *The Thomist* 24 (1961), pp. 163–74

O'Meara, Thomas F. *Thomas Aquinas: Theologian* (Notre Dame, Ind., 1997)

Pasnau, Robert *Thomas Aquinas on Human Nature: A Philosophical Study of* Summa Theologiae *Ia 75–89* (Cambridge, 2002)

Pegis, Anton Charles *St. Thomas and the Problem of the Soul in the Thirteenth Century* (Toronto, 1934)

Perler, Dominik 'Intentionality and action. Medieval discussions on the cognitive capacities of animals', in Maria Cândida Pacheco and José F. Meirinhos (eds.), *Intellect et imagination dans la philosophie médiévale* (Turnhout, 3 vols., 2006), vol. 1, pp. 73–98

Perler, Dominik 'Why is the sheep afraid of the wolf? Medieval debates on animal passions', in Martin Pickavé and Lisa Shapiro (eds.), *Emotion and Cognitive Life in Medieval and Early Modern Philosophy* (Oxford, 2012), pp. 32–52

Resl, Brigitte (ed.), *A Cultural History of Animals in the Medieval Age* (Oxford, 2007)

Resnick, Irven M. 'Albert the Great: biographical introduction', in Irven M. Resnick (ed.), *A Companion to Albert the Great: Theology, Philosophy, and the Sciences* (Leiden, 2013), pp. 1–11

Resnick, Irven M. and Kenneth F. Kitchell, 'Albert the Great on the "language" of animals', *American Catholic Philosophical Quarterly* 70 (1996), pp. 41–61

Roling, Bernd *Drachen und Sirenen: Die Rationalisierung und Abwicklung der Mythologie an den europäischen Universitäten* (Leiden, 2010)

Ronnick, Michele V. *Cicero's 'Paradoxa Stoicorum': A Commentary, an Interpretation and a Study of its Influence*, Studien zur klassischen Philologie 62 (Frankfurt am Main, 1991)

Smalley, Beryl 'William of Auvergne, John of La Rochelle and St. Thomas Aquinas on the Old Law', reprinted in her *Studies in Medieval Thought and Learning from Abelard to Wyclif* (London, 1981), pp. 121–81 [first published in *St. Thomas Aquinas, 1274–1974: Commemorative Studies* (Toronto, 2 vols., 1974), vol. 2, pp. 11–72]

Smith, Lesley 'William of Auvergne and the law of the Jews and the Muslims', in Thomas J. Heffernan and Thomas E. Burman (eds.), *Scripture and Pluralism: Reading the Bible in the Religiously Plural Worlds of the Middle Ages and Renaissance* (Leiden, 2005), pp. 123–42

Sobol, Peter G. 'The shadow of reason: explanations of intelligent animal behaviour in the thirteenth century', in Joyce E. Salisbury (ed.), *The Medieval World of Nature: A Book of Essays* (New York, 1993), pp. 109–28

Steel, Karl *How to Make a Human: Animals and Violence in the Middle Ages* (Columbus, Ohio, 2011)

Teske, Roland J. 'The will as king over the powers of the soul: uses and sources of an image in the thirteenth century', *Vivarium* 32 (1994), pp. 62–71

Teske, Roland J. 'Introduction', in William of Auvergne, *The Universe of Creatures: Selections Translated from the Latin with an Introduction and Notes*, trans. Roland J. Teske (Milwaukee, Wis., 1998), pp. 13–29

Teske, Roland J. 'William of Auvergne', in Jorge J. E. Gracia and Timothy N. Noone (eds.), *A Companion to Philosophy in the Middle Ages* (Oxford, 2002), pp. 680–7

Teske, Roland J. 'William of Auvergne on the various states of our nature', *Traditio* 58 (2003), pp. 201–18

Thijssen, J. M. M. H. 'Reforging the great chain of being: the medieval discussion of the human status of "pygmies" and its influence on Edward Tyson', in Raymond Corbey and Bert Theunissen (eds.), *Ape, Man, Apeman: Changing Views since 1800* (Leiden, 1995), pp. 43–50

Torrell, Jean-Pierre *Saint Thomas Aquinas*, trans. Robert Royal (Washington, D.C., 2 vols., 2005), vol. 1: *The Person and his Work*

Torrell, Jean-Pierre *Aquinas's Summa: Background, Structure, and Reception*, trans. Benedict M. Guevin (Washington, D.C., 2005)

Turner, Denys *Julian of Norwich, Theologian* (New Haven, Conn., 2011)

Valois, Noël *Guillaume d'Auvergne, évêque de Paris (1228–1249): sa vie et ses ouvrages* (Paris, 1880)

Voisenet, Jacques *Bêtes et hommes dans le monde médiéval: le bestiaire des clercs du ve au xiie siècle* (Turnhout, 2000)

Waddell, Michael M. 'Wisdom, fittingness and the relational transcendentals', in Jan A. Aertsen and Andreas Speer (eds.), *Was ist Philosophie im Mittelalter?* (Berlin, 1998), pp. 538–42

Weber, Hubert Philipp 'Alexander of Hales's theology in his authentic texts (Commentary on the *Sentences* of Peter Lombard, various disputed questions)', in Michael J. P. Robson (ed.), *The English Province of the Franciscans (1224–c.1350)* (Leiden, 2017), pp. 273–93

Wei, Ian P. 'The self-image of the masters of theology at the university of Paris in the late thirteenth and early fourteenth centuries', *Journal of Ecclesiastical History* 46 (1995), pp. 398–431

Wei, Ian P. 'Predicting the future to judge the present: Paris theologians and attitudes to the future', in John A. Burrow and Ian P. Wei (eds.), *Medieval Futures: Attitudes to the Future in the Middle Ages* (Woodbridge, 2000), pp. 19–36

Wei, Ian P. 'Gender and sexuality in medieval academic discourse: marriage problems in Parisian quodlibets', *Mediaevalia* 31 (2010), pp. 5–34

Wei, Ian P. 'Discovering the moral value of money: usurious money and medieval academic discourse in Parisian quodlibets', *Mediaevalia* 33 (2012), pp. 5–46

Wei, Ian P. *Intellectual Culture in Medieval Paris: Theologians and the University c.1100–1330* (Cambridge, 2012)

Weisheipl, James A. *Friar Thomas d'Aquino: His Life, Thought and Works* (New York, 1974)

Wright, John H. *The Order of the Universe in the Theology of St Thomas Aquinas* (Rome, 1957)

Young, Spencer E. *Scholarly Community at the Early University of Paris: Theologians, Education and Society, 1215–1248* (Cambridge, 2014)

Index

For EU product safety concerns, contact us at Calle de José Abascal, 56–1°,
28003 Madrid, Spain or eugpsr@cambridge.org.

www.ingramcontent.com/pod-product-compliance
Ingram Content Group UK Ltd.
Pitfield, Milton Keynes, MK11 3LW, UK
UKHW020353140625

459647UK00020B/2438